HISTORIANS AT WORK

How Did American Slavery Begin?

Readings Selected and Introduced by

Edward Countryman

Southern Methodist University

Selections by

Ira Berlin

Margaret Washington

A. Leon Higginbotham Jr.

Winthrop D. Jordan

Edmund S. Morgan

Bedford / St. Martin's   *Boston • New York*

For Bedford / St. Martin's

History Editor: Katherine E. Kurzman
Developmental Editor: Charisse Kiino
Production Supervisor: Catherine Hetmansky
Marketing Manager: Charles Cavaliere
Editorial Assistant: Molly Kalkstein
Copyeditor: Barbara G. Flanagan
Text Design: Claire Seng-Niemoeller
Cover Design: Peter Blaiwas
Cover Art: Tobacco paper titled *The Virginia Planters Best Tobacco* (detail). Colonial
    Williamsburg
Composition: ComCom
Printing and Binding: Haddon Craftsmen, Inc.

President: Charles H. Christensen
Editorial Director: Joan E. Feinberg
Director of Editing, Design, and Production: Marcia Cohen
Managing Editor: Elizabeth M. Schaaf

Library of Congress Catalog Card Number: 98-87525

3   2   1   0

f   e   d   c

For information, write: Bedford / St. Martin's, 75 Arlington Street, Boston, MA 02116
                (617-426-7440)

ISBN: 0–312–18261–9 (paperback)
      0–312–21820–6 (hardcover)

Acknowledgments

IRA BERLIN, "From Creole to African: Atlantic Creoles and the Origins of African-
    American Society in Mainland North America," *William and Mary Quarterly* 53
    (April 1996): 251–88.
A. LEON HIGGINBOTHAM JR., From *Shades of Freedom: Racial Politics and Presumptions
    of the American Legal Process* by A. Leon Higginbotham Jr. Copyright © 1996 by A.
    Leon Higginbotham Jr. Used by permission of Oxford University Press, Inc.
WINTHROP D. JORDAN, "American Chiaroscuro: The Status and Definition of Mu-
    lattoes in the British Colonies," *William and Mary Quarterly*, 3rd ser., 19 (April
    1962): 183–200.
EDMUND S. MORGAN, "Slavery and Freedom: The American Paradox," *Journal of
    American History* 59 (June 1972): 5–29.
MARGARET WASHINGTON, "Gullah Roots," in *"A Peculiar People": Slave Religion and
    Community-Culture among the Gullahs.* Copyright © 1988 by New York University
    Press. Reprinted by permission of the publisher and the author.

Foreword

The short, inexpensive, and tightly focused books in the Historians at Work series set out to show students what historians do by turning closed specialist debate into an open discussion about important and interesting historical problems. These volumes invite students to confront the issues historians grapple with while providing enough support so that students can form their own opinions and join the debate. The books convey the intellectual excitement of "doing history" that should be at the core of any undergraduate study of the discipline. Each volume starts with a contemporary historical question that is posed in the book's title. The question focuses on either an important historical document (the Declaration of Independence, the Emancipation Proclamation) or a major problem or event (the beginnings of American slavery, the Pueblo Revolt of 1680) in American history. An introduction supplies the basic historical context students need and then traces the ongoing debate among historians, showing both how old questions have yielded new answers and how new questions have arisen. Following this two-part introduction are four or five interpretive selections by top scholars, reprinted in their entirety from journals and books, including endnotes. Each selection is either a very recent piece or a classic argument that is still in play and is headed by a question that relates it to the book's core problem. Volumes that focus on a document reprint it in the opening materials so that students can read arguments alongside the evidence and reasoning on which they rest.

One purpose of these books is to show students that they *can* engage with sophisticated writing and arguments. To help them do so, each selection includes apparatus that provides context for engaged reading and critical thinking. An informative headnote introduces the angle of inquiry that the reading explores and closes with Questions for a Closer Reading, which invite students to probe the selection's assumptions, evidence, and argument. At the end of the book, Making Connections questions offer students ways to read the essays against one another, showing how interesting problems emerge from the debate. Suggestions for Further Reading conclude each book, pointing interested students toward relevant materials for extended study.

Historical discourse is rarely a matter of simple opposition. These volumes show how ideas develop and how answers change, as minor themes turn into major considerations. The Historians at Work volumes bring together thoughtful statements in an ongoing conversation about topics that continue to engender debate, drawing students into the historical discussion with enough context and support to participate themselves. These books aim to show how serious scholars have made sense of the past and why what they do is both enjoyable and worthwhile.

EDWARD COUNTRYMAN

Preface

From the very moment that Europeans started crossing the Atlantic in large numbers, Africans were migrating too. Many more black people than white ones endured the journey to the Western Hemisphere between Christopher Columbus's first voyage in 1492 and United States independence in 1776. Without Africans and their American-born progeny, colonial America would have been a very different place. Their role in building it was as central as that of Native Americans, New England Puritans, the Hudson Valley Dutch, Pennsylvania Quakers, Virginia planters, or back-country Scotch-Irish and Germans.

Yet virtually all black colonists were slaves. Their America was a place of hopeless captivity and of forced labor till death. Their story is no "exception" to what was otherwise a tale of success—it is absolutely fundamental to the history of colonial America. Without appreciating their story, we cannot begin to understand either how Africans became African Americans or how the bitter dialectic between American slavery and American freedom got under way. If the *Mayflower* Pilgrims at Plymouth and white Virginians like Captain John Smith at Jamestown tell Americans today something fundamental about themselves, so do the Africans who began arriving at almost the same time.

The Plymouth and Jamestown stories are well known. Until recently, the history of African American beginnings on this continent has been obscure, except to a very few specialists. Recovering that story and making it a part of the main colonial narrative has been one of American historians' major recent achievements. This collection of essays introduces what historians have discovered about the black beginnings of America's unique society. Knowing about those early days changes our sense of both African American history and colonial America. Those beginnings speak directly to the larger question of which elements have shaped American identity.

Acknowledgments

This book is among the first volumes in the Historians at Work series. I owe thanks for help both in assembling the book itself and in working out the series template to my collaborators at Bedford/St. Martin's: Publisher Chuck Christensen, Associate Publisher Joan Feinberg, Sponsoring Editor Katherine Kurzman, Developmental Editor Charisse Kiino, Managing Editor Elizabeth Schaaf, Editorial Assistant Molly Kalkstein, Copyeditor Barbara Flanagan, and Art Director Donna Dennison. The series itself is Katherine's idea, and I'm very honored that she chose me to help her turn that idea into reality. Ross Murfin urged me to work with Bedford on the basis of his own good experience with the people there. Deep thanks go as well to historians Robert Allison, Paul Finkelman, Leslie Harris, and John David Smith. They read my drafts with great care, told me honestly what they thought I was doing wrong, and encouraged me to keep at it until I finally got the book right.

EDWARD COUNTRYMAN

A Note for Students

Every piece of written history starts when somebody becomes curious and asks questions. The very first problem is who, or what, to study. A historian might ask an old question yet again, after deciding that existing answers are not good enough. But brand-new questions can emerge about old, familiar topics, particularly in light of new findings or directions in research, such as the rise of women's history in the late 1970s.

In one sense history is all that happened in the past. In another it is the universe of potential evidence that the past has bequeathed. But written history does not exist until a historian collects and probes that evidence *(research)*, makes sense of it *(interpretation)*, and shows to others what he or she has seen so that they can see it too *(writing)*. Good history begins with respecting people's complexity, not with any kind of preordained certainty. It might well mean using modern techniques that were unknown at the time, such as Freudian psychology or statistical assessment by computer. But good historians always approach the past on its own terms, taking careful stock of the period's cultural norms and people's assumptions or expectations, no matter how different from contemporary attitudes. Even a few decades can offer a surprisingly large gap to bridge, as each generation discovers when it evaluates the accomplishments of those who have come before.

To write history well requires three qualities. One is the courage to try to understand people whom we never can meet—unless our subject is very recent—and to explain events that no one can re-create. The second quality is the humility to realize that we can never entirely appreciate either the people or the events under study. However much evidence is compiled and however smart the questions posed, the past remains too large to contain. It will always continue to surprise.

The third quality historians need is the curiosity that turns sterile facts into clues about a world that once was just as alive, passionate, frightening, and exciting as our own, yet in different ways. Today we know how past events "turned out." But the people taking part had no such knowledge. Good history recaptures those people's fears, hopes, frustrations, failures, and achievements; it tells about people who faced the predicaments and choices that still confront us as we head into the twenty-first century.

All the essays collected in this volume bear on a single, shared problem that the authors agree is important, however differently they may choose to respond to it. On its own, each essay reveals a fine mind coming to grips with a worthwhile question. Taken together, the essays give a sense of just how complex the human situation can be. That point—that human situations are complex—applies just as much to life today as to the lives led in the past. History has no absolute "lessons" to teach; it follows no invariable "laws." But knowing about another time might be of some help as we struggle to live within our own.

EDWARD COUNTRYMAN

Contents

PART ONE

Introduction

The Beginnings of American Slavery

The Beginnings of American Slavery

Africans and Slavery in Colonial America

Virtually all Americans agree that slavery presents one of the greatest blots upon our past. But for many of us, the institution of slavery and the people who endured it seem to have no history. We may recall learning about the arrival of twenty "Negars" at Jamestown, Virginia, in 1619, where they were put to work growing tobacco. Then the story usually jumps to the "Old South" in the decades prior to the Civil War. The number of people involved has grown enormously, and the main crop has become cotton. But aside from that, the standard image suggests, little has changed. Plantations were plantations and slavery was slavery, whether the setting was colonial Virginia or antebellum Mississippi.

Historians of the African American past have learned how inaccurate and inadequate that image is. Consider just a few points regarding those first twenty arrivals. They were not at all the first black migrants to the Western Hemisphere; by 1619 there were Africans all over the Caribbean and Central and South America. We know of at least one, named Esteban, who journeyed into Pueblo Indian country as early as 1539. Nor did those twenty at Jamestown automatically become slaves. On the contrary, it is quite possible that coming to Virginia *ended* the slavery that bound them when they boarded the Dutch vessel that took them there. In 1619 Virginia had no law of slavery and the arrivals became "servants." They went to work in the tobacco fields alongside other servants who were white and had come from England. Conditions were equally hard for both groups, but servitude could end. Early Virginia blacks gained their freedom and a few actually prospered. One, named Anthony Johnson, has become well known to historians. He arrived at Jamestown in 1621, survived his own time of servitude, married, and acquired land and indentured servants of his own. They served him as they would have served any other master, working for no more than their keep until their indentures expired.

Nonetheless, there already was one big difference. The whites had come freely, hoping for better lives once their servitude ended. We have no reason to think that those first twenty blacks entered the colony by their own choice. Many more were to follow. For these, even surviving was a triumph.

We have learned these things because one historian after another has decided that there is an African American past that the stereotypes obscure from sight, that if we ask the right questions we can reveal that past, and that doing so is important. This collection of essays takes us into what historians have discovered about how Africans first came to the British North American colonies and how slavery became the condition that defined their lives.

This book is small. The issue is very large. Esteban and the Jamestown people were among the first of many Africans who came to North America. Those people became just as much "colonists" as *Mayflower* Pilgrims, Pennsylvania Quakers, white Virginians, Louisiana Cajuns, or Spaniards in Santa Fe. By the eve of independence there were enslaved black people in every one of the thirteen British colonies that were rebelling in the name of freedom. The contrast glared so strongly that it provoked Dr. Samuel Johnson of London to ask how it was "that we hear the loudest *yelps* for liberty among the drivers of Negroes." The question stung, as Johnson intended.

The Demography of Early American Slavery

We cannot approach American slavery's beginnings with reference to Africa and North America alone. During the colonial era, slavery developed everywhere from Montreal to Buenos Aires, just as it developed at one time or another in most parts of the world. Historian Philip Curtin estimates that the total slave trade from Africa to the Western Hemisphere amounted to 9,566,000 people, the largest forced migration in all history. The 4,700,000 taken to South America accounted for half of the entire trade. The 4,040,000 who went to the West Indies represented more than 40 percent. By comparison, the British colonies/United States received roughly 399,000. South America imported nearly 12 slaves and the West Indies imported more than 10 slaves for every slave who went to North America. For each of those people, wherever they went, and for the uncounted others who died en route, slavery "began" at the moment of capture.

The degree of suffering that it took to establish New World plantation slavery was very high, as the cases of South Carolina and the West Indies show. There was a black majority in South Carolina as early as the colony's first census in 1708. They were herding cattle, clearing forests, refining pitch and tar, and growing mixed crops. Shortly thereafter Carolinians discovered that rice could be grown in the enormously fertile lowland. As of 1720, at the rice boom's beginning, there were about 12,000 black people in the colony. A fair number of these probably had come from the West Indies. During the ensuing two decades some 32,000 more slaves were brought to South Carolina ports, almost all of them straight from Africa. Yet historian Peter Wood has found that in the year 1740 there were only 39,155 black people in the province. If we add the number present in 1720 and the number imported thereafter, and if we allow for a surplus of births over deaths (as definitely was the case among whites), the result would predict a far larger population. Black Carolinians were dying faster than new Africans could replace them, however fast the slave ships kept coming. The implication is clear: during those first years of Carolina rice slavery, conditions were so bad that only a massive slave trade enabled the black population to grow. Carolina was not alone. Virginia was importing large numbers of slaves about the same time. Conditions there were not as fierce, but 1 in every 4 of those new Africans was dead within a year.

Both of these situations pale by comparison with the Caribbean. Consider Jamaica, whose enormously profitable production of sugar made it the jewel in Britain's American tiara. During the slave-trade era, Jamaica received roughly 748,000 people from Africa. But at the trade's end in 1807, Jamaica's total population stood at no more than 324,000. To state what should be obvious, the conditions of Jamaican slavery were murderous, and those conditions went on for well over a century. Similar ratios between the number who arrived and the number who survived hold for Barbados, the smaller islands, the French and Spanish Caribbean sugar colonies, and Brazil. As long as plantation slavery endured in those places and as long as profitability remained high, the slave trade was "necessary." Without it, the sugar colonies could not have survived and the enormous profits they generated could not have been reaped.

There were times when the mainland colonies were more hungry for slaves even than their rivals. Taken together, Georgia, the Carolinas, Virginia, and Maryland imported more than 69,000 between 1761 and 1770, compared with Jamaica's 62,300. Nonetheless, an important difference developed between slavery in North America and slavery in the West Indies or Brazil. Despite the shock of enslavement, the agony of the journey from Africa, and the hopelessness of lifetime captivity, the Africans who came to North America proved prolific. In contrast to the West Indies, the North American slave population began to sustain itself, and the transatlantic slave trade became less and less necessary to its continuation. In 1790 Africans and their American-born progeny numbered 757,208 in a total U.S. population of 3,929,214, a huge increase on the number of people imported. Yet Wood's South Carolina figures give pause to any simplistic sense that North American slavery was "easier." Wherever plantation slavery was established, it exacted a huge price. The difference is of degree, not kind.

SLAVERY AND THE BEGINNINGS
OF EARLY AMERICAN SOCIETY

During the colonial era most North American slaves lived in the Chesapeake and the Carolina/Georgia low country, growing tobacco, rice, indigo, and sea island cotton on lowland plantations. But black people labored on small farms in the southern backcountry and throughout the middle and northern colonies as well. They helped whites build houses and ships, cobble shoes, bake bread, brew beer, make hats, weave cloth, and sew gowns. They cleaned streets and they hauled heavily laden carts through them. They waited on planters in Virginia mansions and on lawyers, merchants, and public officials in the northern cities. Black men helped turn ore into metal on the "iron plantations" that dotted the interior landscape from Virginia to New York. They loaded and unloaded vessels in colonial ports and they went to sea before the mast. Black women cooked, washed, tended children, and did scullery work in white households everywhere. They also did heavy labor to which no white woman would be subjected. Whatever free white people were doing to build colonial America, enslaved black people were doing it too.

In a vast, sweeping comparison of world slave systems, sociologist Orlando Patterson has likened slavery to "social death." His metaphor offers a way to distinguish slavery from any other kind of subordination or degradation. All societies have some form of hierarchy, and all hierarchies involve different degrees of honor, respect, and reward. Somebody is always at the bottom, even in a society that proclaims equality. A slave, however, is totally dishonored, stripped of all claims to respect, and open to complete exploitation. Slaves live with the knowledge that somebody else is in control of their lives, "without consent or contract."

The Bible tells how the people of ancient Israel were enslaved in Egypt and in Babylon. Greeks enslaved "barbarians," and Romans enslaved Greeks. Slavery happened among some American Indians. "Social death" describes the condition of slaves in Africa, India, China, and the ancient Mediterranean world. The point holds even where slaves could rise to high public office. In Ottoman Turkey it took only a sultan's whim for a high official to find himself in the galleys.

During the Middle Ages, Scandinavian Vikings enslaved people wherever their long ships could sail, from Ireland to Russia. Tatars enslaved Russians and they brought slaves from central Asia to ports on the Black

Sea, where Italian traders purchased them. In the Balkan countries, Latin Christians enslaved both pagan "primitive Slavs" and Christians of non-Latin rites and creeds. The very word *slave* stems from that root. The centuries-long contest between Christianity and Islam saw both sides enslave the losers, even though Islamic law forbade enslaving Jews and Christians who submitted peaceably to Muslim rule. By the age of American colonization, slavery had disappeared from England, the Netherlands, and France. But English, Dutch, and French people who journeyed to eastern or southern Europe were bound to have seen it. They might even have become enslaved themselves. According to Captain John Smith's own account, it happened to him in Turkey before he went to Virginia.

That bare listing of places and situations should break any notion that enslavement happened only to Africans and only in America. Nonetheless, the enslavement of black Africans far outstrips what happened to anybody else. During the Middle Ages slave-trading routes stretched across the Sahara, bringing black slaves to the Ottoman Empire, Arabia, North Africa, and Muslim Spain, where Christians sometimes encountered them. When Iberian seafarers began to explore the West African coast in the fifteenth century, one consequence was to open an oceangoing slave trade straight from Africa to Spain and especially Portugal. According to historian Robin Blackburn, one-tenth of the populations of Lisbon and Seville consisted of black slaves about the year 1500. Slavery did not yet define all relations between Africans and Europeans, however. During the fifteenth and sixteenth centuries, guests from sub-Saharan black African kingdoms were received with honor by European monarchs. Those same kings sent delegates to their African counterparts, especially Kongo, which converted to Catholicism under its king's leadership.

The connection that would bind black captives to Western Hemisphere plantation slavery emerged as the "advanced" world discovered how much it enjoyed luxury crops, beginning with sugar. Sugar cultivation spread from the Levant to the western Mediterranean under Muslim rule. Mediterranean Christians learned about it from Muslims they conquered, and they sometimes enslaved the artisans who knew how to turn the juice of the canes into finished sugar. But most Mediterranean sugar production was done by serfs, who were bound to the soil but not enslaved. The social institution of slavery and the economic institutions we call plantations had not yet come together in European awareness, at least on any large scale.

During the fifteenth, sixteenth, and early seventeenth centuries, sugar growing spread to islands off Africa's Atlantic coast as far south as São Tomé in the West African bight. As Europe discovered its appetite for sweetness, the Atlantic islands began producing sugar in plantation quantities, followed by Brazil and the Caribbean. That meant acquiring African slaves in ever-increasing numbers. It also meant working them ferociously. Slavery may be among the most ancient human institutions. But plantation slavery—growing cash crops on a massive scale for distant markets— developed on a large scale during the early colonization of the Western Hemisphere and became a distinctive New World phenomenon. Although sugar was always the most demanding crop that Western Hemisphere slaves produced, the plantation system proved adaptable to other crops, including tobacco, rice, indigo, cotton, coffee, and hemp.

The conventional Jamestown story may be wrong, then, about the condition of those twenty "Negars," who probably were not slaves. The larger point is that black slavery did arrive in America early. The problem for us is how did the *British* colonies (as opposed to Spanish, Portuguese, French, or Dutch) develop slavery? That raises the general problem of how some people have justified their enslavement of others. It also raises the specific problem of how slave law developed among England's American colonists.

Justifying Enslavement

Throughout slavery's global history, enslavers have offered rationalizations for what they have done. The easiest was simply to invoke God's will: slavery was a fact of life, sanctioned by both the Holy Bible and the Holy Qur'an. Supposedly, the biblical patriarch Noah cursed the children of his son Ham (or *his* son Canaan) into permanent enslavement because Ham had seen Noah drunk and naked. The Apostle Paul enjoined slaves to obey their masters. Christians and Muslims alike maintained that whoever warred against the True Faith deserved enslavement. The ancient philosopher Aristotle posited that some people were naturally slavish and that not speaking Greek was a probable sign of such people. Foreshadowing Patterson's argument about social death, the seventeenth-century English thinker John Locke declared that losers in war had forfeited their lives. If the conqueror chose to enslave them rather than kill them, they still were symbolically dead. Most people probably felt no need to worry about the matter. Enslavement could happen to anyone, whether by divine will or sheer bad luck. The world was structured around the fact of danger and the principle of inequality. Slavery represented both: the danger that anybody might have to face and the bottommost instance of subordination.

How the specific problem of "race" entered the issue is not straightforward. Christopher Columbus knew African slavery firsthand and he brought Indian slaves back to Spain from his voyages, but as an Italian he would also have seen enslaved Slavs and Asians. Massive Indian enslavement took place on the Caribbean islands during the Spanish conquest. But it did not last. During the mid-sixteenth century a fierce debate erupted within the Catholic Church and the Spanish bureaucracy about enslaving the Western Hemisphere's natives. The issue was resolved in favor of the Indians' freedom, although the Indians were still subjected to compulsory mine and *hacienda* labor. The English enslaved Indians too. When Powhatan Indians lost a war against Virginians in 1622, the secretary of the colony gloated that they could "now most justly be compelled to servitude and drudgery." Carolinians enslaved Yamasees, Tuscaroras, and Choctaws and raided the Great Plains to capture distant Pawnees. Puritan New Englanders enslaved the Algonquians whom they defeated in King Philip's War (1675–76) and shipped them off to Carolina and the West Indies. Yet as in Spain's dominions, being Indian ceased to mean being liable to enslavement. During the American Revolution's aftermath, having Indian ancestry became one basis for bringing a lawsuit for freedom.

Unlike Spaniards or Portuguese, English colonists took neither the law nor the practice of enslavement, black or otherwise, with them when they crossed the Atlantic. They developed their slave system, their slave law, and their eventual presumption that in America being black meant being enslaved themselves.

The first legal recognition of slavery in an English colony came on Barbados. The island's slave law of 1636 probably emulated that of the Portuguese and Dutch sugar colonies in Brazil and Guyana. The local assembly passed the law just before "the Barbados planters switched from tobacco and cotton to sugar and from white servants to black slaves." Perhaps the legislators were deliberately preparing for the change. Whatever their reason, the law marked the point when Barbados started to become a "slave society," meaning a place where the entire structure of economy and society rested upon massive enslavement. By 1661 Barbados had a "comprehensive slave code . . . for the better ordering and governing of Negroes," which provided a model for most of the other British island colonies and for South Carolina.

Five years after Barbados first enacted slavery, Massachusetts became the earliest mainland British colony to establish it. The province's initial slave law said nothing about race. Instead it provided that

> there shall never be any bond-slavery, villenage or captivitie amongst us; unless it be lawfull captives taken in just warrs, and such strangers as willingly sell themselves, or are solde to us; and such shall have the libertyes and christian usages which the law of God established in israell concerning such persons doth morally require, provided, this exempts none from servitude who shall be judged thereto by Authoritie.

The "libertyes and christian usages" that the law recognized could be enforced in courts and preached in churches, to a slave's genuine benefit. However, the province's slave population always remained small. There would be no plantations in New England, ever.

Yet the telling phrase "or are solde to us" suggests the forced passivity of people who had been enslaved far away and transported where they never would have gone by their own choice. For all practical purposes, that already meant Africans. New Englanders entered the African trade at first as clandestine "interlopers" during the Royal African Company's seventeenth-century monopoly. After the monopoly ended in 1698, they traded openly. Unlike Massachusetts, Virginia formed its slave law piecemeal, between roughly 1650 and 1700. One of the selections in this book considers how Virginia slid from presuming that anybody within its boundaries was capable of freedom, as the case of Anthony Johnson shows, to assuming that any black person was almost certainly a slave.

Everywhere it is told, the story of the beginnings of American slavery is dismal. Yet it has to be told if the unique, multiracial reality of American life is to be understood. Moreover, it is also a story of lost possibilities, endurance, survival, and creativity, from which African American culture emerged. Let us turn now to the historians who have tried to help us understand what happened, rather than simply dismissing slavery and the people caught within its embrace as having no past worth the knowing.

Historians and the Beginnings of Slavery

Black Americans knew long before white Americans that they had a history. Even in slavery, they preserved their stories each time they named a child after an ancestor. The great black abolitionist Frederick Douglass understood that for his people American history seemed different than it appeared to whites. "What to the Slave is *your* Fourth of July?" he asked a white audience in Rochester, New York, on July 5, 1852. But in that same powerful speech Douglass likened the American Republic to a ship caught in a fearful storm at sea. Regardless of how different people had come to be on board, all stood to drown if the ship foundered. Whether whites liked it or not, Douglass insisted, their history and the history of black Americans were caught up together.

After slavery ended, black scholars went to work to reconstruct the African American past. As Peter Wood has shown, one of the earliest such historians was a former major in the Union army "with the auspicious name of Richard Wright," not to be confused with the twentieth-century writer. Confronted with a flat assertion by a Harvard professor that "'the

Negro [w]as not an 'historical character,' " Wright went " 'to England and made researches in the Bodleian Library at Oxford and in the British Museum' " where he " 'did the best I could for my day.' "

A remarkable series of black historians followed the lead set by early inquirers like Wright. Beginning in 1896 with *The Suppression of the African Slave Trade*, W. E. B. Du Bois launched a writing career that lasted for decades and leaped from genre to genre. Du Bois's great strength was to interpret, most powerfully in his masterpiece *The Souls of Black Folk* (1903). For his contemporary Carter G. Woodson, finding and preserving the evidence had to come first. Woodson established the Association for the Study of Negro History and the *Journal of Negro History* for precisely that purpose. In the next generation Benjamin Quarrels, E. Franklin Frazier, and especially John Hope Franklin emerged as the premier scholars of the black American past. Though Franklin eventually reached the peak of the historical profession, they and white colleagues like Herbert Aptheker and Philip Foner had to endure the poor working conditions that went with non-elite jobs, the discomforts and outright hostility that went with working on the subject in the Jim Crow South, and the realization that most of their fellow professionals did not care.

For "mainstream" history, as represented by major graduate schools, high-prestige professional journals, and college-level textbooks, the "Negro" past remained peripheral at best. Until John Hope Franklin joined the University of Chicago in 1964, no black person held a senior rank in a major history department that encouraged research and trained doctoral students. A textbook by two eminent historians began its bare three pages on black people before the Civil War with "As for Sambo, whose wrongs moved the abolitionists to wrath and tears, there is some reason to believe that he suffered less than any other class in the South from its 'peculiar institution' " (Samuel Eliot Morison and Henry Steele Commager, *The Growth of the American Republic* [1937], 1:433).

That offhand dismissal suggests a major part of the problem that historians of black America used to face. It seemed that before the Civil War timeless, unchanging slavery was all there was, despite the enormous efforts of scholars like Du Bois and especially Woodson to recover a fuller story. Perhaps the biggest gain historians have made since the civil rights era of the 1950s and the 1960s has been to destroy that one-dimensional image, showing instead how very complex and rich is black Americans' history between the first Africans' arrival and slavery's end. As Douglass, Wright, Du Bois, and Franklin all understood and as most historians now appreciate, the subject has to be approached from the point of view that black Americans have been the subjects and the makers of their own history, rather than a "problem" with which whites had to contend. The key statement in the development of that understanding is John Blassingame's *The Slave Community* (1972).

The starting point for discussion of slavery's beginnings among "mainstream" (read, "most white") historians remains Oscar Handlin and Mary Flug Handlin's "Origins of the Southern Labor System," published in the *William and Mary Quarterly* in 1950. The time was right. Simply on academic grounds, the scholarship of "Negro" history specialists was becoming too powerful to ignore. Moreover, thinking white Americans like the Handlins could not but see that a racial crisis was coming. Nazi Germany had shown the world the consequences to which racism could lead, and its actions cast a lurid light on white supremacy American-style. Even before the worst was known about the European Holocaust, the Swedish sociologist Gunnar Myrdal's powerful *An American Dilemma* (1944) pitted the Republic's self-image of freedom and equality against its bleak and deep-rooted racial realities. The National Association for the Advancement of Colored People was well along on its campaign of lawsuits aimed at destroying southern segregation. Though the Handlins could not have known it, the young Martin Luther King Jr. was beginning the theological study that would lead to his public career. In such a situation, the "as for Sambo" dismissal of slavery was bound to come under challenge.

Half a century after its publication, the Handlins' essay still reads like a template for further study. Perhaps it does remain seminal, since most of the themes that subsequent scholars would develop appear in it. The essay notes both the nonexistence of formal slavery in English law and the presence of free black people in seventeenth-century Virginia. There is a commonplace notion that American historical experience purified and simplified European institutions. The Handlins suggested instead that American slavery degenerated out of European-style servitude, as blacks found themselves more and more oppressed while the condition of whites improved. Allowing for the work of Du Bois on the slave trade, the Handlins turned American slavery's origins from a given into a problem. Not the least of their arguments was that racism emerged from slavery, rather than preceding it and justifying it. Not every scholar has agreed, although the "which came first" dimension of the issue perhaps is impossible to resolve.

Nonetheless, most 1950s scholarship remained focused on the much older question of whether slavery was "mild" or "harsh" in some timeless way. This was the central issue at stake between the Old South apologist Ulrich B. Phillips (*American Negro Slavery: A Survey of the Supply, Employment, and Control of Negro Labor as Determined by the Plantation Regime* [1918]) and his civil rights–era critic Kenneth M. Stampp (*The Peculiar Institution: Slav-*

ery in the Ante-Bellum South [1956]). Not until the 1960s did the issues of time, place, and the variety of black people's historical experience turn into a major subject of debate.

Then, as often happens in scholarship, the subject opened up with a rush. Winthrop D. Jordan's essay in this collection, published in 1962, is one of the earliest statements, pointing toward his major book *White over Black: American Attitudes toward the Negro, 1550–1812* (1968). In 1967, David Brion Davis published *The Problem of Slavery in Western Culture,* the first in an as yet uncompleted series of volumes exploring the idea of slavery from the ancient world to the present. Both Jordan and Davis dealt primarily with the attitudes of oppressors toward the people they oppressed. Early in the 1970s, a remarkable trio of books reversed the perspective, turning specifically on what oppressed people had to endure during the unfree beginnings of American labor. Richard S. Dunn's *Sugar and Slaves* (1972) explored the Caribbean islands' demographic disaster. Peter Wood's *Black Majority* (1974) extended the issue of demography to South Carolina, the mainland colony that was most "like a Negro Country." In 1975, Edmund S. Morgan's *American Slavery, American Freedom* broadened the discussion to include Virginia, dealing with the demography of white tobacco servitude and asking whether slavery and freedom were closely bound together rather than just parallel in some regrettable way. A capsule statement of Morgan's argument is also included as a selection in this book.

The best measure of how rapidly the field then expanded is the historiographical essay that Peter Wood published in the *William and Mary Quarterly* in 1978, " 'I Did the Best I Could for My Day.' " Since Wood's essay, the field has continued to grow. The selections by Ira Berlin, A. Leon Higginbotham, and Margaret Washington in this volume provide some sense of the different directions that scholars have taken. Some of the most important contributions by recent historians are noted in Suggestions for Further Reading at the end of this book.

Despite the enormous gains historians have made, early African American history remains open to exploration. The near simultaneous publication of three large and important books that deal with the subject, Robin Blackburn's *The Making of New World Slavery* (1997), Philip D. Morgan's *Slave Counterpoint* (1998), and Ira Berlin's *Many Thousands Gone: The First Two Centuries of Slavery in North America* (1998), are evidence of the subject's continuing intellectual significance. Perhaps some students who begin to encounter the subject here will be among its future explorers. The best may be yet to come.

PART TWO

Some Current Questions

The selections that follow deal with some of the issues about the earliest stages of American slavery that now interest historians. Other questions and other selections could have been chosen, but these show the development of the conversation. Each selection is preceded by a headnote that introduces both its specific subject and its author. After the headnote come Questions for a Closer Reading. The headnote and the questions offer signposts that will allow you to understand more readily what the author is saying. The selections are uncut and they include the original notes. The notes are also signposts for further exploration. If an issue that the author raises intrigues you, use the notes to follow it up. At the end of all the selections are more questions, under the heading Making Connections. Turn to these after you have read the selections, and use them to bring the whole discussion together. In order to answer them, you may find that you need to reread. But no historical source yields up all that is within it to a person content to read it just once.

Ira Berlin

From Creole to African: Atlantic Creoles and the Origins of African-American Society in Mainland North America

This essay by Ira Berlin is the most recently published piece in this volume. It is a study toward his *Many Thousands Gone: The First Two Centuries of Slavery in North America* (1998), which was published as this book was in the final process of assembly. Berlin starts with the assumption that sixteenth- and early seventeenth-century Africans who wandered the Atlantic were not necessarily slaves, and he takes the arrival of Africans as a problem rather than a given.

Berlin reveals a network of part-African places that spanned the Atlantic basin in the seventeenth century. He also complicates our understanding of "African." The "Creoles" of whom he writes were the offspring of African/European sexual unions, which may sometimes have been legal marriages. The Creoles were caught between Africa and Europe. Quite possibly, Berlin's account tells us a great deal about the original black Virginians of 1619. Berlin's opening vignette of Virginia's Robert "King" Carter renaming his new slaves one by one demonstrates the total power that a planter could claim over slaves by the eighteenth century. The historical issue is how a person like Carter became able to claim such power, if, as Berlin argues, he never could have exercised it a century earlier.

Berlin's essay represents a return to the problems that Oscar and Mary Handlin first posed in their 1950 article "Origins of the Southern Labor System." Perhaps there is truth in the saying that although history does not repeat itself, historians do repeat one another. In the case of his article and theirs, however, the relationship is not one of repetition but rather of deepening and enriching a set of insights that were ahead of their time when the Handlins first offered them.

Ira Berlin received his Ph.D. from the University of Wisconsin. He is professor of history and dean of the College of Arts and Humanities at the University of Maryland and is the author of many studies of black Americans in the slavery era. He founded the ongoing Freedom Project, which is reconstructing slavery's final destruction from records long buried in the National Archives. The article reprinted here won the *William and Mary Quarterly* prize for its best contribution in 1996.

Questions for a Closer Reading

1. What does Berlin mean by the "charter generations" of African people in the Western Hemisphere? How did these people's situation differ from that of the slaves who came afterward?

2. Why, in Berlin's view, does it make sense to understand Nieuw Amsterdam (New York) as being just as much an "African" place in the New World as a "European" one? How does this perspective alter our understanding of "early America"?

3. What part did Creole Africans play in the emergence of the Atlantic slave trade?

4. What was the historical difference between the "Creoles" and the "Africans" about whom Berlin writes?

5. Berlin pays little attention to Jamestown. Nonetheless, does his essay help us understand the issues presented by the arrival there of a Dutch ship bearing "Negroes" for sale in 1619?

From Creole to African: Atlantic Creoles and the Origins of African-American Society in Mainland North America

In 1727, Robert "King" Carter, the richest planter in Virginia, purchased a handful of African slaves from a trader who had been cruising the Chesapeake. The transaction was a familiar one to the great planter, for Carter owned hundreds of slaves and had inspected many such human cargoes, choosing the most promising from among the weary, frightened men and women who had survived the transatlantic crossing. Writing to his overseer from his plantation on the Rappahannock River, Carter explained the process by which he initiated Africans into their American captivity. "I name'd them here & by their names we can always know what sizes they are of & I am sure we repeated them so often to them that every one knew their name & would readily answer to them." Carter then forwarded his slaves to a satellite plantation or quarter, where his overseer repeated the process, taking "care that the negros both men & women I sent . . . always go by the names we gave them." In the months that followed, the drill continued, with Carter again joining in the process of stripping newly arrived Africans of the signature of their identity.[1]

Renaming marked Carter's initial endeavor to master his new slaves by separating them from their African inheritance. For the most part, he designated them by common English diminutives—Tom, Jamey, Moll, Nan—as if to consign them to a permanent childhood. But he tagged some with names more akin to barnyard animals—Jumper, for example—as if to represent their distance from humanity, and he gave a few the names of some ancient deity or great personage like Hercules or Cato as a kind of cosmic jest: the most insignificant with the greatest of names. None of his

Ira Berlin, "From Creole to African: Atlantic Creoles and the Origins of African-American Society in Mainland North America," *William and Mary Quarterly,* 3rd ser., 53 (1996): 251–88.

slaves received surnames, marks of lineage that Carter sought to obliterate and of adulthood that he would not admit.[2]

The loss of their names was only the first of the numerous indignities Africans suffered at the hands of planters in the Chesapeake. Since many of the skills Africans carried across the Atlantic had no value to their new owners, planters disparaged them, and since the Africans' "harsh jargons" rattled discordantly in the planters' ears, they ridiculed them. Condemning new arrivals for the "gross bestiality and rudeness of their manners, the variety and strangeness of their languages, and the weakness and shallowness of their minds," planters put them to work at the most repetitive and backbreaking tasks, often on the most primitive, frontier plantations. They made but scant attempt to see that slaves had adequate food, clothing, or shelter, because the open slave trade made slaves cheap and the new disease environment inflated their mortality rate, no matter how well they were tended. Residing in sex-segregated barracks, African slaves lived a lonely existence, without families or ties of kin, isolated from the mainstream of Chesapeake life.[3]

So began the slow, painful process whereby Africans became African-Americans. In time, people of African descent recovered their balance, mastered the circumstances of their captivity, and confronted their owners on more favorable terms. Indeed, resistance to the new regime began at its inception, as slaves clandestinely maintained their African names even as they answered their owner's call.[4] The transition of Africans to African-Americans or creoles[5]—which is partially glimpsed in the records of Carter's estate— would be repeated thousands of times, as African slavers did the rough business of transporting Africa to America. While the transition was different on the banks of the Hudson, Cooper, St. Johns, and Mississippi rivers than on the Rappahannock, the scenario by which "outlandish" Africans progressed from "New Negroes" to assimilated African-Americans has come to frame the history of black people in colonial North America.[6]

Important as that story is to the development of black people in the plantation era, it embraces only a portion of the history of black life in colonial North America, and that imperfectly. The assimilationist scenario assumes that "African" and "creole" were way stations of generational change rather than cultural strategies that were manufactured and remanufactured and that the vectors of change moved in only one direction— often along a single track with Africans inexorably becoming creoles. Its emphasis on the emergence of the creole—a self-sustaining, indigenous population—omits entirely an essential element of the story: the charter generations, whose experience, knowledge, and attitude were more akin to that of confident, sophisticated natives than of vulnerable newcomers.[7] Such men and women, who may be termed "Atlantic creoles"[8] from their broad experience in the Atlantic world, flourished prior to the triumph of plantation production on the mainland—the tobacco revolution in the Chesapeake in the last third of the seventeenth century, the rice revolution in the Carolina lowcountry in the first decades of the eighteenth century, the incorporation of the northern colonies into the Atlantic system during the eighteenth century, and finally the sugar revolution in the lower Mississippi Valley in the first decade of the nineteenth century. Never having to face the cultural imposition of the likes of Robert "King" Carter, black America's charter generations took a different path—despite the presence of slavery and the vilification of slave masters and their apologists. The Atlantic creole's unique experience reveals some of the processes by which race was constructed and reconstructed in early America.

Black life in mainland North America originated not in Africa or America but in the netherworld between the continents. Along the periphery of the Atlantic—first in Africa, then in Europe, and finally in the Americas—African-American society was a product of the momentous meeting of Africans and Europeans and of their equally fateful encounter with the peoples of the Americas. Although the countenances of these new people of the Atlantic—Atlantic creoles—might bear the features of Africa, Europe, or the Americas in whole or in part, their beginnings, strictly speaking, were in none of those places. Instead, by their experiences and sometimes by their persons, they had become part of the three worlds that came together along the Atlantic littoral. Familiar with the commerce of the Atlantic, fluent in its new languages, and intimate with its trade and cultures, they were cosmopolitan in the fullest sense.

Atlantic creoles originated in the historic meeting of Europeans and Africans on the west coast of Africa. Many served as intermediaries, employing their linguistic skills and their familiarity with the Atlantic's diverse commercial practices, cultural conventions, and diplomatic etiquette to mediate between African merchants and European sea captains. In so doing, some Atlantic creoles identified with their ancestral homeland (or a portion of it)—be it African, European, or American—and served as its representatives in negotiations with others. Other Atlantic creoles had been won over by the power and largesse of one party or another, so that Africans entered the employ of European trading companies and Europeans traded with African potentates. Yet others played fast and loose with their diverse heritage, employing whichever identity paid best. Whatever strategy they adopted, Atlantic creoles began the process of integrating the icons and ideologies of the Atlantic world into a new way of life.[9]

The emergence of Atlantic creoles was but a tiny outcropping in the massive social upheaval that accompanied the joining of the peoples of the two hemispheres. But it represented the small beginnings that initiated this monumental transformation, as the new people of the Atlantic made their presence felt. Some traveled widely as blue-water sailors, supercargoes, shipboard servants, and interpreters—the last particularly important because Europeans showed little interest in mastering the languages of Africa. Others were carried—sometimes as hostages—to foreign places as exotic trophies to be displayed before curious publics, eager for firsthand knowledge of the lands beyond the sea. Traveling in more dignified style, Atlantic creoles were also sent to distant lands with commissions to master the ways of newly discovered "others" and to learn the secrets of their wealth and knowledge. A few entered as honored guests, took their places in royal courts as esteemed councilors, and married into the best families.[10]

Atlantic creoles first appeared at the trading *feitorias* or factories that European expansionists established along the coast of Africa in the fifteenth century. Finding trade more lucrative than pillage, the Portuguese crown began sending agents to oversee its interests in Africa. These official representatives were succeeded by private entrepreneurs or *lançados*, who established themselves with the aid of African potentates, sometimes in competition with the crown's emissaries. European nations soon joined in the action, and coastal factories became sites of commercial rendezvous for all manner of transatlantic traders. What was true of the Portuguese enclaves (Axim and Elmina) held for those later established or seized by the Dutch (Fort Nassau and Elmina), Danes (Fredriksborg and Christiansborg), Swedes (Karlsborg and Cape Apolina), Brandenburgers (Pokoso), French (St. Louis and Gorée), and English (Fort Kormantse and Cape Coast).[11]

The transformation of the fishing villages along the Gold Coast during the sixteenth and seventeenth centuries suggests something of the change wrought by the European traders. Between 1550 and 1618, Mouri (where the Dutch constructed Fort Nassau in 1612) grew from a village of 200 people to 1,500 and to an estimated 5,000–6,000 at the end of the eighteenth century. In 1555, Cape Coast counted only twenty houses; by 1680, it had 500 or more. Axim, with 500 inhabitants in 1631, expanded to between 2,000 and 3,000 by 1690.[12] Small but growing numbers of Europeans augmented the African fishermen, craftsmen, village-based peasants, and laborers who made up the population of these villages. Although mortality and transiency rates in these enclaves were extraordinarily high, even by the standards of early modern ports, permanent European settlements developed from a mobile body of the corporate employees (from governors to surgeons to clerks), merchants and factors, stateless sailors, skilled craftsmen, occasional missionaries, and sundry transcontinental drifters.[13]

Established in 1482 by the Portuguese and captured by the Dutch in 1637, Elmina was one of the earliest factories and an exemplar for those that followed. A meeting place for African and European commercial ambitions, Elmina—the Castle São Jorge da Mina and the town that surrounded it—became headquarters for Portuguese and later Dutch mercantile activities on the Gold Coast and, with a population of 15,000 to 20,000 in 1682, the largest of some two dozen European outposts in the region.[14]

The peoples of the enclaves—both long-term residents and wayfarers—soon joined together genetically as well as geographically. European men took African women as wives and mistresses, and, before long, the offspring of these unions helped people the enclave. Elmina sprouted a substantial cadre of Euro-Africans (most of them Luso-Africans)*—men and women of African birth but shared African and European parentage, whose combination of swarthy skin, European dress and deportment, knowledge of local customs, and multilingualism gave them inside understanding of both African and European ways while denying them full acceptance in either culture. By the eighteenth century, they numbered several hundred in Elmina. Farther south along the coast of Central Africa, they may have been even more numerous.[15]

People of mixed ancestry and tawny complexion composed but a small fraction of the population of the coastal factories, yet few observers failed to note their existence—which suggests something of the disproportionate significance of their presence. Africans and Europeans alike sneered at the creoles' mixed lineage (or lack of lineage) and condemned them as knaves, charlatans, and shameless self-promoters. When they adopted African ways, wore African dress and amulets, and underwent ritual circumcision and scarification, Europeans declared them outcasts (*tangomãos*, renegades, to the Portuguese). When they adopted European ways, wore European clothing and crucifixes, employed European names or titles, and comported themselves in the manner of "white men," Africans denied them the right to hold land, marry, and inherit property. Yet, although *tangomãos* faced reproach and proscription, all parties conceded that they were shrewd traders, attested to their mastery of the fine points of intercultural negotiations, and found advantage in dealing with them. Despite their defamers, some rose to positions of wealth and power, compensating for their lack of lineage with knowledge, skill, and entrepreneurial derring-do.[16]

Not all *tangomãos* were of mixed ancestry, and not all people of mixed ancestry were *tangomãos*. Color was only one marker of this culture-in-the-

Luso-Africans: Luso- refers to Portugal; from its Latin name, *Lusitania.*

making, and generally the least significant.[17] From common experience, conventions of personal behavior, and cultural sensibilities compounded by shared ostracism and mercantile aspirations, Atlantic creoles acquired interests of their own, apart from their European and African antecedents. Of necessity, Atlantic creoles spoke a variety of African and European languages, weighted strongly toward Portuguese. From the seeming babble emerged a pidgin that enabled Atlantic creoles to communicate widely. In time, their pidgin evolved into creole, borrowing its vocabulary from all parties and creating a grammar unique unto itself. Derisively called *"fala de Guine"* or *"fala de negros"*—"Guinea speech" or "Negro Speech"—by the Portuguese and "black Portuguese" by others, this creole language became the lingua franca of the Atlantic.[18]

Although jaded observers condemned the culture of the enclaves as nothing more than "whoring, drinking, gambling, swearing, fighting, and shouting," Atlantic creoles attended church (usually Catholic), married according to the sacraments, raised children conversant with European norms, and drew a livelihood from their knowledge of the Atlantic commercial economy. In short, they created societies of their own, *of* but not always *in,* the societies of the Africans who dominated the interior trade and the Europeans who controlled the Atlantic trade.

Operating under European protection, always at African sufferance, the enclaves developed governments with a politics as diverse and complicated as the peoples who populated them and a credit system that drew on the commercial centers of both Europe and Africa. Although the trading castles remained under the control of European metropoles, the towns around them often developed independent political lives—separate from both African and European domination. Meanwhile, their presence created political havoc, enabling new men and women of commerce to gain prominence and threatening older, often hereditary elites. Intermarriage with established peoples allowed creoles to construct lineages that gained them full membership in local elites, something that creoles eagerly embraced. The resultant political turmoil promoted state formation along with new class relations and ideologies.[19]

New religious forms emerged and then disappeared in much the same manner, as Europeans and Africans brought to the enclaves not only their commercial and political aspirations but all the trappings of their cultures as well. Priests and ministers sent to tend European souls made African converts, some of whom saw Christianity as both a way to ingratiate themselves with their trading partners and a new truth. Missionaries sped the process of christianization and occasionally scored striking successes. At the beginning of the sixteenth century, the royal house of Kongo converted to Christianity. Catholicism, in various syncretic forms, infiltrated the posts along the Angolan coast and spread northward. Islam filtered in from the north. Whatever the sources of the new religions, most converts saw little cause to surrender their own deities. They incorporated Christianity and Islam to serve their own needs and gave Jesus and Mohammed a place in their spiritual pantheon. New religious practices, polities, and theologies emerged from the mixing of Christianity, Islam, polytheism, and animism. Similar syncretic formations influenced the agricultural practices, architectural forms, and sartorial styles as well as the cuisine, music, art, and technology of the enclaves.[20] Like the stone fortifications, these cultural innovations announced the presence of something new to those arriving on the coast, whether they came by caravan from the African interior or sailed by caravel from the Atlantic.

Outside the European fortifications, settlements—the town of Elmina as opposed to Castle São Jorge da Mina, for example—expanded to provision and refresh the European-controlled castles and the caravels and carracks that frequented the coast. In time, they developed economies of their own, with multifarious systems of social stratification and occupational differentiation. Residents included canoemen who ferried goods between ships and shore; longshoremen and warehousemen who unloaded and stored merchandise; porters, messengers, guides, interpreters, factors, and brokers or *makelaers* (to the Dutch) who facilitated trade; inn keepers who housed country traders; skilled workers of all sorts; and a host of peddlers, hawkers, and petty traders. Others chopped wood, drew water, prepared food, or supplied sex to the lonely men who visited these isolated places. African notables occasionally established residence, bringing with them the trappings of wealth and power: wives, clients, pawns, slaves, and other dependents. In some places, small manufactories grew up, like the salt pans, boatyards, and foundries on the outskirts of Elmina, to supply the town and service the Atlantic trade. In addition, many people lived outside the law; the rough nature and transient population of these crossroads of trade encouraged roguery and brigandage.[21]

Village populations swelled into the thousands. In 1669, about the time the English were ousting the Dutch from the village of New Amsterdam, population 1,500, a visitor to Elmina noted that it contained some 8,000 residents. During most of the eighteenth century, Elmina's population was between 12,000 and 16,000, larger than Charleston, South Carolina—mainland North America's greatest slave port at the time of the American Revolution.[22]

The business of the creole communities was trade, brokering the movement of goods through the Atlantic world. Although island settlements such as Cape Verde, Principé, and São Tomé developed indigenous agricultural and sometimes plantation economies, the comings and goings of

African and European merchants dominated life even in the largest of the creole communities, which served as both field headquarters for great European mercantile companies and collection points for trade between the African interior and the Atlantic littoral. Depending on the location, the exchange involved European textiles, metalware, guns, liquor, and beads for African gold, ivory, hides, pepper, beeswax, and dyewoods. The coastal trade or cabotage added fish, produce, livestock, and other perishables to this list, especially as regional specialization developed. Everywhere, slaves were bought and sold, and over time the importance of commerce-in-persons grew.[23]

As slaving societies, the coastal enclaves were also societies with slaves. African slavery in its various forms—from pawnage to chattel bondage—was practiced in these towns. Both Europeans and Africans held slaves, employed them, used them as collateral, traded them, and sold them to outsiders. At Elmina, the Dutch West India Company owned some 300 slaves in the late seventeenth century, and individual Europeans and Africans held others. Along with slaves appeared the inevitable trappings of slave societies—overseers to supervise slave labor, slave catchers to retrieve runaways, soldiers to keep order and guard against insurrections, and officials to adjudicate and punish transgressions beyond a master's reach. Freedmen and freedwomen, who had somehow escaped bondage, also enjoyed a considerable presence. Many former slaves mixed Africa and Europe culturally and sometimes physically.[24]

Knowledge and experience far more than color set the Atlantic creoles apart from the Africans who brought slaves from the interior and the Europeans who carried them across the Atlantic, on one hand, and the hapless men and women on whose commodification the slave trade rested, on the other. Maintaining a secure place in such a volatile social order was not easy. The creoles' genius for intercultural negotiation was not simply a set of skills, a tactic for survival, or an attribute that emerged as an "Africanism" in the New World. Rather, it was central to a way of life that transcended particular venues.

The names European traders called Atlantic creoles provide a glimpse of the creole's cosmopolitan ability to transcend the confines of particular nations and cultures. Abee Coffu Jantie Seniees, a leading African merchant and politico of Cape Coast on the Gold Coast in the late seventeenth century, appears in various European accounts and account books as "Jan Snees," "Jacque Senece," "Johan Sinesen," and "Jantee Snees." In some measure, the renderings of his name—to view him only from the perspective of European traders—reflect phonic imperialism or, more simply, the variability of transnational spelling. Seniees probably did not know or care how his trading partners registered his name, which he may have employed for commercial reasons in any case. But the diverse renderings reveal something of Abee Coffu Jantie Seniees's ability to trade with the Danes at Fredriksborg, the Dutch at Elmina, and the English at Cape Coast, as well as with Africans deep in the forested interior.[25]

The special needs of European traders placed Atlantic creoles in a powerful bargaining position, which they learned to employ to their own advantage. The most successful became principals and traded independently. They played one merchant against another, one captain against another, and one mercantile bureaucrat against another, often abandoning them for yet a better deal with some interloper, all in the hope of securing a rich prosperity for themselves and their families. Success evoked a sense of confidence that observers described as impertinence, insolence, and arrogance, and it was not limited to the fabulously wealthy like Jantie Seniees or the near sovereign John Claessen (the near-ruler of Fetu), who rejected a kingship to remain at trade, or the merchant princes John Kabes (trader, entrepreneur, and dominant politico in Komenda) and John Konny (commanding ruler in Pokoso).[26] Canoemen, for example, became infamous among European governors and sea captains for their independence. They refused to work in heavy surf, demanded higher wages and additional rations, quit upon insult or abuse, and abandoned work altogether when enslavement threatened. Attempts to control them through regulations issued from Europe or from local corporate headquarters failed utterly. "These canoemen, despicable thieves," sputtered one Englishman in 1711, "think that they are more than just labour."[27]

Like other people in the middle, Atlantic creoles profited from their strategic position. Competition between and among the Africans and European traders bolstered their stock, increased their political leverage, and enabled them to elevate their social standing while fostering solidarity. Creoles' ability to find a place for themselves in the interstices of African and European trade grew rapidly during periods of intense competition among the Portuguese, Dutch, Danes, Swedes, French, and English and an equally diverse set of African nationals.

At the same time and by the same token, the Atlantic creoles' liminality, particularly their lack of identity with any one group, posed numerous dangers. While their middling position made them valuable to African and European traders, it also made them vulnerable: they could be ostracized, scapegoated, and on occasion enslaved. Maintaining their independence amid the shifting alliances between and among Europeans and Africans was always difficult. Inevitably, some failed.

Debt, crime, immortality, or official disfavor could mean enslavement— if not for great men like Jantie Seniees, Claessen, Kabes, or Konny—at least for those on the fringes of the creole community.[28] Placed in captivity,

Atlantic creoles might be exiled anywhere around the Atlantic—to the interior of Africa, the islands along the coast, the European metropoles, or the plantations of the New World. In the seventeenth century and the early part of the eighteenth, most slaves exported from Africa went to the sugar plantations of Brazil and the Antilles. Enslaved Atlantic creoles might be shipped to Pernambuco, Barbados, or Martinique. Transporting them to the expanding centers of New World staple production posed dangers, however, which American planters well understood. The characteristics that distinguished Atlantic creoles—their linguistic dexterity, cultural plasticity, and social agility—were precisely those qualities that the great planters of the New World disdained and feared. For their labor force they desired youth and strength, not experience and sagacity. Indeed, too much knowledge might be subversive to the good order of the plantation. Simply put, men and women who understood the operations of the Atlantic system were too dangerous to be trusted in the human tinderboxes created by the sugar revolution. Thus rejected by the most prosperous New World regimes, Atlantic creoles were frequently exiled to marginal slave societies where would-be slaveowners, unable to compete with the great plantation magnates, snapped up those whom the grandees had disparaged as "refuse" for reasons of age, illness, criminality, or recalcitrance. In the seventeenth century, few New World slave societies were more marginal than those of mainland North America.[29] Liminal peoples were drawn or propelled to marginal societies.

During the seventeenth century and into the eighteenth, the Dutch served as the most important conduit for transporting Atlantic creoles to mainland North America. Through their control of the sea, they dominated the commerce of the Atlantic periphery. Stretching mercantile theory to fit their commercial ambitions, the Dutch traded with all comers, commissioned privateers to raid rival shipping, and dealt openly with pirates. The Dutch West India Company, whose 1621 charter authorized it to trade in both the Americas and west Africa, cast its eye on the lucrative African trade in gold, ivory, copper, and slaves even as it began to barter for furs and pelts in the North Atlantic and for gold and sugar in the South Atlantic. In 1630, the Dutch captured Portuguese *capitanias* in northeastern Brazil, including Pernambuco, the site of the New World's first sugar boom. About the same time, the West India Company established bases in Curaçao and St. Eustatius. To supply their new empire, the Dutch turned to Africa, supplementing their outposts at Mouri on the Gold Coast and Gorée in Senegambia by seizing the Portuguese enclaves of Elmina and Axim in 1637, Luanda and Principé in 1641, and São Tomé in 1647. They then swept the Angolan coast, establishing trading factories at Cabinda, Loango, and Mpinda.[30]

Although ousted from the Gold Coast, the Portuguese never abandoned their foothold in central Africa, and they and their Brazilian successors regrouped and counterattacked. In 1648, the Portuguese recaptured Luanda and forced the Dutch to evacuate Angola. They expelled the Dutch from Pernambuco in 1645 and completed the reconquest of Brazil in 1654.

Still, the short period of Dutch dominance—roughly, 1620 to 1670—had a powerful impact on the Atlantic world. During those years, the Dutch took control of Portuguese enclaves in Africa, introduced their commercial agents, and pressed their case for Dutch culture and Calvinist religion on the ruling Kongolese Catholics and other remnants of Portuguese imperialism. Although unsuccessful for the most part, the Dutch established ties with the Atlantic creoles and preserved these linkages even after the Portuguese reconquest, keeping alive their connections along the African coast and maintaining their position as the most active agents in slavery's transatlantic expansion during the seventeenth century.[31]

The Dutch transported thousands of slaves from Africa to the New World, trading with all parties, sometimes directly, sometimes indirectly through their base in Curaçao. Most of these slaves came from the interior of Angola, but among them were Atlantic creoles whose connections to the Portuguese offended the Dutch. Following the Portuguese restoration, those with ties to the Dutch may have found themselves in similar difficulties. During the Dutch invasions, the subsequent wars, and then civil wars in which the Portuguese and the Dutch fought each other directly and through surrogates, many creoles were clapped into slavery. Others were seized in the Caribbean by Dutch men-of-war, privateers sailing under Dutch letters of marque, and freebooting pirates.[32] While such slaves might be sent anywhere in the Dutch empire between New Netherland and Pernambuco, West India Company officers in New Amsterdam, who at first complained about "refuse" slaves, in time made known their preference for such creoles—deeming "Negroes who had been 12 or 13 years in the West Indies" to be "a better sort of Negroes."[33] A perusal of the names scattered through archival remains of New Netherland reveals something of the nature of this transatlantic transfer: Paulo d'Angola and Anthony Portuguese, Pedro Negretto and Francisco Negro, Simon Congo and Jan Guinea, Van St. Thomas and Francisco Cartagena, Claes de Neger and Assento Angola, and—perhaps most telling—Carla Criole, Jan Creoli, and Christoffel Crioell.[34]

These names trace the tumultuous experience that propelled their owners across the Atlantic and into slavery in the New World. They suggest that whatever tragedy befell them, Atlantic creoles did not arrive in the New World as deracinated chattel stripped of their past and without resources to meet the future. Unlike those who followed them into slavery in succeeding generations, transplanted creoles were not designated by diminutives, tagged with names more akin to barnyard animals, or given the name of an ancient notable or a classical deity. Instead, their names provided concrete evidence that they carried a good deal more than their dignity to the Americas.

To such men and women, New Amsterdam was not radically different from Elmina or Luanda, save for its smaller size and colder climate. A fortified port controlled by the Dutch West India Company, its population was a farrago of petty traders, artisans, merchants, soldiers, and corporate functionaries, all scrambling for status in a frontier milieu that demanded intercultural exchange. On the tip of Manhattan Island, Atlantic creoles rubbed elbows with sailors of various nationalities, Native Americans with diverse tribal allegiances, and pirates and privateers who professed neither nationality nor allegiance. In the absence of a staple crop, their work—building fortifications, hunting and trapping, tending fields and domestic animals, and transporting merchandise of all sorts—did not set them apart from workers of European descent, who often labored alongside them. Such encounters made a working knowledge of the creole tongue as valuable on the North American coast as in Africa. Whereas a later generation of transplanted Africans would be linguistically isolated and de-skilled by the process of enslavement, Atlantic creoles found themselves very much at home in the new environment. Rather than losing their skills, they discovered that the value of their gift for intercultural negotiation appreciated. The transatlantic journey did not break creole communities; it only transported them to other sites.[35]

Along the edges of the North American continent, creoles found slaves' cultural and social marginality an asset. Slaveholders learned that slaves' ability to negotiate with the diverse populace of seventeenth-century North America was as valuable as their labor, perhaps more so. While their owners employed creoles' skills on their own behalf, creoles did the same for themselves, trading their knowledge for a place in the still undefined social order. In 1665, when Jan Angola, accused of stealing wood in New Amsterdam, could not address the court in Dutch, he was ordered to return the following day with "Domingo the Negro as interpreter," an act familiar to Atlantic creoles in Elmina, Lisbon, San Salvador, or Cap Françis.[36]

To be sure, slavery bore heavily on Atlantic creoles in the New World. As in Africa and Europe, it was a system of exploitation, subservience, and debasement that rested on force. Yet Atlantic creoles were familiar with servitude in forms ranging from unbridled exploitation to corporate familialism. They had known free people to be enslaved, and they had known slaves to be liberated; the boundary between slavery and freedom on the African coast was permeable. Servitude generally did not prevent men and women from marrying, acquiring property (slaves included), enjoying a modest prosperity, and eventually being incorporated into the host society; creoles transported across the Atlantic had no reason to suspect they could not do the same in the New World.[37] If the stigma of servitude, physical labor, uncertain lineage, and alien religion stamped them as outsiders, there were many others—men and women of unblemished European pedigree prominent among them—who shared those taints. That black people could and occasionally did hold slaves and servants and employ white people suggested that race—like lineage and religion—was just one of many markers in the social order.

If slavery meant abuse and degradation, the experience of Atlantic creoles provided strategies for limiting such maltreatment—contrary to notions that they were libidinous heathens without family, economy, or society—and even for winning to freedom. Freedom meant not only greater independence but also identification with the larger group. Although the routes to social betterment were many, they generally involved reattachment to a community through the agency of an influential patron or, better yet, an established institution that could broker a slave's incorporation into the larger society.[38] Along the coast of Africa, Atlantic creoles often identified with the appendages of European or African power—be they international mercantile corporations or local chieftains—in hopes of relieving the stigma of otherness—be it enslavement, bastard birth, paganism, or race. They employed this strategy repeatedly in mainland North America, as they tried to hurdle the boundaries of social and cultural difference and establish a place for themselves. By linking themselves to the most important edifices of the nascent European-American societies, Atlantic creoles struggled to become part of a social order where exclusion or otherness—not subordination—posed the greatest dangers. To be inferior within the sharply stratified world of the seventeenth-century Atlantic was understandable by its very ubiquity; to be excluded posed unparalleled dangers.

The black men and women who entered New Netherland between 1626 and the English conquest in 1664 exemplified the ability of people of African descent to integrate themselves into mainland society during the first century of settlement, despite their status as slaves and the contempt of the colony's rulers. Far more than any other mainland colony during the first half of the seventeenth century, New Netherland rested on slave labor. The prosperity of the Dutch metropole and the opportunities presented to ambitious men and women in the far-flung Dutch empire denied New Netherland its share of free Dutch immigrants and limited its access to indentured servants. To populate the colony, the West India Company scoured the Atlantic basin for settlers, recruiting German Lutherans, French Huguenots, and Sephardic Jews. These newcomers did little to meet the colony's need for men and women to work the land, because, as a company officer reported, "agricultural laborers who are conveyed thither at great expense . . . sooner or later apply themselves to trade, and neglect agriculture altogether." Dutch officials concluded that slave labor was an absolute necessity for New Netherland. Although competition for slaves with Dutch outposts in Brazil (whose sugar economy was already drawing slaves from the African interior) placed New Netherland at a disadvantage, authorities in the North American colony imported all the slaves they could, so that in 1640 about 100 blacks lived in New Amsterdam, composing roughly 30 percent of the port's population and a larger portion of the labor force. Their proportion diminished over the course of the seventeenth century but remained substantial. At the time of the English conquest, some 300 slaves composed a fifth of the population of New Amsterdam, giving New Netherland the largest urban slave population on mainland North America.[39]

The diverse needs of the Dutch mercantile economy strengthened the hand of Atlantic creoles in New Netherland during the initial period of settlement. Caring only for short-term profits, the company, the largest slaveholder in the colony, allowed its slaves to live independently and work on their own in return for a stipulated amount of labor and an annual tribute. Company slaves thus enjoyed a large measure of independence, which they used to master the Dutch language, trade freely, accumulate property, identify with Dutch Reformed Christianity, and — most important — establish families. During the first generation, some twenty-five couples took their vows in the Dutch Reformed Church in New Amsterdam. When children arrived, their parents baptized them as well. Participation in the religious life of New Netherland provides but one indicator of how quickly Atlantic creoles mastered the intricacies of life in mainland North America. In 1635, less than ten years after the arrival of the first black people, black New Netherlanders understood enough about the organization of the colony and the operation of the company to travel to the company's headquarters in Holland and petition for wages.[40]

Many slaves gained their freedom. This was not easy in New Netherland, although there was no legal proscription on manumission. Indeed, gaining freedom was nearly impossible for slaves owned privately and difficult even for those owned by the company. The company valued its slaves and was willing to liberate only the elderly, whom it viewed as a liability. Even when manumitting such slaves, the company exacted an annual tribute from adults and retained ownership of their children. The latter practice elicited protests from both blacks and whites in New Amsterdam. The enslavement of black children made "half-freedom," as New Netherland authorities denominated the West India Company's former slaves who were unable to pass their new status to their children, appear no freedom at all.[41]

Manumission in New Netherland was calculated to benefit slave owners, not slaves. Its purposes were to spur slaves to greater exertion and to relieve owners of the cost of supporting elderly slaves. Yet, however compromised the attainment of freedom, slaves did what was necessary to secure it. They accepted the company's terms and agreed to pay its corporate tribute. But they bridled at the fact that their children's status would not follow their own. Half-free blacks pressed the West India Company to make their status hereditary. Hearing rumors that baptism would assure freedom to their children, they pressed their claims to church membership. A Dutch prelate complained of the "worldly and perverse aims" of black people who "wanted nothing else than to deliver their children from bodily slavery, without striving for piety and Christian virtues."[42] Although conversion never guaranteed freedom in New Netherland, many half-free blacks secured their goal. By 1664, at the time of the English conquest, about one black person in five had achieved freedom in New Amsterdam, a proportion never equalled throughout the history of slavery in the American South.[43]

Some free people of African descent prospered. Building on small gifts of land that the West India Company provided as freedom dues, a few entered the landholding class in New Netherland. A small group of former slaves established a community on the outskirts of the Dutch settlement on Manhattan, farmed independently, and sold their produce in the public market. Others purchased farmsteads or were granted land as part of the Dutch effort to populate the city's hinterland. In 1659, the town of Southampton granted "Peeter the Neigro" three acres. Somewhat later John Neiger, who had "set himself up a house in the street" of Easthampton, was given "for his own use a little quantity of land above his house for him to make a yard or garden." On occasion, free blacks employed whites.[44]

By the middle of the seventeenth century, black people participated in almost every aspect of life in New Netherland. They sued and were sued in Dutch courts, married and baptized their children in the Dutch Reformed Church, and fought alongside Dutch militiamen against the colony's enemies. Black men and women—slave as well as free—traded on their own and accumulated property. Black people also began to develop a variety of institutions that reflected their unique experience and served their special needs. Black men and women stood as godparents to each others' children, suggesting close family ties, and rarely called on white people—owners or not—to serve in this capacity. At times, established black families legally adopted orphaned black children, further knitting the black community together in a web of fictive kinship.[45] The patterns of residence, marriage, church membership, and godparentage speak not only to the material success of Atlantic creoles but also to their ability to create a community among themselves.

To be sure, the former slaves' prosperity was precarious at best. As the Dutch transformed their settlement from a string of trading posts to a colony committed to agricultural production, the quality of freedpeople's freedom deteriorated. The Dutch began to import slaves directly from Africa (especially after the Portuguese retook Brazil), and the new arrivals — sold mostly to individual planters rather than to the company — had little chance of securing the advantages earlier enjoyed by the company's slaves.[46]

The freedpeople's social standing eroded more rapidly following the English conquest in 1664, demonstrating the fragility of their freedom in a social order undergirded by racial hostility. Nonetheless, black people continued to enjoy the benefits of the earlier age. They maintained a secure family life, acquired property, and participated as communicants in the Dutch Reformed Church, where they baptized their children in the presence of godparents of their own choosing. When threatened, they took their complaints to court, exhibiting a fine understanding of their legal rights and a steely determination to defend them. Although the proportion of the black population enjoying freedom shrank steadily under English rule, the small free black settlement held its own. Traveling through an area of modest farms on the outskirts of New York City in 1679, a Dutch visitor observed that "upon both sides of this way were many habitations of negroes, mulattoes and whites. These negroes were formerly the property of the (West India) company, but, in consequence of the frequent changes and conquests of the country, they have obtained their freedom and settled themselves down where they thought proper, and thus on this road, where they have ground enough to live on with their families."[47]

Dutch vessels were not the only ones to transport Atlantic creoles from Africa to North America. The French, who began trading on the Windward Coast of Africa soon after the arrival of the Portuguese, did much the same. Just as a creole population grew up around the Portuguese and later Dutch factories at Elmina, Luanda, and São Tomé, so one developed around the French posts on the Senegal River. The Compagnie du Sénégal, the Compagnie des Indes Occidentales, and their successor, the Compagnie des Indes — whose charter, like that of the Dutch West India Company, authorized it to trade in both Africa and the Americas — maintained headquarters at St. Louis with subsidiary outposts at Galam and Fort d'Arguin.[48]

As at Elmina and Luanda, shifting alliances between Africans and Europeans in St. Louis, Galam, and Fort d'Arguin also ensnared Atlantic creoles, who found themselves suddenly enslaved and thrust across the Atlantic. One such man was Samba, a Bambara,[49] who during the 1720s worked for the French as an interpreter—*maître de langue*—at Galam, up the Senegal River from St. Louis. "Samba Bambara"—as he appears in the records—traveled freely along the river between St. Louis, Galam, and Fort d'Arguin. By 1722, he received permission from the Compagnie des Indes for his family to reside in St. Louis. When his wife dishonored him, Samba Bambara called on his corporate employer to exile her from St. Louis and thereby bring order to his domestic life. But despite his reliance on the company, Samba Bambara allegedly joined with African captives in a revolt at Fort d'Arguin, and, when the revolt was quelled, he was enslaved and deported. Significantly, he was not sold to the emerging plantation colony of Saint Domingue, where the sugar revolution stoked a nearly insatiable appetite for slaves. Instead, French officials at St. Louis exiled Samba Bambara to Louisiana, a marginal military outpost far outside the major transatlantic sea lanes and with no staple agricultural economy.[50]

New Orleans on the Mississippi River shared much with St. Louis on the Senegal in the 1720s. As the headquarters of the Compagnie des Indes in mainland North America, the town housed the familiar collection of corporate functionaries, traders, and craftsmen, along with growing numbers of French *engagés** and African slaves. New Orleans was frequented by Indians, whose canoes supplied it much as African canoemen supplied St. Louis. Its taverns and back alley retreats were meeting places for sailors of various nationalities, Canadian *coureurs de bois*,† and soldiers—the latter no more pleased to be stationed on the North American frontier than their counterparts welcomed assignment to an African factory.[51] Indeed, soldiers' status in this rough frontier community differed little from that on the coast of Africa.

In 1720, a French soldier stationed in New Orleans was convicted of theft and sentenced to the lash. A black man wielded the whip. His work was apparently satisfactory, because five years later, Louis Congo, a recently arrived slave then in the service of the Compagnie des Indes, was offered the job. A powerful man, Congo bargained hard before accepting such grisly employment; he demanded freedom for himself and his wife, regular rations, and a plot of land he could cultivate independently. Louisiana's Superior Council balked at these terms, but the colony's attor-

engagés: Indentured servants.
†*coureurs de bois:* Trappers.

ney general urged acceptance, having seen Congo's *"chef d'oeuvre."** Louis Congo gained his freedom and was allowed to live with his wife (although she was not free) on land of his own choosing. His life as Louisiana's executioner was not easy. He was assaulted several times, and he complained that assassins lurked everywhere. But he enjoyed a modest prosperity, and he learned to write, an accomplishment that distinguished him from most inhabitants of eighteenth-century Louisiana.[52]

Suggesting something of the symmetry of the Atlantic world, New Orleans, save for the flora and fauna, was no alien terrain to Samba Bambara or Louis Congo. Despite the long transatlantic journey, once in the New World, they recovered much of what they had lost in the Old, although Samba Bambara never escaped slavery. Like the Atlantic creoles who alighted in New Netherland, Samba Bambara employed on the coast of North America skills he had learned on the coast of Africa; Louis Congo's previous occupation is unknown. Utilizing his knowledge of French, various African languages, and the ubiquitous creole tongue, the rebel regained his position with his old patron, the Compagnie des Indes, this time as an interpreter swearing on the Christian Bible to translate faithfully before Louisiana's Superior Council. Later, he became an overseer on the largest "concession" in the colony, the company's massive plantation across the river from New Orleans.[53] Like his counterparts in New Amsterdam, Samba Bambara succeeded in a rugged frontier slave society by following the familiar lines of patronage to the doorstep of his corporate employer. Although the constraints of slavery eventually turned him against the company on the Mississippi, just as he had turned against it on the Senegal River, his ability to transfer his knowledge and skills from the Old World to the New, despite the weight of enslavement, suggests that the history of Atlantic creoles in New Amsterdam—their ability to escape slavery, form families, secure property, and claim a degree of independence—was no anomaly.

Atlantic creoles such as Paulo d'Angola in New Netherland and Samba Bambara in New Orleans were not the only products of the meeting of Africans and Europeans on the coast of Africa. By the time Europeans began to colonize mainland North America, communities of creoles of African descent similar to those found on the West African *feitorias* had established themselves all along the rim of the Atlantic. In Europe—particularly Portugal and Spain—the number of Atlantic creoles swelled, as trade with Africa increased. By the mid-sixteenth century, some 10,000 black people lived in Lisbon, where they composed about 10 percent of the population. Seville had

*chef d'oeuvre: Literally, "masterpiece"; the term refers to the quality of Congo's work.

a slave population of 6,000 (including a minority of Moors and Moriscos).[54] As the centers of the Iberian slave trade, these cities distributed African slaves throughout Europe.[55]

With the settlement of the New World, Atlantic creoles sprouted in such places as Cap Françis, Cartagena, Havana, Mexico City, and San Salvador. Intimate with the culture of the Atlantic, they could be found speaking pidgin and creole and engaging in a familiar sort of cultural brokerage. Men drawn from these creole communities accompanied Columbus to the New World; others marched with Balboa, Cortés, De Soto, and Pizarro.[56] Some Atlantic creoles crisscrossed the ocean several times, as had Jerónimo, a Wolof slave, who was sold from Lisbon to Cartagena and from Cartagena to Murica, where he was purchased by a churchman who sent him to Valencia. A *"mulâtress"* wife and her three slaves followed her French husband, a gunsmith in the employ of the Compagnie des Indes, from Gorée to Louisiana, when he was deported for criminal activities.[57] Other Atlantic creoles traveled on their own, as sailors and interpreters in both the transatlantic and African trades. Some gained their freedom and mixed with Europeans and Native Americans. Wherever they went, Atlantic creoles extended the use of the distinctive language of the Atlantic, planted the special institutions of the creole community, and propagated their unique outlook. Within the Portuguese and Spanish empires, Atlantic creoles created an intercontinental web of *cofradias* (*confradias* to the Spanish), so that, by the seventeenth century, the network of black religious brotherhoods stretched from Lisbon to São Tomé, Angola, and Brazil.[58] Although no comparable institutional linkages existed in the Anglo- and Franco-American worlds, there were numerous informal connections between black people in New England and Virginia, Louisiana and Saint Domingue. Like their African counterparts, Atlantic creoles of European, South American, and Caribbean origins also found their way to mainland North America, where they became part of black America's charter generations.

The Dutch were the main conduit for carrying such men and women to the North American mainland in the seventeenth century. Juan (Jan, in some accounts) Rodrigues, a sailor of mixed racial ancestry who had shipped from Hispaniola in 1612 on the *Jonge Tobias,* offers another case in point. The ship, one of the several Dutch merchant vessels vying for the North American fur trade before the founding of the Dutch West India Company, anchored in the Hudson River sometime in 1612 and left Rodrigues either as an independent trader or, more likely, as ship's agent. When a rival Dutch ship arrived the following year, Rodrigues promptly shifted his allegiance, informing its captain that, despite his color, "he was a free man." He served his new employer as translator and agent collecting furs from the native population. When the captain of the *Jonge Tobias* returned to the Hudson River, Rodrigues changed his allegiance yet again, only to be denounced as a turncoat and "that black rascal." Barely escaping with his life, he took up residence with some friendly Indians.[59]

Atlantic creoles were among the first black people to enter the Chesapeake region in the early years of the seventeenth century, and they numbered large among the "twenty Negars" the Dutch sold to the English at Jamestown in 1619 as well as those who followed during the next half century.[60] Anthony Johnson, who was probably among the prizes captured by a Dutch ship in the Caribbean, appears to have landed in Jamestown as "Antonio a Negro" soon after the initial purchase. During the next thirty years, Antonio exited servitude, anglicized his name, married, began to farm on his own, and in 1651 received a 250-acre headright. When his Eastern Shore plantation burned to the ground two years later, he petitioned the county court for relief and was granted a substantial reduction of his taxes. His son John did even better than his father, receiving a patent for 550 acres, and another son, Richard, owned a 100-acre estate. Like other men of substance, the Johnsons farmed independently, held slaves, and left their heirs sizable estates. As established members of their communities, they enjoyed rights in common with other free men and frequently employed the law to protect themselves and advance their interests. When a black man claiming his freedom fled Anthony Johnson's plantation and found refuge with a nearby white planter, Johnson took his neighbor to court and won the return of his slave along with damages from the white man.[61]

Landed independence not only afforded free people of African descent legal near-equality in Virginia but also allowed them a wide range of expressions that others termed "arrogance"—the traditional charge against Atlantic creoles. Anthony Johnson exhibited an exalted sense of self when a local notable challenged his industry. Johnson countered with a ringing defense of his independence: "I know myne owne ground and I will worke when I please and play when I please." Johnson also understood that he and other free black men and women were different, and he and his kin openly celebrated those differences. Whereas Antonio a Negro had anglicized the family name, John Johnson—his grandson and a third-generation Virginian—called his own estate "Angola."[62]

The Johnsons were not unique in Virginia. A small community of free people of African descent developed on the Eastern Shore. Their names, like Antonio a Negro's, suggest creole descent: John Francisco, Bashaw Ferdinando (or Farnando), Emanuel Driggus (sometimes Drighouse; probably Rodriggus), Anthony Longo (perhaps Loango), and "Francisco a Negroe" (soon to become Francis, then Frank, Payne and finally Paine).[63]

They, like Antonio, were drawn from the Atlantic littoral and may have spent time in England or New England before reaching the Chesapeake. At least one, "John Phillip, A negro Christened in *England* 12 yeeres since," was a sailor on an English ship that brought a captured Spanish vessel into Jamestown; another, Sebastian Cain or Cane, gained his freedom in Boston, where he had served the merchant Robert Keayne (hence probably his name). Cain also took to the sea as a sailor, but, unlike Phillip, he settled in Virginia as a neighbor, friend, and sometimes kinsman of the Johnsons, Drigguses, and Paynes.[64]

In Virginia, Atlantic creoles ascended the social order and exhibited a sure-handed understanding of Chesapeake social hierarchy and the complex dynamics of patron-client relations. Although still in bondage, they began to acquire the property, skills, and social connections that became their mark throughout the Atlantic world. They worked provision grounds, kept livestock, and traded independently. More important, they found advocates among the propertied classes—often their owners—and identified themselves with the colony's most important institutions, registering their marriages, baptisms, and children's godparents in the Anglican church and their property in the county courthouse. They sued and were sued in local courts and petitioned the colonial legislature and governor. While relations to their well-placed patrons—former masters and mistresses, landlords, and employers—among the colony's elite were important, as in Louisiana, the creoles also established ties among themselves, weaving together a community from among the interconnections of marriage, trade, and friendship. Free blacks testified on each other's behalf, stood as godparents for each other's children, loaned each other small sums, and joined together for after-hours conviviality, creating a community that often expanded to the larger web of interactions among all poor people, regardless of color. According to one historian of black life in seventeenth-century Virginia, "cooperative projects . . . were more likely in relations between colored freedmen and poor whites than were the debtor-creditor, tenant-landlord, or employee-employer relations that linked individuals of both races to members of the planter class."[65] The horizontal ties of class developed alongside the vertical ones of patronage.

Maintaining their standing as property-holding free persons was difficult, and some Atlantic creoles in the Chesapeake, like those in New Netherland, slipped down the social ladder, trapped by legal snares— apprenticeships, tax forfeitures, and bastardy laws—as planters turned from a labor system based on indentured Europeans and Atlantic creoles to raw Africans condemned to perpetual slavery. Anthony Johnson, harassed by white planters, fled his plantation in Virginia to establish the more modest "Tonies Vineyard" in Maryland. But even as they were pushed out, many of the Chesapeake's charter generations continued to elude slavery. Some did well, lubricating the lifts to economic success with their own hard work, their skills in a society that had "an unrelenting demand for artisanal labor," and the assistance of powerful patrons. A few of the landholding free black families on Virginia's Eastern Shore maintained their propertied standing well into the eighteenth century. In 1738, the estate of Emanuel Driggus's grandson—including its slaves—was worth more than those of two-thirds of his white neighbors.[66]

Atlantic creoles also entered the lowcountry of South Carolina and Florida, carried there by the English and Spanish, respectively. Like the great West Indian planters who settled in that "colony of a colony," Atlantic creoles were drawn from Barbados and other Caribbean islands, where a full generation of European and African cohabitation had allowed them to gain a knowledge of European ways. Prior to the sugar revolution, they worked alongside white indentured servants in a variety of enterprises, none of which required the discipline of plantation labor. Like white servants, some exited slavery, as the line between slavery and freedom was open. An Anglican minister who toured the English islands during the 1670s noted that black people spoke English "no worse than the natural born subjects of that Kingdom."[67] Although Atlantic creole culture took a different shape in the Antilles than it did on the periphery of Africa or Europe, it also displayed many of the same characteristics.

On the southern mainland, creoles used their knowledge of the New World and their ability to negotiate between the various Native American nations and South Carolina's European polyglot—English, French Huguenots, Sephardic Jews—to become invaluable as messengers, trappers, and cattle minders. The striking image of slave and master working on opposite sides of a sawbuck suggests the place of blacks during the early years of South Carolina's settlement.[68]

Knowledge of their English captors also provided knowledge of their captors' enemy, some two hundred miles to the South. At every opportunity, Carolina slaves fled to Spanish Florida, where they requested Catholic baptism. Officials at St. Augustine—whose black population was drawn from Spain, Cuba, Hispaniola, and New Spain—celebrated the fugitives' choice of religion and offered sanctuary. They also valued the creoles' knowledge of the countryside, their ability to converse with English, Spanish, and Indians, and their willingness to strike back at their enslavers. Under the Spanish flag, former Carolina slaves raided English settlements at Port Royal and Edisto and liberated even more of their number. As part of the black militia, they, along with other fugitives from Carolina, fought against the English in the Tuscarora and Yamasee wars.[69]

Florida's small black population mushroomed in the late seventeenth and early eighteenth centuries, as the small but steady stream of fugitives grew with the expansion of lowcountry slavery. Slaves from central Africa—generally deemed "Angolans"—numbered large among the new arrivals, as the transatlantic trade carried thousands of Africans directly to the lowlands. Although many were drawn from deep in the interior of Africa, others were Atlantic creoles with experience in the coastal towns of Cabinda, Loango, and Mpinda. Some spoke Portuguese, which, as one Carolinian noted, was "as near Spanish as Scotch is to English," and sub-scribed to an African Catholicism with roots in the fifteenth-century conversion of Kongo's royal house. They knew their catechism, celebrated feasts of Easter and All Saint's Day or Hallowe'en, and recognized Christian saints.

These men and women were particularly attracted to the possibilities of freedom in the Spanish settlements around St. Augustine. They fled from South Carolina in increasing numbers during the 1720s and 1730s, and, in 1739, a group of African slaves—some doubtless drawn from the newcomers—initiated a mass flight. Pursued by South Carolina militia-men, they confronted their owners' soldiers in several pitched battles that became known as the Stono Rebellion.[70] Although most of the Stono rebels were killed or captured, some escaped to Florida, from where it be-came difficult to retrieve them by formal negotiation or by force. The newcomers were quickly integrated into black life in St. Augustine, since they had already been baptized, although they prayed—as one Miguel Domingo informed a Spanish priest—in Kikongo.[71]

Much to the delight of St. Augustine's Spanish rulers, the former Car-olina slaves did more than pray. They fought alongside the Spanish against incursions by English raiders. An edict of the Spanish crown promising "Liberty and Protection" to all slaves who reached St. Augustine boosted the number of fugitives—most from Carolina—especially after reports circulated that the Spanish received runaways "with great Honors" and gave their leaders military commissions and "A Coat Faced with Velvet." In time, Spanish authorities granted freedom to some, but not all, of the black soldiers and their families.[72]

Among the unrewarded was Francisco Menéndez, a veteran of the Ya-masee War and leader of the black militia. Frustrated by the ingratitude of his immediate superiors, Menéndez petitioned the governor of Florida and the bishop of Cuba for his liberty, which he eventually received. In 1738, when a new governor established Gracia Real de Santa Teresa de Mose, a fortified settlement north of St. Augustine, to protect the Spanish capital from the English incursions, he placed Menéndez in charge. Under Captain Menéndez, Mose became the center of black life in colonial Florida and a base from which former slaves—sometimes joined by Indians—raided South Carolina. The success of the black militia in repelling an English attack on Mose in 1740 won Menéndez a special commendation from the governor, who declared that the black captain had "distinguished himself in the establishment, and cultivation of Mose." Not one to lose an opportunity, the newly literate Menéndez promptly requested that the king remunerate him for the "loyalty, zeal and love I have always demonstrated in the royal service" and petitioned for a stipend worthy of a militia captain.[73]

To secure his reward, Menéndez took a commission as a privateer, with hopes of eventually reaching Spain and collecting his royal reward. Instead, a British ship captured the famous "Signior Capitano Francisco." Although stretched out on a cannon and threatened with emasculation for alleged atrocities during the siege of Mose, Menéndez had become too valuable to mutilate. His captors gave him 200 lashes, soaked his wounds in brine, and commended him to a doctor "to take Care of his Sore A-se." Menéndez was then carried before a British admiralty court on New Providence Island, where "this Francisco that Cursed Seed of Cain" was ordered sold into slavery. Even this misadventure hardly slowed the irrepressible Menéndez. By 1752, perhaps ransomed out of bondage, he was back in his old position in Mose.[74]

Meanwhile, members of the fugitive community around St. Augustine entered more fully into the life of the colony as artisans and tradesmen as well as laborers and domestics. They married among themselves, into the Native American population, and with slaves as well, joining as husband and wife before their God and community in the Catholic church. They baptized their children in the same church, choosing godparents from among both the white and black congregants. Like the Atlantic creoles in New Amsterdam about a century earlier, they became skilled in identifying the lever of patronage, in this case royal authority. Declaring themselves "vassals of the king and deserving of royal protection," they continually placed themselves in the forefront of service to the crown with the expectations that their king would protect, if not reward, them. For the most part, they were not disappointed. When Spain turned East Florida over to the British in 1763, black colonists retreated to Cuba with His Majesty's other subjects, where the crown granted them land, tools, a small subsidy, and a slave for each of their leaders.[75]

In the long history of North American slavery, no other cohort of black people survived as well and rose as fast and as high in mainland society as the Atlantic creoles. The experience of the charter generations contrasts markedly with what followed: when the trauma of enslavement, the violence of captivity, the harsh conditions of plantation life left black people unable to reproduce themselves; when the strange language of their enslavers muted the tongues of newly arrived Africans; and when the slaves' skills and knowledge were submerged in the stupefying labor of plantation production. Rather than having to face the likes of Robert Carter and the imposition of planter domination, Paulo d'Angola, Samba Bambara, Juan Rodrigues, Antonio a Negro, and Francisco Menéndez entered a society not markedly different from those they had left.[76] There, in New Netherland, the Chesapeake, Louisiana, and Florida, they made a place for themselves, demonstrating confidence in their abilities to master a world they knew well. Many secured freedom and a modest prosperity, despite the presumption of racial slavery and the contempt of their captors.

The charter generations' experience derived not only from who they were but also from the special circumstances of their arrival. By their very primacy, as members of the first generation of settlers, their experience was unique. While they came as foreigners, they were no more strange to the new land than were those who enslaved them. Indeed, the near simultaneous arrival of migrants from Europe and Africa gave them a shared perspective on the New World. At first, all saw themselves as outsiders. That would change, as European settlers gained dominance, ousted native peoples, and created societies they claimed as their own. As Europeans became European-Americans and then simply Americans, their identification with—and sense of ownership over—mainland society distinguished them from the forced migrants from Africa who continued to arrive as strangers and were defined as permanent outsiders.

The charter generations owed their unique history to more than just the timing of their arrival. Before their historic confrontation with their new owner, the men and women Robert Carter purchased may have spent weeks, even months, packed between the stinking planks of slave ships. Atlantic creoles experienced few of the horrors of the Middle Passage. Rather than arriving in shiploads totaling into the hundreds, Atlantic creoles trickled into the mainland singly, in twos and threes, or by the score. Most were sent in small consignments or were the booty of privateers and pirates. Some found employment as interpreters, sailors, and *grumetes* on the very ships that transported them to the New World.[77] Although transatlantic travel in the seventeenth and eighteenth centuries could be a harrowing experience under the best of circumstances, the profound disruption that left the men and women Carter purchased physically spent and psychologically traumatized was rarely part of the experience of Atlantic creoles.

Most important, Atlantic creoles entered societies-with-slaves, not, as mainland North America would become, slave societies—that is, societies in which the order of the plantation shaped every relationship.[78] In North America—as in Africa—Atlantic creoles were still but one subordinate group in societies in which subordination was the rule. Few who arrived before the plantation system faced the dehumanizing and brutalizing effects of gang labor in societies where slaves had become commodities and nothing more. Indeed, Atlantic creoles often worked alongside their owners, supped at their tables, wore their hand-me-down clothes, and lived in the back rooms and lofts of their houses. Many resided in towns, as did Paulo d'Angola, Samba Bambara, and Francisco Menéndez. The proportion of the mainland's black population living in places such as New Amsterdam, Philadelphia, Charleston, St. Augustine, and New Orleans was probably higher during the first generations of settlement than it would ever be again. Urban slaves, for better or worse, lived and worked in close proximity to their owners. The regimen imposed the heavy burdens of continual surveillance, but the same constant contact prevented their owners from imagining people of African descent to be a special species of beings, an idea that only emerged with the radical separation of master and slave and the creation of the worlds of the Big House and the Quarters. Until then, the open interaction of slave and slaveowner encouraged Atlantic creoles, and others as well, to judge their enslavement by its older meaning, not by its emerging new one.

The possibility of freedom had much the same effect. So long as some black people, no matter how closely identified with slavery, could still wriggle free of bondage and gain an independent place, slavery may have carried the connotation of otherness, debasement, perhaps even transgression, iniquity, and vice, but it was not social death. The success of Atlantic creoles in rising from the bottom of mainland society contradicted the logic of hereditary bondage and suggested that what had been done might be undone.

The rise of plantation slavery left little room for the men and women of the charter generations. Their efforts to secure a place in society were put at risk by the new order, for the triumph of the plantation régime threatened not inequality—which had always been assumed, at least by Europeans—but debasement and permanent ostracism of the sort Robert "King" Carter delivered on that Virginia wharf. With the creation of a world in which peoples of African descent were presumed slaves and those of European descent free, people of color no longer had a place. It became easy to depict black men and women as uncivilized heathens outside the bounds of society or even humanity.[79]

Few Atlantic creoles entered the mainland after the tobacco revolution in the Chesapeake, the rice revolution in lowcountry Carolina, and the sugar revolution in Louisiana. Rather than being drawn from the African littoral, slaves increasingly derived from the African interior. Such men and women possessed little understanding of the larger Atlantic world: no apprenticeship in negotiating with Europeans, no knowledge of Christianity or other touchstone of European culture, no acquaintance with western law, and no open fraternization with sailors and merchants in the Atlantic trade—indeed, no experience with the diseases of the Atlantic to provide a measure of immunity to the deadly microbes that lurked everywhere in the New World. Instead of speaking a pidgin or creole that gave them access to the Atlantic, the later arrivals were separated from their enslavers and often from each other by a dense wall of language. Rather than see their skills and knowledge appreciate in value, they generally discovered that previous experience counted for little on the plantations of the New World. Indeed, the remnants of their African past were immediately expropriated by their new masters.

In the stereotypes that demeaned slaves, European and European-American slaveholders inadvertently recognized the difference between the Atlantic creoles and the men and women who followed them into bondage, revealing how the meaning of race was being transformed with the advent of the plantation. Slaveholders condemned creoles as roguish in the manner of Juan Rodrigues the "black rascal," or arrogant in the manner of Antonio a Negro, who knew his "owne ground," or swaggering in the manner of "Signior Capitano Francisco," who stood his ground against those who threatened his manhood. They rarely used such epithets against the postcreole generations that labored on the great plantations. Instead, slaveholders and their apologists scorned such slaves as crude primitives, devoid of the simple amenities of refined society. The failings of plantation slaves were not those of calculation or arrogance, but of stark ignorance and dense stupidity. Plantation slaves were denounced, not for a desire to convert to Christianity for "worldly and perverse aims" as were the half-free blacks in New Netherland or because they claimed the "True Faith" as did the Carolinians who fled to St. Augustine, but because they knew nothing of the religion, language, law, and social etiquette that Europeans equated with civilization. The unfamiliarity of the post-Atlantic creole cohort with the dynamics of Atlantic life made them easy targets for the slaveholders' ridicule. Like the Virginia planters who slammed Africans for the "gross bestiality and rudeness of their manners," an eighteenth-century chronicler of South Carolina's history declared lowcountry slaves to be "as great strangers to Christianity, and as much under the influence of Pagan darkness, idolatry and superstition, as they were at their first arrival from Africa." Such a charge, whatever its meaning on the great lowcountry rice plantations, could have no relevance to the runaways who sought the True Faith in St. Augustine.[80]

In time, stereotypes made were again remade. During the late eighteenth century, planters and their apologists rethought the meaning of race as more than a century and a half of captivity remolded people of African descent. As a new generation of black people emerged—familiar with the American countryside, fluent in its languages, and conversant in its religions—the stereotype of the artful, smooth-talking slave also appeared. Manipulative to the point of insolence, this new generation of African-Americans peopled the slave quarter, confronted the master on their own terms, and, in the midst of the Revolution, secured freedom. African-Americans reversed the process of enslavement—among other things, taking back the naming process (although not the names) that "King" Carter had usurped.[81]

Their story—whereby Africans became creoles—was a great one and one that Americans would repeat many times in the personages of men as different as David Levinsky, the Godfather, or Kunta Kinte—as greenhorns became natives. Historians, like novelists and film makers, have enjoyed retelling the tale, but in so doing, they lost the story of another founding generation and its transit from immigrant to native. While the fathers (and sometimes the mothers) of European America, whether Puritan divines or Chesapeake adventurers, would be celebrated by their posterity, members of black America's charter generations disappeared into the footnotes of American history. Generations of Americans lived in the shadow of John Winthrop and William Byrd, even Peter Stuyvesant and Jean Baptiste Bienville, but few learned of Paulo d'Angola, Samba Bambara, Juan Rodrigues, Antonio a Negro, and Francisco Menéndez. If Atlantic creoles made any appearance in the textbook histories, it would be as curiosities and exceptions to the normal pattern of American race relations, examples of false starts, mere tokens.

The story of how creoles became Africans was lost in a chronicle that presumed American history always moved in a single direction. The assimilationist ideal could not imagine how the diverse people of the Atlantic could become the sons and daughters of Africa. The possibility that a society-with-slaves was a separate and distinct social formation, not a stage in the development of slave society, was similarly inconceivable in a nation in which wealth and power rested upon plantation slavery.

The causes of creole anonymity ran deep. While Carter initiated newly arrived Africans to the world of the plantation, the descendants of the charter generations struggled to maintain the status they had earlier achieved. To that end, many separated themselves from the mass of Africans on whom the heavy weight of plantation bondage fell. Some fled as a group, as did the creole community in St. Augustine that retreated with the Spanish from Florida to Cuba following the British takeover in 1764.[82]

Others merged with Native American tribes and European-American settlers to create unique biracial and triracial combinations and established separate identities. In the 1660s, the Johnson clan fled Virginia for Maryland, Delaware, and New Jersey. John Johnson and John Johnson, Jr., the son and grandson of Anthony Johnson, took refuge among the Nanticoke Indians and so-called Moors, among whom the Johnson name has loomed large into the twentieth century. Near one Nanticoke settlement in Delaware stands the small village of "Angola," the name of John Johnson's Virginia plantation and perhaps Anthony Johnson's ancestral home. Similar "Indian" tribes could be found scattered throughout the eastern half of the United States, categorized by twentieth-century ethnographers as "tri-racial isolates."[83]

Others moved west to a different kind of autonomy. Scattered throughout the frontier areas of the eighteenth century were handfuls of black people eager to escape the racially divided society of plantation America. White frontiersmen, with little sympathy for the nabobs of the tidewater, sometimes sheltered such black men and women, employing them with no questions asked. People of African descent also found refuge among the frontier banditti, whose interracial character—a "numerous Collection of outcast Mulattoes, Mustees, free Negroes, all Horse-Thieves," by one account—was the subject of constant denunciation by the frontier's aspiring planters.[84]

While some members of the charter generations retreated before the expanding planter class, a few moved toward it. At least one male member of every prominent seventeenth-century free black family on the Eastern Shore of Virginia married a white woman, so the Atlantic creoles' descendants would, perforce, be lighter in color. Whether or not this was a conscious strategy, there remains considerable, if necessarily incomplete, evidence that these light-skinned people employed a portion of their European inheritance—a pale complexion—to pass into white society.[85]

Retreat—geographic, social, and physical—was not the only strategy members of the charter generations adopted in the face of the emergent plantation régime. Some stood their ground, confronting white authorities and perhaps setting an example for those less fortunate than themselves. In 1667, claiming "hee was a Christian and had been severall years in England," a black man named Fernando sued for his freedom in a Virginia court. The case, initiated just as tidewater planters were consolidating their place atop Virginia society, sent Virginia lawmakers into a parox-ysm that culminated in the passage of a new law clarifying the status of black people: they would be slaves for life and their status would be heredi-tary. In succeeding years, such Atlantic creoles—men and women of African descent with long experience in the larger Atlantic world—would continue as Fernando continued to bedevil planters and other white Americans in and out of the court room, harboring runaway slaves, provid-ing them with free papers, and joining together matters slaveholders viewed as subversive. In 1671, New York authorities singled out Domingo and Manuel Angola, warning the public "that the free negroes were from time to time entertaining sundry of the servants and negroes belonging to the Burghers . . . to the great damage of their owners." It appears that the warning did little to limit black people from meeting, for several years later New York's Common Council again complained about "the frequent randivozing of Negro Slaves att the houses of free negroes without the gates hath bin occasion of great disordr." As slaveholders feared, the line between annoyance and subversion was a thin one. Atlantic creoles were among the black servants and slaves who stood with Nathaniel Bacon against royal authority in 1676.[86]

The relentless engine of plantation agriculture and the transformation of the mainland colonies from societies-with-slaves to slave societies sub-merged the charter generations in a régime in which African descent was equated with slavery. For the most part, the descendants of African creoles took their place as slaves alongside newly arrived Africans. Those who maintained their freedom became part of an impoverished free black mi-nority, and those who lost their liberty were swallowed up in an oppressed slave majority.[87] In one way or another, Atlantic creoles were overwhelmed by the power of the plantation order.

Even so, the charter generations' presence was not without substance. During the American Revolution, when divisions within the planter class gave black people fresh opportunities to strike for liberty and equality, long-suppressed memories of the origins of African life on the mainland bubbled to the surface, often in lawsuits in which slaves claimed freedom as a result of descent from a free ancestor, sometimes white, sometimes Indian, sometimes free black, more commonly from some mixture of these elements.[88] The testimony summoned by such legal contests reveals how the hidden history of the charter generations survived the plantation revolution and suggests the mechanisms by which it would be maintained in the centuries that followed. It also reveals how race had been con-structed and reconstructed in mainland North America over the course of two centuries of African and European settlement and how it would be remade.

Notes

1. Carter to Robert Jones, Oct. 10, 1727 [misdated 1717], Oct. 24, 1729, quoted in Lorena S. Walsh, "A 'Place in Time' Regained: A Fuller History of Colonial Chesapeake Slavery through Group Biography," in Larry E. Hudson, Jr., ed., *Working toward Freedom: Slave Society and the Domestic Economy in the American South* (Rochester, N.Y., 1994), 14.

2. For the names of Carter's slaves see the Carter Papers, Alderman Library, University of Virginia, Charlottesville. The naming of Chesapeake slaves is discussed in Allan Kulikoff, *Tobacco and Slaves: The Development of Southern Cultures in the Chesapeake, 1680–1800* (Chapel Hill, 1986), 325–26, and John Thornton, "Central African Names and African-American Naming Patterns," *William and Mary Quarterly*, 3rd Ser., 50 (1993), 727–42. For surnames see Walsh, "A 'Place in Time' Regained," 26–27 n. 18. The pioneering work on this subject is Peter H. Wood, *Black Majority: Negroes in Colonial South Carolina from 1670 through the Stono Rebellion* (New York, 1974), 181–86. Henry Laurens, the great South Carolina slave trader and planter, followed a similar routine in naming his slaves; Philip Morgan, "Three Planters and Their Slaves: Perspectives on Slavery in Virginia, South Carolina, and Jamaica, 1750–1790," in Winthrop D. Jordan and Sheila L. Skemp, eds., *Race and Family in the Colonial South* (Jackson, Miss., 1987), 65.

3. Gerald W. Mullin, *Flight and Rebellion: Slave Resistance in Eighteenth-Century Virginia* (New York, 1972), chaps. 1–3; Kulikoff, *Tobacco and Slaves*, esp. 319–34; Russell R. Menard, "The Maryland Slave Population, 1658 to 1730: A Demographic Profile of Blacks in Four Counties," *WMQ*, 3rd Ser., 32 (1975), 29–54; Lois Green Carr and Walsh, "Economic Diversification and Labor Organization in the Chesapeake, 1650–1820," in Stephen Innes, ed., *Work and Labor in Early America* (Chapel Hill, 1988), 144–88. Quotation in Hugh Jones, *The Present State of Virginia, from Whence Is Inferred a Short View of Maryland and North Carolina*, ed. Richard L. Morton (Chapel Hill, 1956), 36–38, and Philip Alexander Bruce, *Institutional History of Virginia in the Seventeenth Century . . .* , 2 vols. (New York, 1910), 1:9. See a slightly different version in "The Journal of the General Assembly of Virginia," June 2, 1699, in W. N. Sainsbury et al., eds., *Calendar of State Papers, Colonial Series, America and West Indies*, 40 vols. (London, 1860–1969), 17:261.

4. In the summer of 1767, when two slaves escaped from a Georgia plantation, their owner noted that one "calls himself GOLAGA," although "the name given him [was] ABEL," and the other "calls himself ABBROM, the name given him here BENNET." For evidence that the practice had not ended by 1774 see Lathan A. Windley, comp., *Runaway Slave Advertisements: A Documentary History from the 1730s to 1790*, 4 vols. (Westport, Conn., 1983), 4:22 ([*Savannah*] *Georgia Gazette*, June 3, 1767), 62 (ibid., Apr. 19, 1775).

5. "Creole" derives from the Portuguese *crioulo*, meaning a person of African descent born in the New World. It has been extended to native-born free people of many national origins, including both Europeans and Africans, and of diverse social standing. It has also been applied to people of partly European but mixed racial and national origins in various European colonies and to Africans who entered Europe. In the United States, creole has also been specifically applied to people of mixed but usually non-African origins in Louisiana. Staying within the bounds of the broadest definition of creole and the literal definition of African American, I use both terms to refer to black people of native American birth; John

A. Holm, *Pidgins and Creoles: Theory and Structure,* 2 vols. (Cambridge, 1988–1989), 1:9. On the complex and often contradictory usage in a single place see Gwendolyn Midlo Hall, *Africans in Colonial Louisiana: The Development of Afro-Creole Culture in the Eighteenth Century* (Baton Rouge, 1992), 157–59, and Joseph G. Tregle Jr., "On that Word 'Creole' Again: A Note," *Louisiana History,* 23 (1982), 193–98.

6. See, for example, Mullin, *Flight and Rebellion,* and Mullin, *Africa in America: Slave Acculturation and Resistance in the American South and the British Caribbean, 1736–1831* (Urbana, Ill., 1992), 268, which examines the typology of "African" and "creole" from the perspective of resistance. See also the 3 stages of black community development proposed by Kulikoff, "The Origins of Afro-American Society in Tidewater Maryland and Virginia, 1700–1790," *WMQ,* 3rd Ser., 35 (1978), 226–59, esp. 229, and expanded in his *Tobacco and Slaves,* chaps. 8–10. Although the work of Sidney Mintz and Richard Price, which has provided the theoretical backbone for the study of African acculturation in the New World, begins by breaking with models of cultural change associated with "assimilation" and, indeed, all notions of social and cultural change that have a specific end point, it too frames the process as a progression from African to creole; *Anthropological Approach to the Afro-American Past: A Caribbean Perspective,* Institute for the Study of Human Issues Occasional Papers in Social Change (Philadelphia, 1976). Others have followed, including those sensitive to the process of re-Africanization. See, for example, Wood, *Black Majority;* Kulikoff, *Tobacco and Slaves;* Ira Berlin and Ronald Hoffman, eds., *Slavery and Freedom in the Age of Revolution* (Charlottesville, 1983); and Berlin, "Time, Space, and the Evolution of Afro-American Society on British Mainland North America," *American Historical Review,* 85 (1980), 44–78. Thornton's work represents an important theoretical departure. He distinguishes between the African and the Atlantic experiences, maintaining the "Atlantic environment was . . . different from the African one." He extends the Atlantic environment to the African littoral as well as the Americas, in *Africa and Africans in the Making of the Atlantic World, 1440–1680* (Cambridge, 1992), quotation on 211.

7. The use of charter groups draws on T. H. Breen, "Creative Adoptions: Peoples and Cultures," in Jack P. Greene and J. R. Pole, eds., *Colonial British America: Essays in the New History of the Early Modern Era* (Baltimore, 1984), 203–08. Breen, in turn, borrowed the idea from anthropologist John Porter.

8. "Atlantic creole," employed herein, designates those who by experience or choice, as well as by birth, became part of a new culture that emerged along the Atlantic littoral — in Africa, Europe, or the Americas — beginning in the 16th century. It departs from the notion of "creole" that makes birth definitive (see n. 5 above). Circumstances and volition blurred differences between "African" and "creole" as defined only by nativity, if only because Africans and creoles were connected by ties of kinship and friendship. They worked together, played together, intermarried, and on occasion stood together against assaults on their freedom. Even more important, men and women could define themselves in ways that transcended nativity. "African" and "creole" were as much a matter of choice as of birth. The term "Atlantic creole" is designed to capture the cultural transformation that sometimes preceded generational change and sometimes was unaffected by it. Insightful commentary on the process of creolization is provided by Mintz, "The Socio-Historical Background to Pidginization and Creolization," in Dell Hymes, ed., *Pidginization and Creolization of Languages: Proceedings of a Conference Held at the University of the West Indies, Mona, Jamaica, April 1968* (Cambridge, 1971), 481–96.

9. For ground-breaking works that argue for the unity of working peoples in the Atlantic world see Peter Linebaugh, "All the Atlantic Mountains Shook," *Labour/Le Travailleur,* 10 (1982), 82–121, and Linebaugh and Marcus Rediker, "The Many-Headed Hydra: Sailors, Slaves, and the Atlantic Working Class in the Eighteenth Century," *Journal of Historical Sociology,* 3 (1990), 225–52. Thornton, *Africa and Africans in the Making of the Atlantic World,* adopts a similar perspective in viewing the making of African-American culture. A larger Atlantic perspective for the formation of black culture is posed in Paul Gilroy, *The Black Atlantic: Modernity and Double Consciousness* (Cambridge, Mass., 1993).

10. A. C. de C. M. Saunders, *A Social History of Black Slaves and Freedmen in Portugal, 1441–1555* (Cambridge, 1982), 11–12, 145, 197 n. 52, 215 n. 73 (for black sailors and interpreters in the African trade); P. E. H. Hair, "The Use of African Languages in Afro-European Contacts in Guinea, 1440–1560," *Sierra Leone Language Review,* 5 (1966), 7–17 (for black interpreters and Europeans' striking lack of interest in mastering African languages); George E. Brooks, *Landlords and Strangers: Ecology, Society, and Trade in West Africa, 1000–1630* (Boulder, Colo., 1993), chap. 7 (particularly for the role of *grumetes*), 124, 136–37; Wyatt MacGaffey, "Dialogues of the Deaf: Europeans on the Atlantic Coast of Africa," in Stuart B. Schwartz, ed., *Implicit Understandings: Observing, Reporting, and Reflecting on the Encounters between Europeans and Other Peoples in the Early Modern Era* (Cambridge, 1994), 252 (for hostages); Kwame Yeboa Daaku, *Trade and Politics on the Gold Coast, 1600–1720: A Study of the African Reaction to European Trade* (Oxford, 1970), chap. 5, esp. 96–97 (for ambassadors to the United Provinces in 1611); Anne Hilton, *The Kingdom of Kongo* (Oxford, 1985), 64; Paul Edwards and James Walvin, "Africans in Britain, 1500–1800," in Martin L. Kilson and Robert I. Rotberg, eds., *The African Diaspora: Interpretive Essays* (Cambridge, Mass., 1976), 173–205 (for African royalty sending their sons to be educated in Europe). See also Shelby T. McCloy, "Negroes and Mulattoes in Eighteenth-Century France," *Journal of Negro History,* 30 (1945), 276–92. For the near-seamless, reciprocal relationship between the Portuguese and the Kongolese courts in the 16th century see Thornton, "Early Kongo-Portuguese Relations, 1483–1575: A New Interpretation," *History in Africa,* 8 (1981), 183–204.

11. For an overview see Thornton, *Africa and Africans in the Making of the Atlantic World,* chap. 2, esp. 59–62. See also Daaku, *Trade and Politics on the Gold Coast,* chap. 2; Brooks, *Landlords and Strangers,* chaps. 7–8 (see the Portuguese crown's penalties against *lançados* for illegal trading, 152–54); Philip D. Curtin, *Economic Change in Precolonial Africa: Senegambia in the Era of the Slave Trade* (Madison, Wis., 1975), chap. 3; Ray A. Kea, *Settlements, Trade, and Polities in the Seventeenth-Century Gold Coast* (Baltimore, 1982); John Vogt, *Portuguese Rule on the Gold Coast, 1469–1682* (Athens, Ga., 1979); C. R. Boxer, *Four Centuries of Portuguese Expansion, 1415–1825: A Succinct Survey* (Johannesburg, 1961); and Boxer, *The Dutch Seaborne Empire, 1600–1800* (New York, 1965). *Lançados* comes from a contraction of *lançados em terra* (to put on shore); Curtin, *Economic Change in Precolonial Africa,* 95. As the influence of the Atlantic economy spread to the interior, Atlantic creoles appeared in the hinterland, generally in the centers of trade along rivers.

12. Kea, *Settlements, Trade, and Polities,* chap. 1, esp. 38.

13. Ibid.; Vogt, *Portuguese Rule on the Gold Coast;* Harvey M. Feinberg, *Africans and Europeans in West Africa: Elminans and Dutchmen on the Gold Coast during the Eighteenth Century,* American Philosophical Society, *Transactions,* 79, No. 7 (Philadelphia, 1989). For mortality see Curtin, "Epidemiology and the Slave Trade," *Political*

Science Quarterly, 83 (1968), 190–216, and K. G. Davies, "The Living and the Dead: White Mortality in West Africa, 1684–1732," in Stanley L. Engerman and Eugene D. Genovese, eds., *Race and Slavery in the Western Hemisphere: Quantitative Studies* (Princeton, 1975), 83–98.

14. Kea, *Settlements, Trade, and Polities*, chap. 1, esp. 38–50, 133–34; Vogt, *Portuguese Rule on the Gold Coast;* Feinberg, *Africans and Europeans in West Africa.* Eveline C. Martin, *The British West African Settlements, 1750–1821: A Study in Local Administration* (New York, 1927), and Margaret Priestley, *West African Trade and Coast Society: A Family Study* (London, 1969), describe the English enclaves in the 18th and 19th centuries, casting light on their earlier development.

15. Brooks, *Landlords and Strangers*, chaps. 7–9, esp. 188–96, and Brooks, "Luso-African Commerce and Settlement in the Gambia and Guinea-Bissau Region," *Boston University African Studies Center Working Papers* (1980), for the connection of the Luso-Africans with the Cape Verde Islands; Daaku, *Trade and Politics on the Gold Coast*, chaps. 5–6; Vogt, *Portuguese Rule on the Gold Coast*, 154; Feinberg, *Africans and Europeans in West Africa*, 32, 88–90; Curtin, *Economic Change in Precolonial Africa*, 95–100, 113–21 (for Afro-French). For the development of a similar population in Angola see Joseph C. Miller, *Way of Death: Merchant Capitalism and the Angolan Slave Trade, 1730–1830* (Madison, Wis., 1988), esp. chaps. 8–9, and Miller, "A Marginal Institution on the Margin of the Atlantic System: The Portuguese Southern Atlantic Slave Trade in the Eighteenth Century," in Barbara L. Solow, ed., *Slavery and the Rise of the Atlantic System* (Cambridge, Mass., 1991), 125, 128–29. By the mid-17th century, the hierarchy of Kongolese Catholics was largely mixed African and European ancestry or *pombeiros;* Hilton, *Kingdom of Kongo*, 140–41, 154. See also Allen F. Isaacman, *Mozambique: The Africanization of a European Institution: The Zambezi Prazos, 1750–1902* (Madison, Wis., 1972). The number of such individuals in west Africa is difficult to estimate. Brooks, in his study of the Grain Coast and its interior, estimates "hundreds of Portuguese and Cabo Verdean traders were admitted to western African communities by the close of the fifteenth century." Probably the same could be said for other portions of the African coast at that time. By the middle of the 16th century, Atlantic creoles were more numerous. In 1567, when the English adventurer John Hawkins launched a raid on an African settlement on the Cacheu River, he was repulsed by a force that included "about a hundred" *lançados;* Brooks, *Landlords and Strangers,* 137, 230–31. By the 19th century, the Afro-Europeans had become to a "remarkable extent soundly and politically integrated" and "occupied their own 'quarter' of the town" of Elmina; Larry W. Yarak, "West African Coastal Slavery in the Nineteenth Century: The Case of Afro-European Slaveowners of Elmina," *Ethnohistory,* 36 (1989), 44–60, quotation on 47; J. T. Lever, "Mulatto Influence on the Gold Coast in the Early Nineteenth Century: Jan Nieser of Elmina," *African Historical Studies,* 3 (1970), 253–61.

16. Daaku, *Trade and Politics on the Gold Coast*, chaps. 4–5; Brooks, *Landlords and Strangers,* chaps. 7–9, esp. 188–96; Curtin, *Economic Change in Precolonial Africa,* 95–100. See also Miller's compelling description of Angola's Luso-Africans in the 18th and 19th centuries that suggests something of their earlier history, in *Way of Death,* 246–50. Brooks notes the term *tangomãos* passed from use at the end of the 17th century, in "Luso-African Commerce and Settlement in the Gambia and Guinea-Bissau," 3.

17. Speaking of the Afro-French in Senegambia in the 18th century, Curtin emphasizes the cultural transformation in making this new people, noting that "the important characteristic of this community was cultural mixture, not racial mix-

ture, and the most effective of the traders from France were those who could cross the cultural line between Europe and Africa in their commercial relations," in *Economic Change in Precolonial Africa,* 117.

18. Holm, *Pidgins and Creoles;* Thornton, *Africa and Africans in the Making of the Atlantic World,* 213–18; Saunders, *Black Slaves and Freedman in Portugal,* 98–102 (see special word—*ladinhos*—for blacks who could speak "good" Portuguese, 101); Brooks, *Landlords and Strangers,* 136–37. See also Robert A. Hall Jr., *Pidgin and Creole Languages* (Ithaca, 1966); David Dalby, "The Place of Africa and Afro-America in the History of the English Language," *African Language Review,* 9 (1971), 280–98; Hair, "Use of African Languages in Afro-European Contacts in Guinea," 5–26; Keith Whinnom, "Contacts De Langues et Emprunts Lexicaux: The Origin of the European-Based Pidgins and Creoles," *Orbis,* 14 (1965), 509–27, Whinnom, "Linguistic Hybridization and the 'Special Case' of Pidgins and Creoles," in Hymes, ed., *Pidginization and Creolization of Languages,* 91–115, and Whinnom, "The Context and Origins of Lingua Franca," in Jürgen M. Meisel, ed., *Langues en Contact—Pidgins—Creoles* (Tübingen, 1975); and J. L. Dillard, "Creole English and Creole Portuguese: The Early Records," in Ian F. Hancock, ed., *Readings in Creole Studies* (Ghent, 1979), 261–68. For another theory on the origins of the west African pidgin see Anthony J. Naro, "The Origins of West African Pidgin," in Claudia Corum, T. Cedric Smith-Stark, and Ann Weiser, eds., *Papers from the Ninth Regional Meeting,* Chicago Linguistic Society (1973), 442–49.

19. Daaku, *Trade and Politics on the Gold Coast,* chaps. 3–4; Feinberg, *Africans and Europeans in West Africa,* chap. 6, quotation on 86; Kea, *Settlements, Trade, and Polities,* esp. pt. 2; Curtin, *Economic Change in Precolonial Africa,* 92–93.

20. Vogt, *Portuguese Rule on the Gold Coast,* 54–58; Daaku, *Trade and Politics on the Gold Coast,* 99–101; Thornton, "The Development of an African Catholic Church in the Kingdom of Kongo, 1491–1750," *Journal of African History,* 25 (1984), 147–67; Hilton, *Kingdom of Kongo,* 32–49, 154–61, 179, 198; MacGaffey, *Religion and Society in Central Africa: The BaKongo of Lower Zaire* (Chicago, 1986), 191–216, and MacGaffey, "Dialogues of the Deaf," 249–67. Pacing the cultural intermixture of Africa and Europe was the simultaneous introduction of European and American plants and animals, which compounded and legitimated many of the cultural changes; Alfred W. Crosby, *Ecological Imperialism: The Biological Expansion of Europe, 900–1900* (Cambridge, 1986).

21. The history of one element of this population, the canoemen; is discussed in Peter C. W. Gutkind, "The Boatmen of Ghana: The Possibilities of a Pre-Colonial African Labor History," in Michael Hanagan and Charles Stephenson, eds., *Confrontation, Class Consciousness, and the Labor Process: Studies in Proletarian Class Formation* (Westport, Conn., 1986), 123–66, and Gutkind, "Trade and Labor in Early Precolonial African History: The Canoemen of Southern Ghana," in Catherine Coquery-Vidrovitch and Paul E. Lovejoy, eds., *The Workers of African Trade* (Beverly Hills, Calif., 1985), 25–49; Robert Smith, "The Canoe in West African History," *J. African Hist.,* 11 (1970), 515–33; and Robin Law, "Trade and Politics behind the Slave Trade: The Lagoon Traffic and the Rise of Lagos," ibid., 24 (1983), 321–48. See also Daaku, *Trade and Politics on the Gold Coast,* 103–04, 121–22. For an overview of the coastal towns see Kea, *Settlements, Trade, and Polities,* esp. chap. 2; Daaku, *Trade and Politics on the Gold Coast,* chap. 4; and Curtin, *Economic Change in Precolonial Africa,* 119–20, for the relation between European trading communities and African towns. Since Africans would not rent outsiders more land than needed for a house or a store, food production and other services re-

mained in African hands; Brooks, *Landlords and Strangers*, 189–90. For bandits see Kea, "'I Am Here to Plunder on the General Road': Bandits and Banditry in the Pre-Nineteenth Century Gold Coast," in Donald Crummey, ed., *Banditry, Rebellion, and Social Protest in Africa* (London, 1986), 109–32.

22. Feinberg, *Africans and Europeans in West Africa*, 84–85 (for Elmina); Joyce D. Goodfriend, *Before the Melting Pot: Society and Culture in Colonial New York City, 1664–1730* (Princeton, 1992), 13 (for New Amsterdam); Peter A. Coclanis, *The Shadow of a Dream: Economic Life and Death in the South Carolina Low Country, 1670–1920* (New York, 1989), 115 (for Charleston).

23. Kea, *Settlements, Trade, and Polities,* esp. chap. 6.

24. Feinberg, *Africans and Europeans in West Africa,* 65, 82–83; Kea, *Settlements, Trade, and Polities,* 197–202, 289–90. On the Cape Verde Islands, free blacks obtained the right to hold public office in 1546. Racial distinctions did not appear until the emergence of a plantation society in the mid-16th century, when the preoccupation with skin color and hair texture emerged along with racially exclusionary policies; Brooks, *Landlords and Strangers*, 158–59, 186–87; Dierdre Meintel, *Race, Culture, and Portuguese Colonialism in Cabo Verde* (Syracuse, N.Y., 1984), 96–103.

25. Kea, *Settlements, Trade, and Polities,* 233–35, 315–16, 319–20. Daaku notes that "difficulties arise in establishing the exact nationalities" of Gold Coast traders, as European "writers tended to 'Europeanize' the names of some of the Africans with whom they traded and those in their service, while some of the Africans fancifully assumed European names," in *Trade and Politics on the Gold Coast*, 96.

26. Daaku, *Trade and Politics on the Gold Coast,* chaps. 5–6; David Henige, "John Kabes of Komenda: An Early African Entrepreneur and State Builder," *J. African Hist.,* 18 (1977), 1–19.

27. Gutkind, "Boatmen of Ghana," 131–39, quotation on 137, and Gutkind, "Trade and Labor in Early Precolonial African History," 40–41 (for canoemen who pawned themselves and later became successful traders).

28. For enslavement of canoemen for violation of Portuguese regulations see Gutkind, "Trade and Labor in Early Precolonial African History," 27–28, 36. Okoyaw, a canoeman who pawned himself to the Royal African Company in 1704 to redeem a debt, agreed in return "to attend Dayly the Company's Work"; cited in Kea, *Settlements, Trade, and Polities,* 243. Because there was no established system of commercial law, creditors might seize the slaves or even the fellow townsmen of their debtors to satisfy an obligation; Curtin, *Economic Change in Precolonial Africa,* 302–08.

29. The northern North American colonies often received "refuse" slaves. For complaints and appreciations see Goodfriend, "Burghers and Blacks: The Evolution of a Slave Society at New Amsterdam," *New York History,* 59 (1978), 139; Sainsbury et al., eds., *Calendar of State Papers, Colonial Series, 1708–1709,* 24:110; Lorenzo J. Greene, *The Negro in Colonial New England, 1620–1776* (New York, 1942), 35; Jeremias van Rensselaer to Jan Baptist van Rensselaer, ca. 1659, in A.J.F. Van Laer, ed., *Correspondence of Jeremias Van Rensselaer, 1651–1674* (Albany, 1932), 167–68, 175; William D. Pierson, *Black Yankees: The Development of an Afro-American Subculture in Eighteenth-Century New England* (Amherst, Mass., 1988), 4–5; Edgar J. McManus, *Black Bondage in the North* (Syracuse, N.Y., 1973), 18–25, and McManus, *A History of Slavery in New York* (Syracuse, N.Y., 1966), 23–39; James G. Lydon, "New York and the Slave Trade, 1700 to 1774," *WMQ,* 3rd Ser., 35 (1978), 275–79, 281–90; Darold D. Wax, "Negro Imports into Pennsylvania, 1720–1766," *Pennsylvania History,* 32

(1965), 254–87, and Wax, "Preferences for Slaves in Colonial America," *J. Negro Hist.*, 58 (1973), 374–76, 379–87; and Sharon V. Salinger, *"To Serve Well and Faithfully": Labour and Indentured Servitude in Pennsylvania, 1682–1800* (Cambridge, 1987), 75–78.

30. Boxer, *The Dutch in Brazil, 1624–1654* (Oxford, 1957); Johannes Menne Postma, *The Dutch in the Atlantic Slave Trade* (Cambridge, 1990), chaps. 2–3, 8; Cornelis C. Goslinga, *The Dutch in the Caribbean and on the Wild Coast, 1580–1680* (Gainesville, Fla., 1971).

31. Boxer, *Four Centuries of Portuguese Expansion*, 48–51, and Boxer, *Dutch in Brazil;* P. C. Emmer, "The Dutch and the Making of the Second Atlantic System," in Solow, ed., *Slavery and the Rise of the Atlantic System*, 75–96, esp. 83–84; Thornton, *Africa and Africans in the Making of the Atlantic World*, 64–65, 69–77. Albert van Danzig, ed. and trans., *The Dutch and the Guinea Coast, 1674–1742: A Collection of Documents from the General State Archives at the Hague* (Accra, 1978), provides insight into the operation of the Dutch West India Company and the role of the Dutch on the Gold and Slave coasts.

32. Thornton, *The Kingdom of Kongo: Civil War and Transition, 1641–1718* (Madison, Wis., 1983), esp. 72–74, chaps. 6–7 passim; Hilton, *Kingdom of Kongo*, chaps. 6–7; Ernst Van Den Boogaart and Pieter C. Emmer, "The Dutch Participation in the Atlantic Slave Trade, 1596–1650," in Henry A. Gemery and Jan S. Hogendorn, eds., *The Uncommon Market: Essays in the Economic History of the Atlantic Slave Trade* (New York, 1979), 353–71. The best survey of the Dutch trade is Postma, *Dutch in the Atlantic Slave Trade*.

33. Goslinga, *Dutch in the Caribbean and on the Wild Coast;* Van Laer, ed., *Correspondence of Jeremias Van Rensselaer*, 167–68, 175, quotation on 167; Elizabeth Donnan, ed., *Documents Illustrative of the History of the Slave Trade to America*, 4 vols. (Washington, D.C., 1930–1935), 3:421; Goodfriend, "Burghers and Blacks," 139.

34. Names are drawn from E. B. O'Callaghan, comp., *The Documentary History of the State of New-York*, 4 vols. (Albany, 1849–1851); O'Callaghan, ed., *Documents Relative to the Colonial History of the State of New-York*, 15 vols. (Albany, 1853–1887) (hereafter *N. Y. Col. Docs.*); O'Callaghan, comp., *Laws and Ordinances of New Netherland, 1638–1674* (Albany, 1868); O'Callaghan, ed., *Calendar of Historical Manuscripts in the Office of the Secretary of State, 1630–1664* (Albany, 1865); Berthold Fernow, ed., *The Records of New Amsterdam from 1653 to 1674*, 7 vols. (New York, 1897); Fernow, ed., *Minutes of the Orphanmasters Court of New Amsterdam, 1655–1663*, 2 vols. (New York, 1907); Kenneth Scott and Kenn Stryker-Rodda, comps., *New York Historical Manuscripts: Dutch*, vols. 1–4 (Baltimore, 1974–); Charles T. Gehring, ed., *New York Historical Manuscripts: Dutch Land Papers* (Baltimore, 1980); New York Genealogical and Biographical Society, Collections, *Marriages from 1639 to 1801 in the Reformed Dutch Church of New York* (New York, 1890); I. N. Phelps Stokes, *Iconography of Manhattan Island, 1498–1909*, 6 vols. (New York, 1914–1928). A few names suggest the subtle transformation as the Atlantic creoles crossed the ocean and assumed a new identity that was unfamiliar to its hosts. For example, Anthony Jansen of Salee or Van Vaes, a man of tawny complexion— "mulatto," per below—who claimed Moroccan birth, became "Anthony the Turk," perhaps because Turks were considered fierce—as Anthony's litigious history indicates he surely was—but, more important, because he was alien in status and brown in pigment; Leo Hershkowitz, "The Troublesome Turk: An Illustration of Judicial Process in New Amsterdam," *N. Y. Hist.*, 46 (1965), 299–310. But if names of new arrivals in New Netherland reflect their lived experience rather than an owner's designation, they also have nothing

of the ring of Africa: no Quaws, Phibbis, or any of the day names that Africans later carried. Such names would become familiar to northern slaveholders when the slave trade reached into the interior of Africa. In Portugal, the names slaves bore do not seem different from those of native Portuguese; Saunders, *Black Slaves and Freedmen in Portugal,* 89–90. The practice of attaching a national modifier to a given name was employed for others besides Africans. See Edmund S. Morgan, *American Slavery, American Freedom: The Ordeal of Colonial Virginia* (New York, 1975), 153–54.

35. Nothing evidenced the creoles' easy integration into the mainland society better than the number who survived into old age. There are no systematic demographic studies of people of African descent during the first years of settlement, and perhaps because the numbers are so small, there can be none. Nevertheless, "old" or "aged" slaves are encountered again and again, sometimes in descriptions of fugitives, sometimes in the deeds that manumit—i.e., discard—superannuated slaves. Before the end of the 17th century, numbers of black people lived long enough to see their grandchildren.

36. Fernow, ed., *Records of New Amsterdam,* 5:337, cited in Goodfriend, *Before the Melting Pot,* 252 n. 25.

37. Suzanne Miers and Igor Kopytoff, eds., *Slavery in Africa: Historical and Anthropological Perspectives* (Madison, Wis., 1977); Paul E. Lovejoy, *Transformations in Slavery: A History of Slavery in Africa* (Cambridge, 1983); Patrick Manning, *Slavery and African Life: Occidental, Oriental, and African Slave Trades* (Cambridge, 1990); Thornton, *Africa and Africans in the Making of the Atlantic World,* chap 3; Claude Meillassoux, *The Anthropology of Slavery: The Womb of Iron and Gold* (Chicago, 1991); Martin A. Klein, "Introduction: Modern European Expansion and Traditional Servitude in Africa and Asia," in Klein, ed., *Breaking the Chains: Slavery, Bondage, and Emancipation in Modern Africa and Asia* (Madison, Wis., 1993), 3–26; Toyin Falola and Lovejoy, "Pawnship in Historical Perspective," in Falola and Lovejoy, eds., *Pawnship in Africa: Debt Bondage in Historical Perspective* (Boulder, Colo., 1994), 1–26. A dated but still useful critical review of the subject is Frederick Cooper, "The Problem of Slavery in African Studies," *J. African Hist.,* 20 (1979), 103–25.

38. Miers and Kopytoff, eds., *Slavery in Africa,* chap. 1, esp. 17.

39. Goodfriend, *Before the Melting Pot,* 10, chap. 6; Van Den Boogaart, "The Servant Migration to New Netherland, 1624–1664," in Emmer, ed., *Colonialism and Migration: Indentured Labour before and after Slavery* (Dordrecht, 1986), 58; O'Callaghan, ed., *N. Y. Col. Docs.,* 1:154.

40. Goodfriend, *Before the Melting Pot,* chap. 6; Goodfriend, "Burghers and Blacks," 125–44; Goodfriend, "Black Families in New Netherland," *Journal of the Afro-American Historical and Genealogical Society,* 5 (1984), 94–107; Morton Wagman, "Corporate Slavery in New Netherland," *J. Negro Hist.,* 65 (1980), 34–42; McManus, *Slavery in New York,* 2–22; Michael Kammen, *Colonial New York: A History* (New York, 1975), 58–60; Van Den Boogaart, "Servant Migration to New Netherland," 56–59, 65–71; Vivienne L. Kruger, "Born to Run: The Slave Family in Early New York, 1626 to 1827" (Ph.D. diss., Columbia University, 1985), chap. 2, esp. 46–48, chap. 6, esp. 270–77; Oliver A. Rink, *Holland on the Hudson: An Economic and Social History of Dutch New York* (Ithaca, 1986), 161 n. 33. Between 1639 and 1652, marriages recorded in the New Amsterdam Church represented 28% of the marriages recorded in that period—also note one interracial marriage. For baptisms see "Reformed Dutch Church, New York, Baptisms, 1639–1800," New York Genealogical

and Biographical Society, *Collections,* 2 vols. (New York, 1901), 1:10–27, 2:10–38; for the 1635 petition see Stokes, *Iconography of Manhattan Island,* 4:82, and No. 14, Notulen W1635, 1626 (19–11–1635), inv. 1.05.01.01. (Oude), Algemeen Rijksarchief, The Hague. A petition by "five blacks from New Netherland who had come here [Amsterdam]" was referred back to officials in New Netherland. Marcel van der Linden of the International Institute of Social History in Amsterdam kindly located and translated this notation in the records of the Dutch West India Company.

41. Petition for freedom, in O'Callaghan, ed., *Calendar of Historical Manuscripts,* 269. White residents of New Amsterdam protested the enslavement of the children of half-free slaves, holding that no one born of a free person should be a slave. The Dutch West India Company rejected the claim; O'Callaghan, ed., *N. Y. Col. Docs.,* 1:302, 343; O'Callaghan, ed., *Laws and Ordinances of New Netherland,* 4:36–37. For the Dutch West India Company's "setting them free and at liberty, on the same footing as other free people here in New Netherland," although children remained property of the company, see Van Den Boogaart, "Servant Migration to New Netherland," 69–70.

42. For black men paying tribute to purchase their families see O'Callaghan, ed., *Calendar of Historical Manuscripts,* 45, 87, 105; O'Callaghan, ed., *N. Y. Col. Docs.,* 1:343; Goodfriend, "Burghers and Blacks," 125–44, and "Black Families in New Netherlands," 94–107; McManus, *Slavery in New York,* 2–22; Wagman, "Corporate Slavery in New Netherland," 38–39; quotation in Gerald Francis DeJong, "The Dutch Reformed Church and Negro Slavery in Colonial America," *Church History,* 40 (1971), 430; Kruger, "Born to Run," chap. 1, esp. 90–92; Henry B. Hoff, "Frans Abramse Van Salee and His Descendants: A Colonial Black Family in New York and New Jersey," *New York Genealogical and Biographical Register,* 121 (1990), 65–71, 157–61.

43. Goodfriend estimates that 75 of New Amsterdam's 375 blacks were free in 1664, in *Before the Melting Pot,* 61.

44. Kruger, "Born to Run," 50–55, 591–606, tells of the creation of a small class of black landowners as a result of gifts from the Dutch West India Company and direct purchase by the blacks themselves (quotation on 592); Goodfriend, *Before the Melting Pot,* 115–16, 253 n. 36; Peter R. Christoph, "The Freedmen of New Amsterdam," *J. Afro-Amer. Hist. Gen. Soc.,* 5 (1984), 116–17. See also Stokes, *Iconography of Manhattan Island,* 2:302, 4:70–78, 100, 104–06, 120–48, 265–66; Gehring, ed., *New York Historical Manuscripts;* and Van Den Boogaart, "Servant Migration to New Netherland," 56–59, 65–71. For the employment of a white housekeeper by a free black artisan see ibid., 69; Fernow, ed., *Minutes of the Orphanmasters Court,* 2: 46; and Roi Ottley and William J. Weatherby, eds., *The Negro in New York: An Informal Social History* (New York, 1967), 12.

45. O'Callaghan, ed., *Calendar of Historical Manuscripts,* 87, 105, 269 (for manumission, dubbed "half slaves"), 222 (adoption), 269 (land grants). See also Goodfriend, *Before the Melting Pot,* chap. 6, and Fernow, ed., *Records of New Amsterdam from 1653 to 1674,* 3:42, 5, 172, 337–40, 7, 11 (for actions in court); Goodfriend, "Burghers and Blacks," 125–44, and "Black Families in New Netherlands," 94–107; Van Den Boogaart, "Servant Migration to New Netherland," 56–59, 65–71; McManus, *Slavery in New York,* 2–22; DeJong, "Dutch Reformed Church and Negro Slavery in Colonial America," 430; Kruger, "Born to Run," 46–48; 270–78; Hoff, "Frans Abramse Van Salee and His Descendants"; Kammen, *New York,* 58–60. For

blacks using Dutch courts early on see Rink, *Holland on the Hudson*, 160–61 — e.g., in 1638, Anthony Portuguese sued Anthony Jansen for damages done his hog; soon after, one Pedro Negretto claimed back wages. For adoption of a black child by a free black family see Scott and Stryker-Rodda, eds., *The Register of Salmon Lachaire, Notary Public of New Amsterdam, 1661–1662* (Baltimore, 1978), 22–23; O'Callaghan, ed., *Calendar of Historical Manuscripts,* 222, 256; and Kruger, "Born to Run," 44–51.

46. Until New Netherland developed an agricultural base, slavery did not seem to take hold, and settlers admitted in 1649 that slaves imported at great cost "just dripped through the fingers" and "were sold for pork and peas"; O'Callaghan, ed., *N. Y. Col. Docs.,* 1:302. For the change that took place during the 1650s and the beginning of direct African importation in 1655 see O'Callaghan, ed., *Calendar of Historical Manuscripts,* 268, 289, 293, 307, 331. New York sharply limited manumission in 1712. Few slaves were freed before then. One careful enumeration counted 8 manumissions between 1669 and 1712; Kruger, "Born to Run," 593.

47. James B. Bartlett and J. Franklin Jameson, eds., *Journal of Jasper Danckaerts, 1679–1680* (New York, 1913), 65. See also Goodfriend, *Before the Melting Pot,* 115–16 (land). After the English conquest, black people continued to present their children for baptism, although they changed to the Anglican church; ibid., 131.

48. Curtin, *Economic Change in Precolonial Africa,* 104–05, 121–27; Jean Mettas, *Répertoire des Expéditions Négrières Françaises au XVIIIe Siècle,* 2 vols. (Paris, 1984); Marcel Giraud, *A History of French Louisiana: The Reign of Louis XIV, 1698–1715,* trans. Joseph C. Lambert (Baton Rouge, 1974); Hall, *Africans in Colonial Louisiana,* chaps. 2–4. For the French slave trade see Robert Louis Stein, *The French Slave Trade in the Eighteenth Century: An Old Regime Business* (Madison, Wis., 1979).

49. The Bambaras had complex relations with the French. Although many Bambaras — usually captives of the tribe whom the French also deemed Bambaras (although they often were not) — became entrapped in the international slave trade and were sold to the New World, others worked for the French as domestics, boatmen, clerks, and interpreters in the coastal forts and slave factories. Their proud military tradition — honed in a long history of warfare against Mandingas and other Islamic peoples — made them ideal soldiers as well as slave catchers. Along the coast of Africa, "Bambara" became a generic word for soldier; Hall, *Africans in Colonial Louisiana,* 42, and Curtin, *Economic Change in Precolonial Africa,* 115, 143, 149, 178–81, 191–92; see the review of Hall in *Africa,* 64 (1994), 168–71.

50. The evidence of Samba's participation in the Fort D'Arguin insurrection is insubstantial and contradictory, but he got himself into enough trouble to be enslaved and deported; Hall, *Africans in Colonial Louisiana,* 109–10; Le Page du Pratz, *Histoire de la Louisiane,* 3 vols. (Paris, 1758), 3:305–17; Daniel H. Usner Jr., "From African Captivity to American Slavery: The Introduction of Black Laborers to Colonial Louisiana," *La. Hist.,* 20 (1979), 37. On the Afro-French community in St. Louis and other enclaves on the Senegal see Curtin, *Economic Change in Precolonial Africa,* 113–21.

51. The first census of the French settlement of the lower Mississippi Valley comes from Biloxi in 1699. It lists 5 naval officers, 5 petty officers, 4 sailors, 19 Canadians, 10 laborers, 6 cabin boys, and 20 soldiers; Hall, *Africans in Colonial Louisiana,* 3, and esp. chap. 5. Usner makes the point in comparing the use of black sailors on the Mississippi and the Senegal, in "From African Captivity to American Slavery," 25–47, esp. 36, and more generally in *Indians, Settlers, and Slaves*

in a Frontier Exchange Economy: The Lower Mississippi Valley before 1783 (Chapel Hill, 1992). See also James T. McGowan, "Planters without Slaves: Origins of a New World Labor System," *Southern Studies*, 16 (1977), 5–20; John G. Clark, *New Orleans, 1718–1812: An Economic History* (Baton Rouge, 1970), chap. 2; and Thomas N. Ingersoll, "Old New Orleans: Race, Class, Sex, and Order in the Early Deep South, 1718–1819" (Ph.D. diss., University of California at Los Angeles, 1990), chaps. 2–3.

52. Hall, *Africans in Colonial Louisiana*, 131–32.

53. Ibid., 106–12; du Pratz, *Histoire de la Louisiane*, 3:305–17; Usner, "From African Captivity to American Slavery," 37, 42.

54. Charles Verlinden, *The Beginnings of Modern Colonization: Eleven Essays with an Introduction* (Ithaca, 1970), 39–40; Saunders, *Black Slaves and Freedmen in Portugal*, chap. 1, esp. 55; Ruth Pike, "Sevillian Society in the Sixteenth Century: Slaves and Freedmen," *Hispanic American Historical Review*, 47 (1967), 344–59, and Pike, *Aristocrats and Traders: Sevillian Society in the Sixteenth Century* (Ithaca, 1972), 29, 170–92; P.E.H. Hair, "Black African Slaves at Valencia, 1482–1516," *History in Africa*, 7 (1980), 119–31; Thornton, *Africa and Africans in the Making of the Atlantic world*, 96–97; A.J.R. Russell-Wood, "Iberian Expansion and the Issue of Black Slavery: Changing Portuguese Attitudes, 1440–1770," *AHR*, 83 (1978), 20. During the first two decades of the 16th century, about 2,000 African slaves annually entered Lisbon and were sold there. By the 1530s, most slaves brought to Lisbon were sent to the New World via Seville.

55. In the mid-16th century, black people entered the periphery of Europe; Verlinden, *Beginnings of Modern Colonization*, chap 2. England developed a small black population that grew with English involvement in the African trade; see James B. Walvin, *Black and White: The Negro and English Society, 1555–1945* (London, 1973), chap. 1, and F. O. Shyllon, *Black Slaves in Britain* (London, 1974), and *Black People in Britain 1555–1833* (London, 1977). For France see William B. Cohen, *The French Encounter with Africans: White Response to Blacks, 1530–1880* (Bloomington, 1980), and Sue Peabody, "'There Are No Slaves in France': Law, Culture, and Society in Early Modern France, 1685–1789" (Ph.D. diss., University of Iowa, 1993).

56. J. Fred Rippy, "The Negro and the Spanish Pioneer in the New World," *J. Negro Hist.*, 6 (1921), 183–89; Leo Wiener, *Africa and the Discovery of America*, 3 vols. (Philadelphia, 1920–1922).

57. Saunders, *Black Slaves and Freedmen in Portugal*, 29; for sailors see 11, 71–72, 145, and Hall, *Africans in Colonial Louisiana*, 128. A sale of 6 slaves in Mexico in 1554 included one born in the Azores, another born in Portugal, another born in Africa, and the latter's daughter born in Mexico; Colin A. Palmer, *Slaves of the White God: Blacks in Mexico, 1570–1650* (Cambridge, Mass., 1976), 31–32; "Abstracts of French and Spanish Documents Concerning the Early History of Louisiana," *Louisiana Historical Quarterly*, 1 (1917), 111.

58. Saunders, *Black Slaves and Freedmen in Portugal*, 152–55; Russell-Wood, "Black and Mulatto Brotherhoods in Colonial Brazil," *Hisp. Amer. Hist. Rev.*, 54 (1974), 567–602, and Russell-Wood, *The Black Man in Slavery and Freedom in Colonial Brazil* (New York, 1982), chap. 8, esp. 134, 153–54, 159–60. See also Pike, *Aristocrats and Traders*, 177–79. In the 16th century, some 7% (2,580) of Portugal's black population was free; Saunders, *Black Slaves and Freedmen in Portugal*, 59.

59. Simon Hart, *The Prehistory of the New Netherland Company: Amsterdam Notarial Records of the First Dutch Voyages to the Hudson* (Amsterdam, 1959), 23–26, 74–75, quotations on 80–82; Thomas J. Condon, *New York Beginnings: The Commercial Ori-*

gins of New Netherland (New York, 1968), chap. 1, esp. 30; Rink, *Holland on the Hudson,* 34, 42; Van Cleaf Bachman, *Peltries or Plantations: The Economic Policies of the Dutch West India Company in New Netherland, 1623–1639* (Baltimore, 1969), 6–7.

60. Wesley Frank Craven's investigation determined that the first black people to arrive at Jamestown were prizes taken by a Dutch man-of-war in consort with an English ship somewhere in the eastern Caribbean. Craven maintains they were born in the West Indies and stolen from there. J. Douglas Deal suggests they may have been taken from a Portuguese or Spanish slaver. Craven, *White, Red, and Black: The Seventeenth-Century Virginian* (Charlottesville, 1971), 77–81; Deal, *Race and Class in Colonial Virginia: Indians, Englishmen, and Africans on the Eastern Shore during the Seventeenth Century* (New York, 1993), 163–64. In 1708, a Virginia planter remembered "that before the year 1680 what negros were brought to Virginia were imported generally from Barbados for it was very rare to have a Negro ship come to this Country directly from Africa"; Donnan, ed., *Documents Illustrative of the Slave Trade,* 4:89.

61. Anthony Johnson's primacy and "unmatched achievement" have made him and his family the most studied members of the charter generation. The best account of Johnson and his family is found in Deal, *Race and Class in Colonial Virginia,* 217–50. Also useful are T. H. Breen and Stephen Innes, *"Myne Owne Ground": Race and Freedom on Virginia's Eastern Shore, 1640–1676* (New York, 1980), chap. 1; Ross M. Kimmel, "Free Blacks in Seventeenth-Century Maryland," *Maryland Magazine of History,* 71 (1976), 22–25; Alden Vaughan, "Blacks in Virginia: A Note on the First Decade," *WMQ,* 3rd Ser., 29 (1972), 475–76; James H. Brewer, "Negro Property Owners in Seventeenth-Century Virginia," ibid., 12 (1955), 576–78; Susie M. Ames, *Studies of the Virginia Eastern Shore in the Seventeenth Century* (Richmond, 1940), 102–05; John H. Russell, *The Free Negro in Virginia, 1619–1865* (Baltimore, 1913); and Russell, "Colored Freemen as Slave Owners in Virginia," *J. Negro Hist.,* 1 (1916), 233–42. Indirect evidence of the baptism of Johnson's children comes from the 1660s, when John Johnson replied to challenges to his right to testify in court by producing evidence of baptism. He may have been baptized as an adult.

62. Quotation in Breen and Innes, *"Myne Owne Ground,"* 6. The statement is generally attributed to Johnson but may have been uttered by Francis Payne. See Deal, *Race and Class in Colonial Virginia,* 266–67. For John Johnson's Angola see Kimmel, "Free Blacks in Maryland," 23.

63. Deal, *Race and Class in Colonial Virginia,* 205–406, 265–67 (for Payne), 305 n. 2 (for the Driggus name), and Deal, "A Constricted World: Free Blacks on Virginia's Eastern Shore, 1680–1750," in Lois Green Carr, Philip D. Morgan, and Jean B. Russo, eds., *Colonial Chesapeake Society* (Chapel Hill, 1989), 275–305; Breen and Innes, *"Myne Owne Ground,"* esp. chap. 4, 69 (names).

64. The nature of the slave trade in the Chesapeake was summarized by Maryland's governor in 1708: "before the year 1698, this province has been supplyd by some small Quantitys of Negro's from Barbados and other her Ma'tys Islands and Plantations, as Jamaica and New England Seaven, eight, nine or ten in a Sloope, and sometymes larger Quantitys, and sometymes, tho very seldom, whole ship Loads of Slaves have been brought here directly from Affrica by Interlopers, or such as have had Lycenses, or otherwise traded there." Most of the latter had arrived in the previous decade; Donnan, ed., *Documents Illustrative of the Slave Trade,* 4:21–23, 88–90; Menard, "From Servants to Slaves: The Transformation of the Chesapeake Labor System," *Southern Studies,* 16 (1977), 363–67; Deal, *Race and Class in Colonial Virginia,* 164–65; Breen and Innes, *"Myne Owne Ground,"* 70–71.

On Phillip see Robert McColley, "Slavery in Virginia, 1619–1660: A Reexamination," in Robert H. Abzug and Stephen E. Mazlish, eds., *New Perspectives on Race and Slavery in America* (Lexington, Ky., 1986), 15–16, and Vaughan, "Blacks in Virginia," 470; on Cain see Deal, *Race and Class in Colonial Virginia,* 254–55, 317–19, and Robert C. Twombly and Robert H. Moore, "Black Puritan: The Negro in Seventeenth-Century Massachusetts," *WMQ,* 3rd Ser., 24 (1967), 236.

65. Deal, *Race and Class in Colonial Virginia,* 205–405, quotation on 209, and Deal, "A Constricted World," 275–305; Michael L. Nicholls, "Passing Through This Troublesome World: Free Blacks in the Early Southside," *Virginia Magazine of History and Biography,* 92 (1984), 50–70.

66. Deal, *Race and Class in Colonial Virginia,* 225–35, quotation on 208, and Deal, "A Constricted World," 290; Breen and Innes, *"Myne Owne Ground,"* 79–82, 86, 90.

67. Morgan Godwyn, *The Negro's and Indian's Advocate* (London, 1680), 101, quoted in Breen and Innes, *"Myne Owne Ground,"* 70, 130 n. 8.

68. Wood, *Black Majority,* chaps. 1, 4, esp. 97, for a reference to a slave master who "worked many days with a Negro man at the Whip saw." See also Clarence L. Ver Steeg, *Origins of a Southern Mosaic: Studies of Early Carolina and Georgia* (Athens, Ga., 1975), 105–07.

69. Jane Landers, "Spanish Sanctuary: Fugitives in Florida, 1687–1790, *Florida Historical Quarterly,* 62 (1984), 296–302, and Landers, "Gracia Real de Santa Teresa de Mose: A Free Black Town in Spanish Colonial Florida," *AHR,* 95 (1990), 9–30; John J. TePaske, "The Fugitive Slave: Intercolonial Rivalry and Spanish Slave Policy, 1687–1764," in Samuel Proctor, ed., *Eighteenth-Century Florida and Its Borderlands* (Gainesville, 1975), 2–12; I. A. Wright, comp., "Dispatches of Spanish Officials Bearing on the Free Negro Settlement of Gracia Real de Santa Teresa de Mose, Florida," *J. Negro Hist.,* 9 (1924), 144–93, quotation on 150; Zora Neale Hurston, "Letters of Zora Neale Hurston on the Mose Settlement, and Negro Colony in Florida," ibid., 12 (1927), 664–67; J. D. Duncan, "Slavery and Servitude in Colonial South Carolina, 1670–1776" (Ph.D. diss., Emory University, 1964), chap. 17, quotation on 664; and J. G. Dunlop, "William Dunlop's Mission to St. Augustine in 1688," *South Carolina Historical and Genealogical Magazine,* 34 (1933), 1–30. Several of the slaves who rejected freedom and Catholicism in St. Augustine and returned to South Carolina were rewarded with freedom, creating a competition between English and Spanish colonies that redounded to the fugitives' advantage. See Duncan, "Slavery and Servitude in Colonial South Carolina," 381–83.

70. Wood, *Black Majority,* chaps. 11–12; Thornton, "African Dimensions of the Stono Rebellion," *AHR,* 96 (1991), 1101–11, quotation on 1102. Thornton makes a powerful case for the Kongolese origins of the Stono rebels in their military organization and the nature of their resistance. For the pretransfer conversion of slaves from central Africa to Christianity see Thornton, "Development of an African Catholic Church in the Kingdom of Kongo," 147–50, and *Kingdom of Kongo,* 63–68; MacGaffey, *Religion and Society in Central Africa,* 198–211; and Hilton, *Kingdom of Kongo,* 179–98.

71. Thornton, "African Dimensions of the Stono Rebellion," 1107; Landers, "Gracia Real de Santa Teresa de Mose," 27; Michael Mullin, ed., *American Negro Slavery: A Documentary History* (New York, 1976), 84.

72. Landers, "Spanish Sanctuary," 296–302; Landers, "Gracia Real de Santa Teresa de Mose," 9–30; Duncan, "Servitude and Slavery in Colonial South Carolina," chap. 17, quotations on 659, 663.

73. Landers, "Gracia Real de Santa Teresa de Mose," 15–21, quotation on 20; Larry W. Kruger and Robert Hall, "Fort Mose: A Black Fort in Spanish Florida," *The Griot*, 6 (1987), 39–40.

74. Landers, "Gracia Real de Santa Teresa de Mose," 21–22, quotations on 22.

75. Ibid., quotations on 21, 23–30; Theodore G. Corbett, "Population Structure in Hispanic St. Augustine," *Florida Historical Quarterly*, 54 (1976), 265, and "Migration to a Spanish Imperial Frontier in the Seventeenth and Eighteenth Centuries: St. Augustine," *Hisp. Amer. Hist. Rev.*, 54 (1974), 420–21.

76. I have been unable to locate female analogues of Paulo d'Angola, Samba Bambara, Juan Rodrigues, Antonio a Negro, and Francisco Menéndez. Their absence does not, however, reflect the experience of Atlantic creoles, as small shards of evidence indicate that women played central roles in the production of creole culture, the transmission of language, the facilitation of trade, and the accumulation of capital. The best study derives from the 18th century. See George E. Brooks Jr., "The *Signares* of Saint-Louis and Gorée: Women Entrepreneurs in Eighteenth-Century Senegal," in Nancy J. Hafkin and Edna G. Bay, eds., *Women in Africa: Studies in Social and Economic Change* (Stanford, Calif., 1976), 19–44. For an interpretation of 17th-century Chesapeake society that stresses the critical role of women in the shaping of race relations and the emergence of slavery see Kathleen Mary Brown, "Gender and the Genesis of a Race and Class System in Virginia, 1630–1750" (Ph.D. diss., University of Wisconsin, 1990).

77. Writing about the forced transfer of Africans to the New World, W. Jeffrey Bolster observes that "many of the slaves who left Africa with no maritime skills acquired rudimentary ones on the Middle Passage, along with some knowledge of European work-routines and social organization," in *Black Jacks: African-American Seamen in the Atlantic World, 1740–1865* (forthcoming).

78. For a useful distinction between societies with slaves and slave societies see Keith Hopkins, *Conquerors and Slaves: Sociological Studies in Roman History*, 2 vols. (Cambridge, 1978), 1:99, and Moses I. Finley, "Slavery," *International Encyclopedia of the Social Sciences* (New York, 1968), and *Ancient Slavery and Modern Ideology* (New York, 1980), 79–80.

79. Jordan, *White over Black: American Attitudes toward the Negro* (Chapel Hill, 1968), chaps. 1–6, traces the initial appearance of such notions among the transplanted English and their later triumph.

80. Quotations in Bruce, *Institutional History of Virginia in the Seventeenth Century*, 1:9, and Alexander Hewatt, *An Historical Account of the Rise and Progress of the Colonies of South Carolina and Georgia*, 2 vols. (London, 1779), 2:100.

81. Their story is told by Mullin, *Flight and Rebellion*, and *Africa in America*. On renaming see Berlin, *Slaves without Masters: The Free Negro in the Antebellum South* (New York, 1974), 51–52; Gary Nash, *Forging Freedom: The Formation of Philadelphia's Black Community, 1720–1840* (Cambridge, Mass., 1988), 79–88, and "Forging Freedom: The Emancipation Experience in the Northern Seaport Cities, 1775–1820," in Berlin and Hoffman, eds., *Slavery and Freedom in the Age of Revolution*, 20–27; and Cheryll Ann Cody, "Kin and community among the Good Hope People after Emancipation," *Ethnohistory*, 41 (1994), 28–33.

82. Corbett, "Migration to a Spanish Imperial Frontier in the Seventeenth and Eighteenth Centuries," 420; Wilbur H. Siebert, "The Departure of the Spaniards and Other Groups from East Florida, 1763–1764," *Florida Historical Quarterly*, 19 (1940), 146; Robert L. Gold, "The Settlement of the East Florida Spaniards in Cuba, 1763–1766," ibid., 42 (1964), 216–17; Landers, "Gracia Real de Santa Teresa

de Mose," 29. For the northward migration of free people of color from the Chesapeake region see Deal, *Race and Class in Colonial Virginia,* 188.

83. The accepted anthropological designation for the these communities is "tri-racial isolates." Scholars have traced their origins to Virginia and North Carolina in the 17th century and then their expansion into South Carolina, Kentucky, and Tennessee with various branches moving north and south. A recent survey by Virginia Easley DeMarce provides an excellent overview; "'Verry Slitly Mixt': Tri-Racial Isolate Families of the Upper South—A Genealogical Study," *National Genealogical Society Quarterly,* 80 (1992), 5–35.

84. Rachel N. Klein, *Unification of a Slave State: The Rise of the Planter Class in the South Carolina Backcountry, 1760–1808* (Chapel Hill, 1990), 18–21, 62–72.

85. For Johnson's whitening see Deal, *Race and Class in Colonial Virginia,* 258–69, esp. 277. See, for example, the case of Gideon Gibson, a mulatto slave-holder who during the mid-18th century was in the process of transforming himself from "black" to "white," in Jordan, *White over Black,* 171–74; Klein, *Unification of a Slave State,* 69–71; Robert L. Meriwether, *The Expansion of South Carolina, 1729–1765* (Kingsport, Tenn., 1940), 90, 96. As a group, free people of color were getting lighter in the Chesapeake during the late 17th century and into the 18th, perhaps as part of a conscious strategy of successful free men who married white women. See, for example, Deal, *Race and Class in Colonial Virginia,* 187, 276 n. 20, and Berlin, *Slaves without Masters,* 3–4.

86. Quotation from William W. Hening, comp., *The Statutes at Large: Being a Collection of All the Laws of Virginia,* 13 vols. (Richmond, 1800–1823) 2:260; Warren M. Billings, "The Cases of Fernando and Elizabeth Key: A Note on the Status of Blacks in Seventeenth-Century Virginia," *WMQ,* 3rd Ser., 30 (1973), 467–74; Billings, ed., *The Old Dominion in the Seventeenth Century: A Documentary History of Virginia, 1606–1689* (Chapel Hill, 1975), 165–69; David W. Galenson, "Economic Aspects of the Growth of Slavery in the Seventeenth-Century Chesapeake," in Solow, ed., *Slavery and the Rise of the Atlantic System,* 271; Fernow, ed., *Records of New Amsterdam,* 6:146, 286; Herbert L. Osgood, ed., *Minutes of the Common Council of the City of New York,* 8 vols. (New York, 1905), 1:134, 276–77; J. B. Lyon, ed., *Colonial Laws of New York from 1664 to the Revolution,* 5 vols. (Albany, 1894–1896), 1:356–57; Goodfriend, *Before the Melting Pot,* 120–21. After warning Domingo and Manuel Angola not to repeat their behavior, the court ordered them to communicate its admonition to "the other remaining free negroes"; ibid.

87. Goodfriend, *Before the Melting Pot,* 116–17; Nicholls, "Passing Through This Troublesome World," 50–53; Deal, "A Constricted World," 275–305; Breen and Innes, *"Myne Owne Ground,"* chaps. 4–5.

88. Berlin, *Slaves without Masters,* 33–34; Shane White, *Somewhat More Independent: The End of Slavery in New York City, 1770–1810* (Athens, Ga., 1991), 117–18; Nash and Jean R. Soderlund, *Freedom by Degrees: Emancipation in Pennsylvania and Its Aftermath* (New York, 1991), 115–36. Also see the papers of the Pennsylvania Society for Promoting the Abolition of Slavery (Historical Society of Pennsylvania), and the New York Manumission Society (New-York Historical Society), for the upsurge of suits for freedom. For naming patterns within free black families that reached from the Revolutionary era back to the mid-17th century see Deal, *Race and Class in Colonial Virginia,* 342.

2. Who enslaved whom?

Margaret Washington

Gullah Roots

From *"A Peculiar People": Slave Religion and Community-Culture among the Gullahs*

One aspect of the rice-boom slave trade in South Carolina was that masters sought not just African labor but also African knowledge. They drew their slaves from areas that already cultivated rice, in contrast to the deliberate mixing of ethnic and language groups that enslavers practiced elsewhere. These Africans brought their material culture, their language, and their folktales with them and continued to use them all in America. They quickly outnumbered whites, and they put down deep roots in the Carolina and Georgia low country. They became the Gullah people, and the culture they developed still survives. Scholars such as Peter Wood (*Black Majority*, 1974), Daniel C. Littlefield (*Rice and Slaves*, 1981), and Charles Joyner (*Down by the Riverside*, 1984) have explored deep into the Gullah world. More than any other, however, Margaret Washington has linked Gullah culture to what its progenitors brought when they crossed the ocean.

This selection from Washington's study of Gullah religion shows the North American slave trade in full operation. Washington is not content with horror stories or with a simple account of white people victimizing black. She demonstrates how aware enslavers were of the complexities of African life and why white Carolinians wanted particular sorts of Africans. She also explores the raging conflict between Muslim and non-Muslim African people as one source of slaves for the trade in the late seventeenth and early eighteenth centuries. In her view it is not good enough to speak simply in general terms like *Africans* or *black people.* The Africa that appears in her pages is just as complex and turmoil-ridden as the Europe from which white colonists came. Moreover, the slave trade did not begin at the African coast but rather deep inside Africa itself.

Margaret Washington received her Ph.D. from the University of California, Davis, and now teaches at Cornell University. In addition to writing *"A Peculiar People,"* she has appeared in several public television productions about the Gullahs.

Questions for a Closer Reading

1. Why did Carolina planters seek African slaves of particular sorts, rather than just any person who could be put to labor? How much knowledge did they have of different sorts of Africans?

2. What qualities did enslavers not want in Africans? What do these tell us about the enslavers and about the Africans?

3. How did African labor and African culture transform the Carolina coast in the eighteenth century?

4. How did Africans maintain and reproduce their culture in lowland South Carolina?

5. What were the differences among the three "phases" that Washington finds in the South Carolina slave trade? How can these differences be explained?

6. What was the place of Islam's expansion into sub-Saharan Africa in the slave trade?

Gullah Roots

The majority of the tribes of the Upper Guinea Coast were active participants in the Atlantic slave-trade. . . . But the Mandingas, Susus and Fulas stood well to the fore—partly because of their own key role in the slaving operations on the Upper Guinea Coast, and partly because they succeeded in reducing many of the littoral peoples and the inhabitants of the Futa Djalon to a state of vassalage, under the banner of Islam.[1]

But I must own to the shame of my own countrymen, that I was first kidnapped and betrayed by my own complexion, who were the first cause of my exile and slavery; but if there were no buyers there would be no sellers.[2]

Ethnic Origins and Carolina Preferences

European traders divided the African shoreline into Upper and Lower Guinea, although opinions differed on where the division occurred. In this study Upper Guinea refers to the area from the Senegal River north, called the Senegambia, to the Cross River south, termed the Slave Coast. Lower Guinea is south of the Slave Coast, to the Kongo-Angola region. Most Africans imported into South Carolina were taken from trading stations in four areas of the Guinea Coast. From Lower Guinea Africans mainly from the Kongo and Angola region comprised black cargoes destined for Charleston. From Upper Guinea they came from the land between the Senegal and Gambia Rivers, present-day Gambia; from the Windward Coast, now Sierra Leone and Liberia; and from the Gold Coast, presently the Republic of Ghana. Few African ethnic

Margaret Washington, "Gullah Roots," in "A Peculiar People": Slave Religion and Community-Culture among the Gullahs (New York: New York University Press, 1988), 29–44.

groups were spared a tribute to slave coffles.* Yet the littoral of the above areas and inhabitants living about 200 miles inland provided the majority of black cargoes destined for the Carolina coast.[3]

Gold Coast Africans were apparently the first black Carolinians. They were preferred by West Indian adventurers who initially settled Carolina and brought about 1,000 slaves with them. Often referred to as Coromantees (or Kromanti), after the coastal factory from which they were first shipped, most of these Africans, generally Akan and Ashanti peoples, were sold into bondage by powerful, coast-dwelling Fanti. Famous on West Indian plantations for their work habits, efficiency, and strength, Akan-Ashanti groups were also said to possess the haughty spirit that planters associated with rebelliousness. "The Coromantees are not only the best and most faithful of our slaves, but are really born heroes," wrote the governor of the Leeward Islands in 1701. He added that:

> there never was a rascal or coward of that nation, intrepid to the last degree. . . . My father, who had studied the genius and temper of all kinds of negroes for forty-five year . . . would say "no man deserved a Coromantee that would not treat him like a friend rather than a slave."[4]

Men who made voyages to the Guinea Coast concurred with and often fostered attitudes expressed toward Gold Coast Africans. John Atkins, a ship's surgeon, considered himself an "authority" on Africans. "Slaves differ in their goodness," he insisted, maintaining that "those from the Gold Coast are accounted best, being cleanest limbed, and more docile by our Settlements than others." But Atkins cautioned that Akan-Ashanti were also "more prompt to Revenge, and murder the Instruments of their Slavery, and also apter in means to compress it."[5]

Charleston merchants paid particular attention to the source of black cargoes. Although Gold Coast Africans sold at a premium, early Carolinian planters were forced to compete for them with West Indian sugar producers who usually got first choice. Second in favor were Africans from Angola. "We wish therefore you would send either to the Gold Coast or Angola," wrote one Charleston factor. "And there will not be this next Year Insuing Negroes Enough especially Gold Coast and Angola, for the Demand."[6] Peter Wood's study of blacks in colonial South Carolina argues effectively for a preponderance, by 1740, of "salt water" Angolans over other ethnic groups. According to Wood, the 1730s was a time of massive slave importation and low natural increase. Over 50 percent of the slaves had

---

slave coffles: Groups of captured Africans en route to the port of embarkation for America.

been in the colony less than ten years, and approximately 70 percent of the black population was originally from Angola where the trade was mainly conducted by the Portuguese.[7]

The diversity of Portuguese slave-trading policy and their concentration on penetrating Africa's interior partly accounts for a paucity of records on their trade.[8] At any rate studies do indicate that while slave traders were not usually compelled to go into the interior in the eighteenth century, they occasionally went as far as Mozambique, largely by sea. Dieudonne Rinchon, a well-known French scholar and sometimes apologist for the slave trade, provided evidence of the expanse of Portuguese activity:

> Les esclaves exportés sont principalement des Ambundus, (Ovimbundu) des gens de Mbamba et de Mbata, et pour le reste des Nègres due Haute-Congo achetés par les Bamfumgunu et les Bateke du Pool [the Stanley Pool]. Quelques-uns de ces esclaves viennent de fort loin dans l'intérieur. Le capitaine négrier Degrandpré achète à Cabinda une Négresse qui lui paraît assez familière avec les Blancs, ou du moins qui ne témoigne à leur vue ni surprise, ni frayeur; frappé de cette sécurité peu ordinaire, le négrier lui en demande la cause. Elle répond qu'elle a vu précédement des Blancs dans une autre terre, où le soleil se lève dans l'eau, et non comme au Congo où il se cache dans la mer; et elle ajoute en montrant le levant *monizi monambu*, j'ai vu le bord de la mer; elle a été en chemin, *gonda cacata*, beaucoup de lune. Ce récit semble confirmer les dires de Dapper que parfois des esclaves du Mozambique sont vendus au Congo.[9]*

Information provided by Rinchon's informant is supported by recent scholarship. Long-distance trade routes in Central Africa were a direct result of the emergence of Portuguese activity according to Jan Vansina. Trade around the Stanley Pool touched a number of regional water networks. Slave recruitment extended as far as what is now Shaba Province in Zaire. Furthermore, scholars investigating African retentions in Gullah dialect identify Ovimbundu, BaKongo, Mbundu, Mayombe, and others as Bantu-speaking peoples who greatly contributed patterns of speech to the Sea Island patois.

---

*The exported slaves are principally Ambundus (Ovimbundu) of the people of Mbamba and Mbata, and for the remainder they are Negroes of the Upper Congo bought by the Bamfumgunu and the Bateke of the region of the [Stanley] Pool [about two hundred miles from the coast]. Some of these slaves come from very far in the interior. The enslaver captain Degrandpré bought a black woman at Cabinda who appeared to him to be familiar with whites, or at least who gave evidence of neither surprise nor fear. Struck by this extraordinary security, the enslaver asked her the reason. She responded that she had seen whites earlier, in another land, where the sun rises from the water, and not as in the Congo where it hides itself in the sea. And she added in showing it rising *"monizi monambu,* I have seen the seashore." She had journeyed [in her words] *gonda cacata,* [meaning] many months. This tale seems to confirm what Dapper says, that sometimes slaves from Mozambique are sold in the Congo.

With the exception of Mozambique(ans), most of these people lived no more than 200 miles from the Coast.[10]

Ethnic characteristics as perceived by white Carolinians labeled Angolan slaves as "docile" and "comely" but not particularly strong. Hence they supposedly made better house slaves than the presumably more sturdy Gold Coast Africans. Bantu-speaking Africans were also considered especially apt at mechanical arts and trades. Categories related to temperament and labor capability were subjective, having more to do with need than reality. At a time when Carolina's economy was diverse and Africans were engaged in numerous occupations, perceptions may have suited availability. Yet the theory that Africans contributed skill and know-how to Carolina's early economy has much validity. In any case, events leading up to the Stono Rebellion of 1739 caused white Carolinians to alter their attitudes toward their servile population. The Bantu family of Africa was ethnically diverse, and from Angola to Mozambique contained a variety of physical types. Yet they possessed many common customs and values. In Carolina, cultural and linguistic homogeneity, coupled with mounting white repression, inspired a reputedly "docile" people to rebel against the "Instruments of their Slavery." Thus to Kongo-Angolans, Carolinians attributed still another adage — the tendency toward flight and rebellion.[11]

At the time of the Stono Rebellion, there were around 39,000 blacks and 20,000 whites in South Carolina. Fear and anxiety followed the uprising, culminating in a prohibitive duty on slave imports. During this nearly ten-year moratorium the trade was reduced to a mere trickle, bringing to a close what can be considered the first of three phases in the history of the African slave trade to the colony and the state.[12]

Cessation of the transatlantic slave trade found the majority of South Carolina's black laborers, between 80–90 percent, concentrated in parishes closest to Charleston. The sparsely settled Sea Island parish of St. Helena, located on the southern frontier, had only forty-two slaves in 1720. Even by the 1730s when settled parishes were bulging with Africans and rice shifted from a competing export to the primary agricultural concern, growth and settlement of the coastal frontier remained minimal. Given the preponderance of Kongo-Angolans in the slave population, most slaves in the Sea Island region were undoubtedly from this group. St. Helena Parish was close to Spanish territory and possible freedom. It was a congregating area for slaves, and a number of bondsmen from there were known to have been involved in the Stono Rebellion.[13] Naturally, as the Sea Islands developed, planters relied on their supply of country-born and more acculturated Africans to oversee labor operation on frontier plantations. Hence early African cultural influences of Akan-Ashanti and Bantu were present. During the next generation, following the slave trade moratorium, two developments added to African cultural patterns. These dual occurrences encouraged rapid settlement of the islands south of Charleston, and created labor demands that brought a resurgence of African importations, ushering in the second phase of the Carolina trade.

First was the geographical change of rice-producing areas. In the 1750s inland swamps, which since the 1720s had been utilized for rice cultivation, were gradually deserted in favor of tidal and river swamps. These were better suited for growing rice because soil was more fertile and irrigation was more easily conducted. This discovery opened the remaining coastal frontier to settlement. Workers were not only needed for rice cultivation but also to clear away dense woods and growth prior to planting. Memory of the Stono Rebellion notwithstanding, large-scale use of white labor was never seriously considered. Not only was such labor scarce and expensive, but tidal swamps were infested with malaria-carrying mosquitos, and the summers there were so hot and unhealthy that whites convinced themselves they could not endure such conditions.[14] Rather than relinquish dependency on African workers, South Carolinians altered their ethnic preferences.

The second factor responsible for renewed interest in forced black labor was the cultivation of indigo in the Sea Islands. Great Britain needed large quantities of indigo for its textile industry and encouraged indigo production in the colony. But despite the prospect of a guaranteed market, and even though indigo was found growing in a wild state in Carolina, no commercial possibilities were realized until 1748. The change was precipitated by a young Sea Island woman, Eliza Lucas (later Eliza Lucas Pinckney), who from 1742 to 1744 engaged in a series of experiments. She crossbred and developed the plant through seed selection and from a West Indian indigo maker learned the difficult process of properly extracting dye from the plant. Indigo grew well in the Sea Islands and soon became the most favored commodity with the British government. Next to rice, indigo was also the most bountiful source of wealth in the province, laying the foundation for many Sea Island fortunes while further enriching British textile capitalists. Commodity output of rice and indigo during this period of economic advancement was matched by heavy African importation. From 1740 to the eve of the War for Independence, South Carolina imported over 50,000 Africans into the colony.[15] This middle period of the slave trade provided the Sea Island region with numerically dominant African ethnic groups who strongly impacted Gullah religious culture and communal organization.

Strong preferences and equally fervent disdain for certain Africans continued to dominate Carolinian rationale, but Kongo-Angolans were no longer considered desirable. Instead, Africans from Senegambia were put on a par with those of the Gold Coast. Newspaper advertisements and private correspondence provide insight into this preference. The most influential Charleston factor was Henry Laurens. Carolina-born and British-educated, Laurens established himself as a successful merchant and planter in his early twenties. Laurens was a "particular friend" of Richard Oswald, a wealthy British merchant. Oswald owned the British slave factory on Bance Island in the Sierra Leone River. During the middle period of the trade (1750–1787), Laurens handled Oswald's Sierra Leone cargoes in Charleston for a 10 percent commission. Laurens was careful and methodical in preserving communications. His records reveal a sense of prevailing attitudes toward African origins. In one correspondence, Laurens urged a West Indian associate to send portions of his cargoes to Carolina where Africans who were "healthy and in good flesh would find a ready market." Laurens cautioned, however, that the quality of the slaves should be high, at least two-thirds of them men eighteen to twenty-five years of age and that "there must not be a Callabar (Igbo) amongst them. Gold Coast and Gambia are best, next to them the Windward Coast are preferred to Angolas. . . . Pray observe that our people like tall slaves best for our business and strong withal."[16]

Cargoes from the Slave Coast (Dahomey and the Ivory Coast) were rarely noted by Laurens or mentioned in newspaper advertisements. When ships from these areas did arrive, an explanation in the announcement was called for: "Just arrived in the ship Marlborough . . . 300 Negroes, directly from Whydah, a country greatly preferred to any other thru-out the West Indies and inferior to none on the Coast of Africa."[17]

Callabar Africans were shunned by Carolinians and consistently rejected by Laurens. "Callabar slaves won't go down when others can be had," Laurens warned a British merchant in 1755. That same year he also wrote to another correspondent discussing the deplorable conditions of the trade for Carolina merchants competing for Africans with West Indian planters. He asked for "stout healthy fellows . . . the country is not material if they are not from Callabar which slaves are quite out of repute from numbers in every cargo that have been sold with us destroying themselves."[18]

Among the many judgments Carolinians made about African ethnic groups—from supposed suicidal and melancholy tendencies of Callabars to the height and strength of Senegambians, one characteristic predominated: the desirability of purchasing slaves familiar with rice cultivation. Upper Guinea and especially Senegambia was visited by Europeans before North American settlement. Some Europeans settled on African coasts and along rivers leading inland. Daniel Littlefield has made a strong case for colonial Carolina preference being based on Africans' knowledge of rice cultivation.[19]

Early explorers were impressed with Upper Guinea Africans' knowledge of grain cultivation, particularly their rice staple. In the Gambia region,

Africans engaged in large-scale planting operations of corn, pepper, grains, and nuts, as well as "superior" cotton and indigo. Present-day Liberia was first called the Malaguetta Coast by the Portuguese because the Africans there cultivated Malaguetta pepper. This pepper supposedly prevented dysentery and was used to season food given to Africans during the journey to America known as the Middle Passage. Later the name Malaguetta Coast was dropped and the term Grain Coast was adopted. Before the end of the eighteenth century the Grain Coast was synonomous with rice producing and referred to as the Rice Coast. Following establishment of the slave trade, some Africans shipped to America had been employed previously at slave factories or in the homes of English businessmen residing on the coasts. These "castle slaves" were often skilled in trades and housekeeping, some even having knowledge of English. A Charleston newspaper provides an example:

> 230 choice Negroes . . . just arrived from Gambia . . . in perfect health, and have been inoculated for the smallpox on the coast. Among them are 20 young men and women with their children in families late servants of a person leaving Gambia R. Most of them can talk English and have been used to attend in a house and go in a craft, who will be kept separate in the yard.[20]

Of course most Africans possessed no rudimentary English and had no experience with white society. Their value was a long familiarity with planting and cultivation of rice and indigo, the quality of which was said to have surpassed that grown in Carolina. This meant that an extensive "breaking in" period and close agricultural supervision of "new" Africans was minimal. Thus while Upper Guinea Africans may have been preferred because they were tall and considered more manageable, evidence also suggests a more sound explanation: knowledge of agriculture made these Africans particularly sought after in coastal Carolina.

Hence, the middle period of the slave trade to Carolina which corresponds to the last half of the eighteenth century, is significant for obtaining additional impressions of African provenance in the coastal and Sea Island region, since this time span corresponded with vigorous economic growth in those areas. Aside from records left by merchants and factors, advertisements in the *South Carolina Gazette,* which, beginning in 1732, is an almost unbroken newspaper file, provide information on the trade. Announcements such as the following from 1756 usually mentioned and frequently emphasized the origin of cargoes:

> To be Sold: on Wednesday . . . a cargo of fine Slaves just arrived in the ship St. Andrew . . . directly from the River Gambia [Wolof, Serer, Mandingo, etc.]; they are perfectly healthy, and have been so the whole passage.

Negroes chiefly from the same country as those which are brought from the River Gambia . . . from the factory in Sierra Leone [Mende, Temne, Vai, etc.] on the Windward Coast of Guiney, where said cargo was picked out of a large parcel.[21]

In the early nineteenth century the South Carolina up-country engaged in large-scale production of short staple cotton, creating a renewed demand for slaves. This brought on the third and final phase of African trading, from 1804 to 1808. The Kongo-Angola area mainly supplied up-country plantations as well as plantations in other states that refused to import. Percentage-wise then, Bantu-speaking peoples apparently comprised the majority of Africans imported to South Carolina. Yet it has generally gone unnoticed that Upper Guinea contributed heavily to the slave populations of the Sea Islands and surrounding coast. Africans of Senegambia figured most prominently in the slave trade to South Carolina prior to and immediately after the War for Independence. Closely following in imports were those of the Windward Coast. Together these two regions' captured inhabitants comprised a large majority of Africans brought to South Carolina even if we make allowances for the fact that Angolan ships were sometimes larger and sometimes brought more Africans to America.[22]

Thus, the middle period of the slave trade represented expanded economic enterprise in the Sea Islands where indigo dominated, and in the hinterlands where rice was almost exclusively cultivated. Africans brought into these areas where chiefly ethnic groups of Upper Guinea and were victims of the "holy war" conducted by Moslem Mandinga, Susu, and Fula peoples.

Moslem Jihad and Ethnic Displacement

European demand for slaves exacerbated a process of ethnic displacement already occurring in Upper Guinea. The mountains of the Futa Djalon were a transitional point between Islamic Western Sudan and the Upper Guinea Coast. The Futa Djalon massif was an irregular triangle, the base of which began at the Upper Gambia River with the apex extending just north of present-day Sierra Leone. Mountainous country extended south of the Futa Djalon so that a continuous range provided a watershed from which a number of Upper Guinea rivers flowed, including the Senegal and the Niger. Previous to European coastal contact, migration, population displacement, and assimilation, mostly the result of efforts to spread Islam, affected geographical ethnic groupings and patterns. Moslem Fula, Susu, and Mandingas occupied the Futa Djalon with some non-Moslem ethnic groups, while other Sudanic groups continued west, settling beside peoples already inhabiting the coast. By the time of Portuguese contact, non-Moslem coastal peoples were virtually surrounded as well as somewhat infiltrated by a large semicircle of Moslem traders with a number of hinterland groups sandwiched in between (in the rain-forest regions).[23]

In Senegambia Mandingas were the most powerful if not most numerous ethnic group and the first to meet Portuguese seamen in the fifteenth century. Hence they began the barter in slaves, gold, and ivory in exchange for European goods. So-called pagans were the first victims of the trade. By the time of British presence in the Gambia region, victims included littoral groups such as Wolofs and to a far greater extent, Djolas. Other smaller, inland non-Moslem ethnic peoples such as the Patcharis in the Middle Gambia Valley, Baasaris in the Upper Valley, and Bambaras were also mentioned in chronicles as contributing to slave coffles. In the seventeenth century the Wolof kingdom was located between the Senegal River south to the Gambia River and extended inland. By the eighteenth century some Wolof leadership accepted Islam while the common people continued their traditional beliefs. Djolas were independent longtime residents of the coastal areas between the Gambia and Cassamance Rivers and their communities spread a distance of one hundred miles inland. Even at the leadership level Djolas physically resisted Mandinga dominance and Islamic religion. They were also among the few groups who refused to be predatory participants in the Atlantic slave trade. Djolas' simple manners and customs, loose tribal organization, and decentralized government made them easy prey for the European-backed, domineering, highly politically structured Moslem Mandingas. Thousands of Djolas filled the holds of British slave ships. Fulani inhabitants of the Gambia were, like Mandingas, followers of the Koran and by the sixteenth century were vassals of the latter. They planted crops, tended Mandinga cattle, leased their territory, and occasionally joined Mandinga merchants in wars against ethnic groups to procure slaves. Mandinga-Fulani interdependency probably goes farther than common religious ties to explain why large numbers of Fulani were not sold into slavery as compared with Djolas and Wolofs. Another large ethnic group of the Senegambia was the Seraculeh. They were actually a northern branch of Mandingas who engaged in slaving in the Upper River Division of the Gambia Valley.[24]

Besides obeying the Koran's edict to make war on "non-believers," black Muslim traders followed a custom of general acquisitiveness stimulated by European labor demands. Moslem Africans were enslaved for petty as well as major crimes and offenses. Walter Rodney has maintained that prior to the Atlantic trade most crimes were punishable by fines and few groups practiced capital punishment. The slave trade heightened rivalries and intensified a pattern of class exploitation.[25] This insight is supported by Francis Moore, a contemporary observer who remained on the Gambia River from 1730 to 1735. Moore noted that some Mandinga merchants journeyed inland and might not return with slaves for twenty days. But in referring to the littoral trade he observed:

> Besides the slaves which merchants bring down, there are many bought along the river. These are either taken in war, as the former are, or else men condemned for crimes, or else stolen, which is very frequent. . . . Since this slave trade has been us'd all punishments are changed into slavery; there being an Advantage on such condemnations, they strain for crimes very hard . . . every trifling crime is punished in the same manner.[26]

Rulers and elites perpetrated the trade against the general population, often whether Islam was professed or not. Occasionally mistakes were made and a noble would be enslaved, as in the case of Job ben Solomon. He was a wealthy Fula of the Gambia region who crossed the river with a coffle of slaves that he intended to sell for his father. Ben Solomon was caught by Mandinga merchants and sold to a Captain Pike of the ship *Arabella,* the same person with whom ben Solomon had bartered for his slaves, although the two could not agree on a price. Job ben Solomon attracted attention in America because of his noble birth and knowledge of Arabic. He was sent to England and later returned to his native Gambia. Europeans made every effort to rectify such situations before the Middle Passage, if a local nobleman inadvertently fell into their hands. Fear of retaliation on the part of the black elite and a desire to protect trading interests dictated this policy.[27] Thus while Djolas, Wolofs, and smaller non-Moslem groups figured most heavily in the Senegambia slave trade during the eighteenth century, all of the major tribes of the region were represented in the slave marts.

In the Sierra Leone littoral, the Temne and Bullom were the largest and most powerful ethnic groups by the sixteenth century. Other peoples included the Baga and the Lokko. Moslems did not wield political or military dominance in this area of the coast in the sixteenth century. However, Portuguese arrival encouraged Moslem Susu and Fula to move closer to the sea. Most of this penetration was peaceful but at times conflicts flared and captives were sold to slaving captains. By the mid eighteenth century, the Susu had carved out a seaway at the expense of the Baga and rivaled Mandinga activity in the Upper Guinea trade.[28]

In the seventeenth century a new wave of Fulani and Mandinga Muslims began settling in the mountainous regions of Sierra Leone, intermingling with non-Moslem Susu and Fula. Initial peaceful contact gave way to violence and the invaders launched the Jihad of the Futa Djalon in 1726, pushing converted and non-converted Susu and their ethnic kinspeople, the Djalonkes, south and west. Hence on the coast, Susu presence was enhanced and speeded up by the coming of refugees from the Jihad, and Islam made inroads among the littoral ruling groups. The Futa Djalon refugees encroached upon the indigenous peoples and sold these "war" captives in the slave trade. The Mandinga contingent, interested primarily in slaves but dispersing their knowledge of Islam as well, backed Fula Moslems who were thrusting singly and in groups from the interior. The victims of Moslem Fula, Mandinga, and Susu traders were primarily the Limba, Lokko, and Gizzi; secondarily, the Kono and Kuranko. But Moslem forces also came to dominate the coastal Baga, Temne, and Bullom. Ultimately an Islamic base was established among the upper class and the Jihad of the sword was rarely necessary against them. Hence harrassment of the common people was practiced on both sides. Bullom and Temne often worked with Susu and Fula traders in supplying their own people, and placing Moslems in positions of authority and influence. Ruling groups became ideologically if not ethnically homogenous.[29]

The result of the Jihad was a "prodigious" trade in slaves in the last half of the seventeenth century. Despite interruptions of the trade to North America caused first by European wars and later by the War for Independence, British and Yankee captains supplied Carolina planters with a large number of "war captives" from factories on the Sierra Leone littoral. While their numbers did not compare with those taken from the Gold Coast by the British, the latter were primarily destined for the West Indies. The Jihad largely created the "startling activity" of slaving on the Upper Guinea coast.[30] It also coincided with coastal Carolina's agricultural expansion and renewed labor demands peopling the Sea Island region with Africans from a common cultural circle.

Another large ethnic group falling within the present geographical boundaries of Sierra Leone and also heavily engaged in the slave trade was the Mende people. Mende were of Mandinga stock but not followers of Islam during the era of the Atlantic trade. They were a warlike people, pushing into occupied territories, killing local rulers, and enslaving villagers. In the eighteenth century Mende occupied a large section of the Sherbro hinterland. Although they remained inland throughout most of the slave-trading period, Mende traders frequented the coast. The Mende preyed upon some of the same groups victimized by Moslem traders. But they also spread havoc and influence into the hinterlands of the Malaguetta Coast, a present-day Liberia. There they sought slaves for European traders and for their own society which was dominated by this type of labor.[31]

Pre-European history of ethnic populations of the Malaguetta or Windward Coast has been largely overshadowed by the long, unsettling presence of black American colonizers since the beginning of the nineteenth century. Yet during the time of South Carolina's coastal expansion slave trading in this region was brisk. Linguistically speaking, people of the region, now called Liberia, can be divided into three groups. Among the lower coast were the Kru group or Kwa-speaking people consisting of the Kru, Bassa, De, and Grebo. Kru were seldom enslaved because they were reportedly so adverse to bondage that they committed suicide if escape was impossible. Actually Kru men were excellent sailors and both African and European traders depended on them to transport cargoes to waiting vessels on the lower coast. The second grouping was farther north and comprised the Mandingas or Mande-speaking people who were the Mandinga, Gbande, Mende, Vai, Kono, Buzi, Loma, Kpelle, Gio, and Mano. Within this group the Vai, Mende, and Mandingas dominated trade and most often infringed upon the liberty of their neighbors. The third group is perhaps most significant because so many of them made the Middle Passage. This group, the Gola, included Gizzis and Golas, and was of the Niger-Congo linguistic family encompassing Temne, Bullom, Fulani, and Wolof—widely separated peoples geographically. In the Malaguetta Coast region Gola and Gizzi were linguistically isolated on the northeast and northwest by Mande-speaking people.[32]

A process similar to what transpired in present-day Sierra Leone occurred in the Malaguetta Coast region of Upper Guinea. Warfare and movements of the Mende, Mandingas, and Fulani stimulated by the slave trade, created pressure situations for interior forest groups. Just as the Temne and Bullom were displaced by more aggressive groups, so was intensive Mandinga activity on the Malaguetta Coast evident by the seventeenth century. A commercial confederacy existed in which Western Sudanic goods were exchanged for slaves. The slaves were then sent to the coast through Vai and De middlemen. This created another series of wars in which Golas and Gizzis, inhabiting the interior northeast, were heavily involved. Golas and Gizzis struck back against Mandingas and Mende, but generally were no match for the two latter groups. Golas and Gizzis were in a state of almost continual warfare from the seventeenth century on. As slaving activity increased in the next century, Golas began stretching out to areas near Cape Mount and placing themselves under Vai and De protection. Other members of the Gola ethnic group moved out of the northeast where they had been heavily preyed upon. In both instances what began as small villages grew to become dominant towns. Hence while Gola numbers were being diminished in the northeast because of the slave trade, in regions near the coast they were thriving numerically. This led to conflict with Vai and De, the nominal rulers, and hence to more wars. The real source of conflict was control of trade. In the eighteenth century access to gunpowder, small arms, and cannon provided a new and more deadly kind of warfare, as well as extreme concentrations of power and wealth. A process of internal alliances and war within Gola chiefdoms and elsewhere created predacious conditions from the old Gola-Gizzi homeland in the interior to the heterogeneous coastal Mandinga confederacy.[33]

Golas never succeeded in wresting a settlement on the littoral from the Vai and hence had no direct commerce with European ships. Yet by the time of the first black American colonists' arrival in Liberia, Golas were a dominant group culturally and economically in the immediate interior. Prior to that however, they were, along with the Gizzi, the eighteenth century's major victims of the Atlantic slave trade in the region known as Liberia. They also succumbed to the defensive act of attacking and enslaving their own ethnic people. Gizzis were apparently transported in such large numbers that a river in Bullom territory was thusly named, although the Gizzi lived nowhere in that vicinity which was part of the Sierra Leone littoral. In 1778 it was reported that victims secured at Idolos, the factory near the Gizzi or Kizzi River, were in poor physical condition from having traveled great distances in slave coffles.[34]

The late Walter Rodney maintained that the scope of the Atlantic slave trade as conducted on the Upper Guinea Coast during the second half of the eighteenth century has not been fully appreciated and that the general level of trading from 1750 onward was high. Developments in South Carolina support his contention. During this period Africans arrived who transferred a medium of culture, communalism, and spirituality that assimilated with the existing African traditions, both of which necessarily adapted to Euro-American ambiance. Ultimately Africa's loss was America's gain. Still the history of the Atlantic slave trade remains a bitter memory, and the tragedy of it is poignantly revealed in the words of Professor Rodney:

> The impression that African society was being overwhelmed by its involvement with the European economy was most strongly conveyed at points when Africans conceded that their slaving activities were the consequences of the fact that nothing but slaves would purchase European goods. Yet European consumer goods contributed nothing to the development of African production. Only the rulers benefited narrowly, by receiving the best cloth, drinking the most alcohol, and preserving the widest collection of durable items for prestige purposes. It is this factor of realized self-interest which goes some way towards explaining the otherwise incomprehensible actions of Africans toward Africans.[35]

In summary, I argue that in the Carolina Lowcountry there was an early cultural dominance of BaKongo peoples of Kongo-Angolan origin, followed by Upper Guinea Africans of the Senegambia and Windward Coasts. Upper Guinea peoples coming to Carolina found a creolized black culture already adjusting and acculturating. But more significantly, the large numbers of

African-born slaves, entrenched into a system of rice production, also reinforced the Old World heritage. The complex formation of African-American Gullah culture involved, in some ways, the concept of "hearth areas," that is, those who arrive earlier may have as strong an impact as latecomers of more numerical strength. This may explain the continued use of Tshi (Gold Coast) names from the colonial era through the Civil War. Still, it was the BaKongo influence that served as incubator for many Gullah cultural patterns, and superceded Akan-Ashanti impact. Yet BaKongo cultural antecedents did not smother the Upper Guinea contribution to African-American culture. Indeed, it appears that each major group left its presence, and the longevity of these influences depended on adaptability. Thus, the "Doctrine of First Effective Settlement"[36] is significantly altered in the case of the Gullahs.

Notes

1. Walter Rodney, "African Slavery and Other Forms of Social Oppression on the Upper Guinea Coast in the Context of the Atlantic Slave-Trade," *Journal of African History* 8, no. 3 (1966): 436.

2. Ottobah Cugoano, *Thoughts and Sentiments on the Evils of Slavery* (London: Dawsons of Pall Mall, 1969; repr. from 1787 ed.), 12.

3. James Pope-Hennessy, *Sins of Our Fathers: A Study of the Atlantic Slave Traders, 1441–1807* (New York: Alfred A. Knopf, 1968), 38; Daniel Littlefield, *Rice and Slaves: Ethnicity and the Slave Trade in Colonial South Carolina* (Baton Rouge: Louisiana State University Press, 1981), 34–36; Basil Davidson, *The African Slave Trade: Precolonial History, 1450–1850,* originally published as *Black Mother* (Boston: Little, Brown, 1961), 105; Melville J. Herskovits, *The Myth of the Negro Past* (Boston: Beacon Press, 1958; repr. from 1941 ed.), 34–40; Philip D. Curtin, *The Atlantic Slave Trade: A Census* (Madison: University of Wisconsin Press, 1969), passim; Daniel P. Mannix and Malcolm Cowley, *Black Cargoes: A History of the Atlantic Slave Trade, 1518–1865* (New York: Viking Press, 1969), 14–20; the term Upper Guinea Coast has altered over centuries. Here our definition is taken from Walter Rodney, *A History of the Upper Guinea Coast, 1545–1800* (Oxford: Clarendon Press, 1970), 2, 7; Elizabeth Donnan, *Documents Illustrative of the History of the Slave Trade to America,* 4 vols. (Washington, D.C.: Carnegie Institution, 1935), vol. 4, *The Southern Colonies,* passim; Roger Anstey, *The Atlantic Slave Trade and British Abolition, 1760–1810* (Atlantic Highlands, N.J.: Humanities Press, 1975), 58–60.

4. Peter H. Wood, *Black Majority: Negroes in Colonial South Carolina from 1670 through the Stono Rebellion* (New York: Alfred A. Knopf, 1974), 131; Curtin, *Atlantic Slave Trade,* 156; Elizabeth Donnan, "The Slave Trade into South Carolina before the Revolution," *American Historical Review* 33 (1927–28): 816–17; William Snelgrave, *A New Account of Some Parts of Guinea and the Slave Trade* (London: James, John and Paul Knapton, 1734; London: Frank Cass, 1971), 173–74; William Smith, *A Voyage to Guinea* (London: John Nourse, 1744; London: Frank Cass, 1967), 135; William Bosman, *A New and Accurate Description of the Coast of Guinea,* trans. John

Ralph Willis (Holland, 1704; 4th English ed., New York: Barnes and Noble, 1967), 56–68; Mannix and Cowley, *Black Cargoes,* 17–18; Herskovits, *Negro Past,* 35; Pope-Hennessy, *Sins of Our Fathers,* 58–59.

5. Donnan, *Documents,* vol. 2, *The Eighteenth Century,* 282.

6. Ibid., II:xxxi–xxxiii, 355; IV:301, 382.

7. Wood, *Black Majority,* 301–04, Appendix C, 333–41.

8. Douglas L. Wheeler and Rene Pelissier, *Angola* (London: Pall Mall Press, 1971), 28–51; Davidson, *African Trade,* 144–52; Donnan, *Documents,* II:xvii–xviii; Herskovits, *Negro Past,* 37. Roger Bastide has written that the official documents concerning the Portuguese trade were burned after slavery was suppressed "in an effort to expunge a blot on the country's escutcheon." See Roger Bastide, *African Religions of Brazil: Toward a Sociology of the Interpretations of Civilizations,* trans. Helen Sebba (Baltimore: Johns Hopkins Press, 1978), 33.

9. Jan Vansina, "Long Distance Trade Routes in Central Africa," *Journal of African History* 3 (1962): 375–90; Walter Rodney, "Slavery and Other Forms of Social Oppression on the Upper Guinea Coast in the Context of the Atlantic Slave Trade," *Journal of African History* 8, no. 3 (1966): 431, 440; Quoted from Herskovits, *Negro Past,* 37–38.

10. Vansina, "Trade Routes," 375–83; Lorenzo D. Turner, *Africanisms in the Gullah Dialect* (New York: Arno Press and New York Times, 1969; repr. from 1949 ed.), passim; Winifred Vass, *The Bantu Speaking Heritage of the United States* (Los Angeles: Center for Afro-American Studies, 1979), 9–19. Wheeler and Pelissier, *Angola,* 6–10; Herskovits, *Negro Past,* 38; Curtin, *Atlantic Slave Trade,* 157, Table 45.

11. Wheeler and Pelissier, *Angola,* 6–10; Placide Tempels, *Bantu Philosophy,* trans. Colin King (Paris: Présence Africaine, 1959), passim; H. P. Junod, *Bantu Heritage* (Johannesburg: Hortors, 1938; Westport, Conn.: Negro University Press, 1970), 59–67, 82–102, 125–33; Robert Farris Thompson, *Flash of the Spirit: African and Afro-American Art and Philosophy* (New York: Vintage Books, 1983), 103; *Gentleman's Magazine* 35 (October 1764): 487; Leila Sellers, *Charleston Business on the Eve of the American Revolution* (Chapel Hill: University of North Carolina Press, 1934), 143; Augustine Smyth et al., *The Carolina Low Country* (New York: Macmillan, 1931) 173; Vass, *Bantu Heritage,* 3–5; Wood, *Black Majority,* 96–130, 195–217, 272–326; Littlefield, *Rice and Slaves,* 11–15.

12. Wood, *Black Majority,* 52–153, 324–35. From 1741 to 1743 a prohibitive duty was imposed. In 1744 four African cargoes arrived. No slave cargoes entered Charleston in 1745 and from 1746 and 1748 another prohibitive duty was in effect. Three African cargoes arrived in 1749 and 1750, respectively. By 1752 the trade was once again in full swing. Donnan, "Slave Trade before the Revolution," 807–08; W. E. B. DuBois, *The Suppression of the African Slave Trade to the United States of America, 1638–1870* (New York: Schocken Books, 1969; repr. from 1896 ed.), 9–10; W. Robert Higgins, "The Geographical Origins of Negro Slaves in Colonial South Carolina," *South Atlantic Quarterly* 70 (1971): 42–43.

13. Wood, *Black Majority,* 148, 323; Frank J. Klingberg, *An Appraisal of the Negro in Colonial South Carolina: A Study in Americanization* (Washington, D.C.: Associated Publishers, 1941), 69–70; 72; Converse D. Clowse, *Economic Beginnings in Colonial South Carolina, 1730–1760* (Columbia: University of South Carolina Press, 1971), 206, 230–32. Rice was never raised to any large extent on the Sea Islands since salt water in poisonous to the rice plant. Some Sea Islands did have a few fresh water ponds where rice was grown, but the amount was small and only for local consumption. Guion G. Johnson, *A Social History of the Sea Islands* (Chapel Hill: University of

the North Carolina Press, 1930), 18; Frederick V. Emerson, "Geographical Influences in American Slavery," *Geographical Society Bulletin* 63 (1911): 108–09.

14. William A. Schaper, *Sectionalism and Representation in South Carolina* (New York: DaCapo Press, 1968), 51; Emerson, "Geographical Influences," 108–11; Edward McCrady, *South Carolina under the Royal Government, 1719–1776* (New York: Macmillan, 1899), 386–88; Higgins, "Geographical Origins of Negro Slaves," 35, 37, 46–47; Robert L. Meriwether, *The Expansion of South Carolina, 1728–1765*, (Kingsport, Tenn.: Southern Publishers, 1940), 37–38; Philip D. Morgan, "Black Society in the Lowcountry, 1760–1810," in Ira Berlin and Ronald Hoffman, *Slavery and Freedom in the Age of the American Revolution* (Charlottesville: University of Virginia Press, 1983), 84; Peter Wood offers interesting evidence which points to Africans' immunity to certain diseases, such as malaria. Yet, as he states, this was not "absolute." Moreover, Todd L. Savitt notes that malaria certainly took its toll in human losses among slaves. He maintains that some blacks did possess an inherited immunity to one or another strain of malaria. But adds that even adult African-born slaves had to go through a "seasoning" period because the "strains of malarial parasites in this country differed from those in their native lands." The "acquired" immunity that blacks reportedly developed was "risky," according to Savitt, since this involved repeated, uninterrupted exposure to malaria over a period of years. Furthermore, we must rely heavily on the words of colonial whites with a vested interest in rationalizing that blacks were more suited to labor in the Carolina swamps and marshes. Africans may have had a varied immunity to certain diseases, but it appears unlikely that this determined white attitudes toward black labor. For Wood, see *Black Majority* 85–88, 90–91. See also Todd L. Savitt, *Medicine and Slavery: The Diseases and Health Care of Blacks in Antebellum Virginia* (Urbana, Ill.: University of Illinois Press, 1978), 21–26.

15. Schaper, *Sectionalism* 55–56; Emerson, "Geographical Influences," 112; Higgins, "Geographical Origins of Negro Slaves," 40–46; Johnson, *Social History*, 18–19; McCrady, *South Carolina under Royal Government*, 267–69; Donnan, *Documents*, IV: passim; See Appendix A.

16. Ellen Gibson Wilson, *The Loyal Blacks* (New York: G. P. Putnam's Sons, 1976), 48; Philip M. Hamer, et al. eds., *Papers of Henry Laurens*, 10 vols. (Columbia: University of South Carolina Press, 1968), IV: 294–95.

17. *SCG,* July 14, 1759.

18. Hamer, *Laurens Papers,* I:252, 331.

19. Littlefield, *Rice and Slaves,* 74–114. Additionally Ian Hancock partly bases his contention of the prevalence of Upper Guinea influence in Gullah dialect on the introduction of creole-speaking slaves brought to South Carolina from this region of Africa. The number of Africans speaking Guinea Coast creole English was small compared to those who spoke no English. Yet the former could have begun the process of spreading creolized English to the latter. Ian F. Hancock, "Gullah and Barbadian—Origins and Relationships," *American Speech* 55 no. 1 (Spring, 1980): 27–30.

20. Richard Jobson, *The Golden Trade or A Discovery of the River Gambia* (London: Nicholas Okes, 1623), 42, 123–25; Francis Moore, *Travels into the Inland Parts of Africa* (London: J. Stagg, 1739), 17–29, 30–32, 38–39, 47–52, 72–73, 80–82, 105–22; Michel Adanson, *A Voyage to Senegal, the Isle of Goree and the River Gambia* (London: J. Nourse and W. Johnston, 1759), 166; Joseph Corry, *Observations upon the Windward Coast of Africa* (London: Frank Cass 1958; repr. from 1807 ed.),

64–66; David McPherson, *Annals of Commerce,* 4 vols. (London: Johnson Reprint Co., 1972; repr. from 1805 ed.), IV: 141–42; Harry Gailey Jr., *A History of the Gambia* (London: Routledge and Kegan Paul, 1964), 6, 11, 13; Sellers, *Charleston Business,* 143; David P. Gamble, *The Wolof of Senegambia* (London: International African Institute, 1957), 31–37; Christopher Fyfe, *A History of Sierra Leone* (London: Oxford University Press, 1962), 1–4; Mannix and Cowley, *Black Cargoes,* 15–16; *SCG,* July 2, 1760, October 11, 1760, August 29, 1761; *South Carolina Gazette and Country Journal,* March 13, 1769, May 8, 1769, June 22, 1769, July 2, 1771, August 13, 1771, December 1, 1772, June 1, 1773, July 18, 1774, January 13, 1785, December 1, 1772.

21. Appendix A; *SCG,* August 19, 1756, June 23, 1756.

22. Donnan, *Documents,* IV: 404 n.; Higgins, "Geographical Origins of Negro Slaves," 41; Morgan, "Black Society in the Lowcountry," 84–85; DuBois, *African Trade,* 90; Schaper, *Sectionalism,* 81–88, 149–62; Sellers, *Charleston Business,* 29–30, 128; Appendix A; Wood, *Black Majority,* 333–41. Higgins states that many slaves, prior to 1775, entered Charleston but were not employed in Carolina. The Sea Island port of Beaufort did some importing as well, although Higgins gives no port-by-port importation breakdown. He believes the "majority of all Negroes in the United States today are descended from blacks brought to North America during the colonial period." This has even stronger implications for the spread of cultural influences by ethnic groups of the middle period of the trade. Higgins, "Geographical Origins of Negro Slaves," 39, 46–47.

23. Rodney, *History of Upper Guinea,* 3–15, 233.

24. Moore, *Travels,* 29–35, 40–51; Jobson, *Golden Trade,* 27–37; Adanson, *Voyage to Senegal,* 57–59; Smith, *Voyage to Guinea,* 32; Rodney, *History of Upper Guinea,* 117; Charlotte Quinn, *Mandingo Kingdoms of the Senegambia* (Evanston: Northwestern University Press, 1972), 1–54; Gailey, *History of Gambia,* 10–17; Henry Fenwick Reeve, *The Gambia: Its History, Ancient, Medieval and Modern* (London: Smith, Elder, 1972), 12, 73, 78–79, 171–79, 180–81, 198–203; Curtin, *Atlantic Slave Trade,* 156–67.

25. Rodney, *History of Upper Guinea,* 112–15, 116–17; Moore, *Travels,* 41–44; Reeve, *Gambia, Ancient Medieval, Modern,* 171–78.

26. Moore, *Travels,* 42–43.

27. Douglas Grant, *The Fortunate Slave* (London: Oxford University Press, 1968), Chapter 4, 156–67; Moore, *Travels,* 205–8; Rodney, *History of Upper Guinea,* 116–17. Curtin, *Atlantic Slave Trade.* For another example of a black nobleman being sold into slavery see Terry Alford, *Prince among Slaves* (New York: Oxford University Press, 1986; repr. from 1977 ed.).

28. Rodney, *History of Upper Guinea,* 111–17, 236–39.

29. John Matthews, *A Voyage to the River Sierra Leone* (London: Frank Cass, 1966; repr. from 1788 ed.), 13, 18, 74–75, 91–95, 141–42; Corry, *Windward Coast,* 94–95; Thomas Winterbottom, *An Account of the Native Africans in the Neighborhood of Sierra Leone,* 2 vols. (London: Frank Cass, 1969; repr. from 1803 ed.), I: 3–7; Rodney, *History of Upper Guinea,* 232–39; Fyfe, *Sierra Leone,* 2–3, 5–6, 9, 65; Robert T. Parsons, *Religion in an African Society* (Leiden: E. J. Brill, 1964), xiv. 226.

30. Rodney, *History of Upper Guinea,* 236–53; Appendix A.

31. Kenneth Little, *The Mende of Sierra Leone* (London: Routledge & Kegan Paul, 1951), 28–29, 37–39; Fyfe, *Sierra Leone,* 5–6.

32. Higgins, "Geographical Origins of Negro Slaves," 41; James L. Sibley and D. Westermann, *Liberia Old and New* (London: James Clarke, 1928), 45–46; Sir Harry

Johnston, *Liberia,* 2 vols. (London: Hutchinson, 1906), I: 107–10; II: 921–24, 947–48, 1095–96: Warren L. d'Azevedo, "The Setting of Gola Society and Culture: Some Theoretical Implications of Variation in Time and Space," *Kroeber Anthropological Society Papers* (Berkeley: University of California, 1959), 21, 51.

33. d'Azevedo, "Gola Society and Culture," 55–59; Rodney, *History of Upper Guinea,* 255.

34. Folkways Research Series, *Tribes of the Western Province and the Denwoin People* (Monrovia: Dept. of Interior 1955) 140–42; and *The Traditional History and Folklore of the Gola Tribe in Liberia,* 2 vols. (Monrovia: Dept. of the Interior, 1961) I: 2–3; Rodney, *History of Upper Guinea,* 255.

35. Rodney, *History of Upper Guinea,* 253.

36. Diary of William F. Allen, 63, in William F. Allen Papers, 1775–1937, State Historical Society of Wisconsin, Madison; Donald R. Kloe, "Buddy Quow: An Anonymous Poem in Gullah-Jamaican Dialect Written Circa 1800," *Southern Folklore Quarterly* 38, no. 2 (June, 1974): 82–84, 87; Wilbur Zelinsky, *The Cultural Geography of the United States* (Englewood Cliffs, N.J.: Prentice-Hall, 1973), 20–21.

A. Leon Higginbotham Jr.

The Ancestry of Inferiority (1619–1662)

From *Shades of Freedom: Racial Politics and Presumptions of the American Legal Process*

Slavery and law have a peculiarly complex relationship. In one sense, slavery overrides law by placing the slaves at the mercy of their masters with little or no appeal. But in any literate, commercial society, slavery cannot exist without law to protect and enforce the claims of the masters over their slaves. Moreover, as the introduction notes, some forms of slave law might be seen as extending protection to the slaves.

In North America, that protection was always minimal. Slaves were not reduced to the actual level of beasts (a slave could be put on trial for a crime; an animal could not). But only Louisiana protected the relationship of a slave mother to her child. No colony or state recognized slaves' marriages or slaves' property. Looking at earliest Virginia, A. Leon Higginbotham Jr. asks how that situation developed.

Higginbotham's specific interest in this selection is whether black people faced legal inferiority and legal discrimination before there was a formal law of slavery. Although he joins in the opinion that the earliest black Virginians were servants, he finds evidence that their condition and that of whites began to diverge early. In many cases his evidence is very subtle, such as the use of a descriptive word in relation to a black person but not to a white one. Central to the essay is his argument that Virginia courts were presuming black inferiority well before the emergence of formal black slavery. This was so even when a court appeared to be recognizing one or another privilege that a black person had come to court to claim. The time was not far away when the law would hold that slaves had almost no rights that a Virginia court would enforce. Higginbotham invites us to watch that situation taking shape.

A. Leon Higginbotham Jr. studied at Yale University Law School and enjoyed a distinguished career as a federal judge, retiring as senior circuit judge of the Third District of the United States Court of Appeals. After leaving the bench, he became a professor in the John F. Kennedy School of Government and the Law School at Harvard University. Higginbotham has taught at many other universities and has written widely on legal history and race relations.

Questions for a Closer Reading

1. Why, in Higginbotham's view, should we suspect that even the earliest black Virginians were not "full equals" within the servant class?

2. In the case of both "John Phillip a Negro" (1624) and Hugh Davis (1630), Higginbotham takes the mention of race as evidence of "the precept of black inferiority." Can you think of another possible reading of this evidence?

3. In what ways did issues of sexuality become mingled with issues of race in seventeenth-century Virginia law cases?

4. How does the case of John Graweere (1641) illustrate the pressures that black Virginians faced as they began to form families?

5. Does Higginbotham demonstrate that a deliberate strategy of making black Virginia servants into social inferiors was under way? Or does he merely describe a pattern whose results nobody could foresee?

6. Does Higginbotham's essay give any help with the problem of whether racism preceded slavery or slavery preceded racism?

The Ancestry of Inferiority
(1619–1662)

Last among Equals

When the first Africans arrived at Virginia in August 1619,[1] they were initially accorded an indentured servant status similar to that of most Virginia colonists. In two letters, John Rolfe, Secretary and Recorder of the Virginia colony, reported on the arrival of the Africans. One letter stated that a Dutch man-of-war "brought not any thing but 20. and odd Negroes, which the Governor and Cape Marchant bought for victualles."[2] The other letter, describing the same event, stated: "[A]bout the last of August, came in a dutch man of warre that sold us twenty Negars."[3] The references in the letters to "buying" and "selling" do not necessarily mean that these Africans were being sold into chattel slavery. During that period, the majority of the population in Virginia consisted of servants.[4] It was common practice to refer to the transaction of acquiring a servant as "buying" a person. Buying in that sense simply meant buying the person's services and not actually buying the person's body.[5] Thus, it would appear that, in 1619, the first Africans became one more group in a majority servant class made up of whites and Native Americans.[6]

There are two reasons, however, why the Africans probably did not join this servant class as full equals. First, most but not all white servants came to the colony voluntarily and engaged in service with a written contract of indenture for a specific period.[7] At the expiration of the period of their indenture, whites were released into freedom. The master of a white indentured servant could not, at his sole desire and discretion, prolong the period of servitude. In fact, court approval was necessary for masters and servants to extend the original indenture.[8] Only if the white servant had

A. Leon Higginbotham Jr., "The Ancestry of Inferiority (1619–1662)," in *Shades of Freedom: Racial Politics and Presumptions of the American Legal Process* (New York: Oxford University Press, 1996), 18–27.

broken the contract of indenture, or if the servant had in some way violated the laws of the colony, could the period of servitude be extended, either as compensation to the master for the servant breaking the contract
or as punishment by society for the servant violating the law.[9] By contrast,
as far as we know, the Africans came involuntarily or under duress,[10] and
presumably were sold into service *without* a written contract of indenture
for a specific period. So, in theory, their period of servitude may have
been for as long as the purchaser desired, or even for life.

The second reason why the new Africans probably did not occupy the
exact same socioeconomic position as other white servants is that—as
Winthrop Jordan has demonstrated—since the fifteenth century, Englishmen had regarded blackness as "the handmaid and symbol of baseness
and evil, a sign of danger and repulsion."[11] There is no reason to suppose
that, in August 1619, the English colonists of Virginia would have immediately abandoned their historical tendency of associating blackness with inferiority in favor of a more enlightened view of seeing these particular
black Africans as fully human. It is more likely that, in the eyes of the English colonists, the Africans represented a dark and inferior quantity. As
members of the servant class they probably were last among equals.

Blackness As Sin

Notwithstanding the colonists' predilection for seeing Africans as less than
human, from 1619 and for approximately two decades thereafter, the legal
system did not appear to actively promote rigid, invidious distinctions between the new African settlers and their European counterparts.[12] The first
reference to a black person in a judicial proceeding occurred in 1624,
when the Council and General Court of Virginia mentioned, in the case of
Re Tuchinge, in sum: "John Phillip A negro Christened in England 12 yeers
since, sworne and exam sayeth, that beinge in a ship with Sir Henry
Maneringe, they took A spanish shipp aboute Cape Sct Mary, and Caryed
her to mamora."[13]

The case apparently involved the trial of a white man, Symon Tuchinge,
for the illegal seizure of a Spanish ship and the kidnapping of various persons. Given that Phillip was referred to specifically by the court as black, it
is logical to assume that the defendant, whose race was not similarly specified, was white. This conclusion is supported by the fact that other wit-
nesses were not identified by race.[14]

Phillip's testimony against the white man was accepted presumably because, as the court explained, Phillip had been "Christened in England."

Prior to 1680, the colonies would often follow the Spanish and English practice that blacks who had been baptized into the Christian religion were to be accorded the privileges of a free person.

Had the legal process in 1624 in Virginia not yet begun to institutionalize the precept of black inferiority, however, one would have expected the case to have been reported quite differently from the way it was actually reported. Specifically, had Virginia law been free of any theory of racial subordination, the case would have been reported as follows: "John Phillip sworne and exam sayeth, that beinge in a ship with Sir Henry Maneringe, they tooke A spanish shipp aboute Cape Sct Mary, and Caryed her to mamora." There would have been no description of Phillip as a "Negro" and having been "Christened," just as there had been no mention of the white defendant's race or his religion. In a jurisdiction where black did *not* carry the stigma of inferiority, Phillip's race and religion would *not* be material to the determination of whether his testimony was admissible in court because the blemish of his race would *not* need to be washed clean by the grace of his Christian religion. In a jurisdiction such as Virginia, however, where black was already the stigma of inferiority, Phillip's race and religion *were* material to the determination of whether his testimony was to be admitted, because in a real sense, his race was a sin for which he could obtain forgiveness only by becoming a Christian.

By explicitly describing Phillip's race and religion, the court implicitly revealed that, in 1624 Virginia, the legal process was ready to perceive and to treat blacks, by reason of the color of their skin, as different from white colonists. Granted, at first, the consequences of that difference were not immutable. If blackness was a sin, at least it could be absolved by Christianity. But the sinner who obtains Christian forgiveness for his sin always pays a price for that forgiveness. The price is that he has to admit that his sin caused him to be, in some way, a less perfect or inferior image of God. For the African, the sin that caused him to be a less perfect or inferior image of God was his race. So, to the African, Christian forgiveness *and all its attendant legal rights and privileges here on earth* came only at the price of admitting to himself and to society that he was inferior. What's more, the legal process, supported by public opinion and cloaked with the mysticism of Christian religion, reinforced this sense of black inferiority by the identification of the black race in judicial decisions and in legislative enactments. In short, by 1624, the legal process had begun to lay the foundation for the precept of black inferiority and white superiority; the process had "crossed," in the words of historian Lerone Bennett, Jr., "a great divide," and had placed white colonists on one side and Africans on the other side.[15]

The case of *Re Davis*, decided in 1630, illustrates that great divide in very stark terms. The full official court report reads as follows: "Sept. 17. 1630 *Hugh Davis* to be soundly whipt before an assembly of negroes & others for abusing himself to the dishon[o]r of God and shame of Christianity by defiling his body in lying with a negro. w[hi]ch fault he is to actk next *Sabbath* day."[16]

This case demonstrates the evolution of the precept of inferiority in at least three ways. First, though the court did not state that Hugh Davis was white, his race may be inferred from the fact that he is not identified as a "Negro," whereas the person with whom he presumably "defiled" his body was specifically identified as a "negro." The very statement that Davis "abused himself," and that "he defiled his body by lying with a negro," means that he engaged in sexual relations with someone inferior, someone less than human. In short, Davis's crime was not fornication, but bestiality. Second, the statement of the court that Davis had abused himself "to the dishon[o]r of God and shame of Christianity" means that the blacks' inferiority was not simply a custom of society, but also a tenet of Christianity. Finally, the court ordered Davis to be "whipt before an assembly of *negroes & others*." One must assume that the "others" referred to most probably were white colonists. Therefore, the only reason why the court specified that the assembly was also to include "negroes" was because generally white colonists were not whipped in front of blacks. For Davis, a white colonist, to be whipped in front of blacks would have been especially humiliating, because he would have been debased in front of individuals who were his legal inferiors.

The *Davis* case, decided a mere six years after the *Tuchinge* case, marked an important step in the development of the precept of black inferiority in the common law of Virginia. In *Tuchinge*, the court had remarked upon Phillip's "otherness" by simply identifying him as a "Negro Christened." The precept that Phillip's race marked him as inferior was not stated, but instead remained implicit in the fact that his race alone was identified. By contrast, in *Davis*, the precept of black inferiority was no longer implied, but stated explicitly in the fact that a white colonist "defiled" his body by engaging in sexual relations with an African. In *Tuchinge*, the court recognized that Phillip's inferiority was not so immutable that it could not be mitigated by his Christianity. Phillip, having become a Christian, was permitted to give testimony in court against a white man. God was the African's savior from inferiority. In *Davis*, however, Christianity, instead of supplying a balm for the injury of black inferiority, provided the very instrument which confirmed its existence. Davis's crime of engaging in sexual relations with a black was a crime against Christianity. God now became witness to the African's inferiority. But in *Tuchinge,* the black man's relative equality was measured by his presence in court as a witness against the white man's transgression. By contrast, in *Davis,* the black person's irredeemable inferiority was measured by his presence as the reason for the white man's punishment.

Ten years later, in 1640, the courts in Virginia took the next step in the development of the precept of black inferiority. In *Re Sweat,* the court considered the case of Robert Sweat, a white colonist who had impregnated a black woman servant belonging to a Lieutenant Sheppard.[17] As punishment for Sweat and the unnamed black woman, the court ruled: "[T]he said negro woman shall be whipt at the whipping post and the said *Sweat* shall tomorrow in the forenoon do public penance for his offence at *James city* church in the time of devine service according to the laws of *England* in that case p[ro]vided."[18]

Sweat, at one level, can be interpreted simply as a case about the invasion of property rights. The black woman servant belonged not to Sweat, but to Lieutenant Sheppard. Sweat impregnated her. During her pregnancy and post-childbirth period, she probably became less valuable to Sheppard.[19] Therefore, Sweat had to pay a price for diminishing the value of Sheppard's property, and the woman servant had to pay a price for allowing her value to Sheppard to be diminished. If the case was, however, only about the invasion of Sheppard's property rights, then Sweat and the woman servant would have been made to pay compensation to Sheppard: Sweat would have had to pay monetary damages to Sheppard, and the woman servant would have had to increase the period of servitude she owed to Sheppard. Instead, Sweat and the woman servant were administered respective forms of punishment, as if this were a criminal prosecution and not a property rights dispute.

That the woman was punished and not made to increase her period of servitude can be explained simply by the fact that she "belonged" to Sheppard and was probably already a servant for life. That Sweat was also not made to pay some form of compensation to Sheppard cannot be easily explained by interpreting the case solely in the context of property rights. Instead, a more complete explanation suggests itself if the case is viewed also as an expression of the precept of black inferiority. By engaging in sexual relations, Sweat and the black woman did much more than diminish Sheppard's property rights. Sweat "defiled his body" and shamed God by sleeping with someone less than human. For that, he needed to be punished by doing public penance in church in order to mortify him and to require him to ask God's forgiveness. The black woman, in turn, defied society and rejected her inferiority by sleeping with her superior.[20] For that, she needed to be punished at the whipping post, so that the mark of her inferiority that she had failed to imprint in her mind would now be whipped into her skin.

For blacks, the lesson of their inferiority was one that was written not only on their own bodies, but also on the bodies of their children. *In Re Graweere* in 1641 described how John Graweere, a black servant belonging to a white colonist named William Evans purchased the freedom of his young child from a Lieutenant Sheppard, the owner of the child's mother.[21] After Graweere purchased his child from Sheppard, it seems that a question arose as to whether the child belonged to him or to Evans, his master.[22] Graweere argued that the child should be freed, so that he would "be made a christian and be taught and exercised in the church of *England.*"[23] The court ruled in Graweere's favor and ordered: "that the child shall be free from the said *Evans* or his assigns and to be and remain at the disposing and education of the said *Graweere* and the child's godfather who undertaketh to see it brought up in the christian religion as aforesaid."[24]

This case is correctly interpreted as significant evidence that, by 1641, the legal process had not contemplated the institution of hereditary slavery. Graweere, himself, may have been a servant for life, but he was able to break the grip of servitude on his posterity by purchasing his child's freedom. Moreover, the facts of the case reveal that Graweere enjoyed certain benefits not usually afforded to slaves. Evans, Graweere's master, permitted him to own and raise hogs under an arrangement whereby Graweere paid half of the profits from his hog business to Evans and kept the other half for himself.[25] However, this case presents more than mere evidence of the ambiguous socioeconomic position of black servants in 1641 Virginia.

In Re Graweere also offers an illustration of how the precept of black inferiority operates. The court sided with Graweere's position, by freeing his child, so that he could be raised as a Christian. But nowhere in the opinion was it stated that Graweere himself was a Christian. A close reading of the opinion reveals that Graweere was probably *not* a Christian. There are two reasons for this conclusion. First, Graweere is described only as "a negro servant unto *William Evans.*"[26] During that period, it was common practice to distinguish between "negroes" and "Christian negroes," since certain rights and privileges flowed from a black person being a Christian.[27] Recall the *Tuchinge* case in which the court accepted a black witness's testimony, because he had been baptized a Christian himself. Yet in this case, which turned almost entirely on the very issue of religion, Graweere's own faith was not explicitly mentioned. Surely, Graweere's position to raise his child as a free Christian would have been strengthened in the mind of the court had he been a Christian. Additionally, the court's decision to free the child would have been even more rational had the court stated that Graweere was a "Christian negro." Graweere presumably did not claim that he was a Christian, and the court did not so state in its opinion.

The second reason for that conclusion is: If Graweere was a Christian, or if he desired to convert to the Christian religion, one would assume that he could have petitioned the court to purchase *his own* freedom from Evans, because the court permitted him to purchase the freedom of his child on the promise the child was to be raised as a Christian. In other words, if, as the opinion clearly suggests, religion was the decisive argument that convinced the court to free the child, the same argument would also presumably be convincing in gaining Graweere his own freedom. The most probable reason why that argument did not apply to Graweere's situation was because, even though he wanted his child raised as a Christian, he himself was *not* a Christian.

If this argument is correct, then it inevitably raises a critical question: Why did the court permit a non-Christian black servant to gain the freedom of his child on the promise that the child would be raised and educated as a Christian? Put more simply, how could the court expect a non-Christian parent to educate a Christian child? The answer is suggested by the cryptic last statement in the court's opinion. The court wrote that the child was to "remain at the disposing and education of the said *Graweere and the child's godfather* who undertaketh to see it brought up in the christian religion as aforesaid."[28] The godfather to whom the court refers was a Christian to be sure, either a black Christian or a white Christian. It is unlikely that the godfather was black, because that would have presented a much too obvious way for black servants to achieve their freedom in 1641. Blacks could have petitioned the court, *en masse,* for freedom by getting themselves baptized with black Christian godfathers and promising to follow in the ways of Christianity. The system of non-indentured black servants could not have possibly survived and flourished for as long as it did had the legal process permitted blacks and their children to gain freedom merely with the help of fellow blacks who were Christians.

The only remaining possibility was that the godfather of Graweere's child was white. As implausible as it may at first sound, this does more completely explain the court's willingness to free the child. After all, if the precept of black inferiority meant anything, it certainly meant that, in the court's estimation, the child's Christian education would have been better safeguarded if entrusted to the care of a white colonist than if placed in the hands of a black servant, Christian or otherwise.

In short, this case exemplifies how the legal process in a subtle but pernicious manner, reinforced the precept of black inferiority and white superiority in the minds and hearts of the colonists. The black parent was not completely denied dominion over his child, but he was made to understand that, alone, he was too inferior to protect the freedom and save the soul of his child. The white godfather, in turn, was given control over the child, not because of any parental rights, but because of the superiority of his race.

The cases of *Tuchinge, Davis, Sweat,* and *Graweere* were not the only judicial decisions in Virginia involving blacks during the first stage in the development of the precept of black inferiority.[29] Moreover, as was characteristic of the first stage, these four decisions were relatively benign in their treatment of blacks in comparison with later developments in Virginia law.[30] While these cases exemplify how the legal process began to recognize the precept of black inferiority, it should also be noted that the common law at that time had not yet evolved a seamless rationale for the principles of racial subordination that would permit judges in successive decisions to apply the precept of black inferiority to different factual scenarios in a consistent fashion. In other words, the legal process had not yet merged the precept of black inferiority with the doctrine of *stare decisis.**

These qualifications notwithstanding, reviewing the decisions in *Tuchinge, Davis, Sweat,* and *Graweere* is crucial to a proper understanding of the precept of black inferiority and white superiority. Taken together, these cases reveal four essential steps that were taken in the first stage of development of the precept of black inferiority and white superiority: establish white superiority; establish black inferiority; enforce the notions publicly; and enforce the notions by way of theology.

First: convince the white colonists, regardless of their social or economic status, that they are superior to the black colonists. In that way, white servants, who may in reality have more in common with black servants, will identify with propertied whites, with whom they may have little in common other than race. For example, in *Davis* and in *Sweat,* the white colonists who engaged in sexual relations with black women were made to understand that they had defiled their own bodies. Had the defendants been propertied whites, it is difficult to imagine that they would have been punished for sleeping with their black servants or their slaves. During the antebellum period, when slavery was certainly firmly rooted in Virginia, a white master had the right to demand sexual compliance from his female slaves, just as surely as he had the right to ride his mares. This practice, encouraged *openly* as a matter of right in 1831 Virginia was, to be sure, already tolerated secretly as a matter of privilege in 1630. This was precisely the position ad-

---

stare decisis: The legal principle that a precedent case normally should not be overturned.

vanced on the floor of the Virginia legislature in 1831 by a Mr. Gholson, in response to statements proposing abolition: "Why, I really have been under the impression that I *owned* my slaves. I lately purchased *four women and ten children,* in whom I thought I obtained a great bargain, for I really supposed they were *my property,* as were my *brood mares.*"[31] The only logical conclusion to be drawn from *Davis* and *Sweat,* then, is that the defendants were probably poor whites or servants who had managed to sleep with black women belonging to others. In spite of their relatively modest socioeconomic positions, the legal process sought to convince these whites that they were superior to blacks.

Second: convince blacks that they are inferior to all others. In that way, they will feel hopeless about their fate, they will become submissive to the propertied whites, and they will not hope to form alliances with white servants. For example, in *Davis,* the simple act of a white man's sleeping with a black woman was described in the space of a single-sentence judicial opinion as the white man abusing himself, dishonoring God, shaming Christianity, and defiling his body. For blacks, the lesson must have been clear: If there was only shame and dishonor and, therefore, no joy or trust in the secret sexual bonding of black and white, then there would have been even more shame and dishonor and, therefore, even less joy or trust in these two groups forging an open political, social, or economic bond.

Third: enforce the inferiority of blacks and the superiority of whites in the most open and public manner. In that way, both blacks and whites will understand the precept as clear evidence of societal custom. For example, in *Davis,* the white defendant was condemned to be whipped "before an assembly of negroes & others." Similarly, in *Sweat* the black woman was sentenced to be whipped "at the whipping post," and the white defendant, to do public penance in church. These forms of public punishment were not only designed to exact retribution from the offenders, but also to deter others from engaging in similar behavior. It must be remembered that, at the time, Virginia had already begun to erect the social and color ladder, with propertied whites at the top, poor and servant whites in the middle, and Native Americans and Africans at the bottom. For a white man to engage in sexual relations with a black woman constituted a private slip down to the bottom-most rung of the ladder. For a white man to be punished publicly for his private fall was society's way of reminding one and all of the terrible cost in status that would accompany any failure to observe the precept of black inferiority.

Fourth: explain the inferiority of blacks and the superiority of whites by reference to Christianity. In that way, both blacks and whites will respect the precept as the natural expression of divine will. For example, in *Tuchinge,* the black witness avoided a disability of inferiority only by the grace of Christianity.

In *Davis,* the white colonist was said to have dishonored God and shamed Christianity by his sexual relations with a black. In *Sweat,* the white offender was sentenced to public penance in church. In *Graweere,* the black child was saved from servitude only by the intervention of a white Christian godfather. The colonists realized that, while a foolish few might be tempted to sacrifice their public status in the service of private desires, almost no one would be willing to set his face against God for the sake of a people whose black color was itself a sin.

In one passage in his *Notes on the State of Virginia,* Thomas Jefferson explained in great detail the various physical and mental differences between blacks and whites that he believed rendered blacks inferior and whites superior. After listing those differences, Jefferson concluded: "I advance it therefore as a suspicion only, that the blacks, whether originally a distinct race, or made distinct by time and circumstances, are inferior to the whites in the endowments both of body and mind."[32] That passage, though written in 1782, best sums up the first stage in the legal development of the precept of black inferiority in Virginia between 1619 and 1662.

During that stage, the colonists seemed to believe, "as suspicion only," that blacks were inferior to whites. Their ambivalence was reflected in the uncertain socioeconomic status of the black servants in the colony, and in the relatively benign manner in which the legal process defined and enforced their condition of servitude. By 1662, however, the legal process would begin to put in place the components of lifetime and hereditary slavery for blacks. With that, Virginia would move into the second stage in the development of the precept of black inferiority.

Notes

1. See A. Leon Higginbotham Jr., *In the Matter of Color: Race and the American Legal Process: The Colonial Period* 20 (1978) [hereinafter *In the Matter of Color*].

2. Alden T. Vaughan, *Blacks in Virginia: A Note on the First Decade,* 29 Wm. & Mary Q. 469, 470 (1972).

3. Id.

4. *In the Matter of Color,* supra note 1, at 21–22 (citing Oscar Handlin and Mary F. Handlin, *Origin of the Southern Labor System,* 7 Wm. & Mary Q. 199, 202–03 (1950) ("almost everyone, even tenants and laborers, bore some sort of servile obligation")).

5. Paul C. Palmer, *Servant into Slave: The Evolution of the Legal Status of the Negro Laborer in Colonial Virginia,* 65 S. Atlantic Q. 355, 356 (1966).

6. See *In the Matter of Color,* supra note 1, at 20–22.

7. Id. at 393; Abbot E. Smith, *Colonists in Bondage: White Servitude and Convict Labor in America 1607–1776,* at 16–21 (1947).

8. *In the Matter of Color,* supra note 1, at 54–55.

9. See, e.g., id. at 28.

10. See, e.g., id. at 20. It should be noted that many indentured servants did not come to America voluntarily. Some were kidnapped, and others were falsely accused of crimes by conspiring shipowners and judicial authorities, who profited from the selling of indentured servants. Id. at 393–95.

11. Winthrop D. Jordan, *White over Black: American Attitudes toward the Negro, 1550–1812*, at 7 (1968).

12. See *In the Matter of Color*, supra note 1, at 21–22, 58.

13. 1 *Judicial Cases Concerning American Slavery and the Negro* 76 (Helen T. Catterall ed., 1926) [hereinafter Catterall] (citing *Minutes of the Council and General Court of Colonial Virginia* 33 (H.R. McIlwaine ed., 2d ed. 1979) (1924) [hereinafter McIlwaine]) (footnote omitted).

14. McIlwaine, supra note 13, at 33–35.

Since *Tuchinge* is the first case discussed, it is appropriate here to set out my approach to evaluating colonial cases. During colonial times judicial opinions tended to be very brief. There is much that we do not know (and may never know) about the complete facts of these cases. The interpretation of the cases in this work draws upon many sources in order to give shape and meaning to the precept of black inferiority. As such, this work takes a more creative approach in interpreting colonial cases by focusing more on what the courts do not say (and their probable reasons for not saying it) than on what they do say. Obviously, this mode of interpretation would not be appropriate for modern cases where courts almost always lay out the background facts and the judicial rationale in their decisions. But it is perfectly appropriate for colonial cases where more often than not one has to "read between the lines" to truly understand the rationale for the holding of the court. After all, it is not possible to understand, for example, how the United States Constitution promoted the institution of slavery by focusing solely on what the Framers wrote. One must also focus on what the Framers did not write about African Americans in the Constitution (and their reasons for not writing it) in order to understand the relationship between the Constitution and slavery.

15. Lerone Bennett Jr., *Before the Mayflower: A History of Black America* 45 (5th ed. 1982).

16. McIlwaine, supra note 13, at 479.

17. Id. at 477.

18. Id.

19. The property rights issue may be viewed in a different way if a system of hereditary slavery had definitely been in place in 1640 Virginia. There exists no conclusive evidence that by 1640 Virginia had already established a system of chattel slavery. Had such system been in place, the woman servant could have possibly been considered more valuable pregnant than not because her child at birth would have belonged to Lieutenant Sheppard. The use of the term "servant" does not negate the possibility that this woman was a slave. *In the Matter of Color*, supra note 1, at 24.

20. Even if, as a servant, she was coerced by Sweat to engage in sexual intercourse, in the context of the precept of black inferiority, the law always assumed that the choice was hers. If the choice had not been hers, the law would have had no cause to punish her.

21. McIlwaine, supra note 13, at 477.

22. Id.

23. Id.

24. Id.

25. Id.

26. Id.

27. See *In the Matter of Color,* supra note 1, at 20–21.

28. McIlwaine, supra note 13, at 477 (emphasis added).

29. See also 1 Catterall, supra note 13, at 76–78.

30. See *In the Matter of Color,* supra note 1, at 32–60.

31. William Goodell, *The American Slave Code* 36 (New York, American and Foreign Anti-Slavery Society, 3rd ed. 1853).

32. Thomas Jefferson, *Notes on the State of Virginia* 150 (Boston, Lily and Wait 1832) (1787).

4. How did North America's absolute racial division begin?

Winthrop D. Jordan

American Chiaroscuro: The Status and Definition of Mulattoes in the British Colonies

Winthrop Jordan's monumental *White over Black: American Attitudes toward the Negro, 1550–1812* was published to wide acclaim in 1968. "American Chiaroscuro: The Status and Definition of Mulattoes in the British Colonies" appeared six years before *White over Black* and announced many of the book's themes. Drawing on the Italian word for the artistic technique of shading dark and light colors, Jordan concentrated on the questions of interracial sexual relations and the offspring it produces. "American Chiaroscuro" turns "race mixing" into a defining historical image. Jordan found his subject wherever black and white people met, from the West Indies to New England. What differed from place to place was how people thought about it, and in Jordan's reading that difference turned on demography.

Caribbean sugar islands were as much British colonies as Virginia or Rhode Island, but they became agricultural machines rather than places of settlement. Nobody stayed who could leave. White men who did stay displayed no compunction about liaisons with black women, and children resulted. One consequence was an elaborate language of racial gradation to describe different ratios of white and black "blood." At the opposite extreme was New England, which saw the development of interracial marriage (rather than concubinage) and of relationships in which the black partner was male.

In between lay the emerging mainland South. If America became a place where a person is either "white" or "black" until the point of "passing" as a white person, colonial Virginia is the place where that formula took shape. Mixing did happen. But as much as possible, nobody wanted to know. South Carolina was like both Virginia and the West Indies. Never as openly tolerant of black concubinage as the Caribbean islands, it still developed a more complex vocabulary and a more complex set of practices about race mixing than the Chesapeake generated. But the pattern that Virginians set came to dominate American attitudes.

Winthrop D. Jordan received his Ph.D. from Brown University and is now professor of history and African American studies at the University of Mississippi. In addition to *White over Black*, he is author of *Tumult and Silence at Second Creek: An Inquiry into a Civil War Slave Conspiracy* (Baton Rouge: Louisiana State University Press, 1993). Both of Jordan's books have won Columbia University's Bancroft Prize as outstanding book of the year in American history.

Questions for a Closer Reading

1. Why did the status of "mulatto" present problems for English colonizers but not for their Spanish counterparts?

2. How can you explain the different ways that different sorts of European colonists responded to the undeniable "mixing" of "races" that developed in early America?

3. What does Jordan mean when he describes a contrast between "hierarchy of status" and absolute racial division?

4. Does the case of the West Indies support the idea that the English colonizers were inherently racist, rigidly separating white from black?

5. How did colonial South Carolina represent a racial middle ground between its northern and southern neighbors?

American Chiaroscuro: The Status and Definition of Mulattoes in the British Colonies

The word *mulatto* is not frequently used in the United States. Americans generally reserve it for biological contexts, because for social purposes a mulatto is termed a *Negro*. Americans lump together both socially and legally all persons with perceptible admixture of Negro ancestry, thus making social definition without reference to genetic logic; white blood becomes socially advantageous only in overwhelming proportion. The dynamic underlying the peculiar bifurcation of American society into only two color groups can perhaps be better understood if some attempt is made to describe its origin, for the content of social definitions may remain long after the impulses to their formation have gone.

After only one generation of European experience in America, colonists faced the problem of dealing with racially mixed offspring, a problem handled rather differently by the several nations involved. It is well known that the Latin countries, especially Portugal and Spain, rapidly developed a social hierarchy structured according to degrees of intermixture of Negro and European blood, complete with a complicated system of terminology to facilitate definition.[1] The English in Maryland, Virginia, and the Carolinas, on the other hand, seem to have created no such system of ranking. To explain this difference merely by comparing the different cultural backgrounds involved is to risk extending generalizations far beyond possible factual support. Study is still needed of the specific factors affecting each nation's colonies, for there is evidence with some nations that the same cultural heritage was spent in different ways by the colonial heirs, depending on varying conditions encountered in the New World. The English, for example, encountered the problem of race mixture in

Winthrop D. Jordan, "American Chiaroscuro: The Status and Definition of Mulattoes in the British Colonies," *William and Mary Quarterly*, 3rd ser., 19 (1962): 183–200.

very different contexts in their several colonies; they answered it in one fashion in their West Indian islands and in quite another in their colonies on the continent.

As far as the continental colonies were concerned, the presence of mulattoes received legislative recognition by the latter part of the seventeenth century. The word itself, borrowed from the Spanish, was in English usage from the beginning of the century and was probably first employed in Virginia in 1666. From about that time, laws dealing with Negro slaves began to add "and mulattoes." In all English continental colonies mulattoes were lumped with Negroes in the slave codes and in statutes governing the conduct of free Negroes:[2] the law was clear that mulattoes and Negroes were not to be distinguished for different treatment—a phenomenon occasionally noted by foreign travelers.[3]

If mulattoes were to be considered Negroes, logic required some definition of mulattoes, some demarcation between them and white men. Law is sometimes less than logical, however, and throughout the colonial period only Virginia and North Carolina grappled with the question raised by continuing intermixture. In 1705 the Virginia legislature defined a mulatto as "the child, grand child, or great grand child of a negro," or, revealingly, merely "the child of an Indian." North Carolina wavered on the matter, but generally pushed the taint of Negro ancestry from one-eighth to one-sixteenth.[4] There is no reason to suppose that these two colonies were atypical, and in all probability something like these rules operated in the other continental colonies. What the matter came down to, of course, was visibility. Anyone whose appearance discernibly connected him with the Negro was held to be such. The line was thus drawn with regard to practicalities rather than logic. Daily practice supplied logic enough.

Another indication of the refusal of the English continental colonies to separate the "mixed breed" from the African was the absence of terminology which could be used to define a hierarchy of status. The colonists did, it is true, seize upon a separate word to describe those of mixed blood. They were forced to do so if they were to deal with the problem at all, even if they merely wished, as they did, to lump "mulattoes" with Negroes. If, however, an infusion of white blood had been regarded as elevating status, then presumably the more white blood the higher the social rank. Had such ranking existed, descriptive terminology would have been required with which to handle shades of distinction. Yet no such vocabulary developed in the American colonies. Only one word besides *mulatto* was used to describe those of mixed ancestry. The term *mustee (mestee, mustize, mestizo, mustizoe)* was used to describe a mixture which was in part Indian, usually Indian-Negro but occasionally Indian-white. The term was in common use only in the Carolinas, Georgia, and to some extent New York, that is, in those colonies where such crosses occurred with some frequency. Its use revealed the colonists' refusal to identify Indians and Negroes as the same sort of people, a refusal underlined by their belief that the two groups possessed a natural antipathy for each other.[5] Yet while the colonists thus distinguished persons of some Indian ancestry by a separate word, they lumped these *mustees* with mulattoes and Negroes in their slave codes.

Although legislative enactments provide a valuable index of community sentiment, they do not always accurately reflect social practice. An extensive search in the appropriate sources—diaries, letters, travel accounts, newspapers, and so on—fails to reveal any pronounced tendency to distinguish mulattoes from Negroes, any feeling that their status was higher and demanded different treatment. The sources give no indication, for instance, that mulattoes were preferred as house servants or concubines. There may well have been a relatively high proportion of mulattoes among manumitted slaves, but this was probably due to the not unnatural desire of some masters to liberate their own offspring. Yet all this is largely negative evidence, and the proposition that mulattoes were not accorded higher status than Negroes is as susceptible of proof as any negative. Perhaps the usual procedure of awaiting disproof through positive evidence may be allowed.

A single exception to these generalizations stands out sharply from the mass of colonial legislation. In 1765 the colony of Georgia not only undertook to encourage immigration of free colored persons (itself a unique step) but actually provided that free mulatto and mustee immigrants might be naturalized as white men by the legislature, complete with "all the Rights, Priviledges, Powers and Immunities whatsoever which any person born of British parents" could have, except the right to vote and sit in the Commons House of Assembly.[6] Thus a begrudging kind of citizenship was extended to free mulattoes. That Georgia should so distinguish herself from her northern neighbors was a measure of the colony's weak and exposed condition. A small population with an increasingly high proportion of slaves and perpetual danger from powerful Indian tribes made Georgians eager for men who might be counted as white and thus strengthen the colony. The legislature went to great lengths in its search—perhaps too far, for it never actually naturalized anyone under the aegis of the 1765 law.

Only rarely in the colonial period did the subject of mulattoes receive any attention from American writers. Mulattoes were so fixed in station that their position apparently did not merit attention. The subject did come up once in the *South-Carolina Gazette,* yet even then it was casually raised in connection with an entirely different topic. An anonymous contributor in 1735 offered the public some strictures on Carolina's *nouveau riche,* the "half Gentry," and attacked especially their imitative and snobbish behavior. For illustration he turned to the character of the mulatto.

> It is observed concerning the Generation of *Molattoes,* that they are seldom well beloved either by the Whites or the Blacks. Their Approach towards Whiteness, makes them look back with some kind of Scorn upon the Colour they seem to have left, while the Negroes, who do not think them better than themselves, return their Contempt with Interest: And the Whites, who respect them no Whit the more for the nearer Affinity in Colour, are apt to regard their Behaviour as too bold and assuming, and bordering upon Impudence. As they are next to Negroes, and but just above them, they are terribly afraid of being thought Negroes, and therefore avoid as much as possible their Company or Commerce: and Whitefolks are as little fond of the Company of *Molattoes.*[7]

The writer's point, of course, was not that mulattoes were in fact superior to Negroes, but that they alone thought they were. Apparently mulattoes thought white blood to be a source of elevation, a proposition which whites (and Negroes as well) were quick to deny. White blood secured one's status only if undiluted.

A somewhat different aspect of this problem came up in 1784 when it was forced on the attention of a Savannah merchant, Joseph Clay. As executor of a will Clay became responsible for the welfare of two young mulattoes, very possibly the children of his deceased friend. Because the young people were both free, Clay's letter to a gentleman in Ireland offers valuable evidence of what a combination of personal freedom and some white ancestry afforded in the way of social position in Georgia. "These young Folks are very unfortunately situated in this Country," Clay wrote, "their descent places them in the most disadvantageous situation, as Free persons the Laws protects them—but they gain no rank in Life White Persons do not commonly associate with them on a footing of equality—so many of their own Colour (say the mixt breed) being Slaves, they too naturally fall in with them, and even the Negro Slaves claim a right to their acquaintance and Society." For Clay the situation was one of unrelieved gloom, even of horror: "thus a little reflection will present to you what their future Prospects here must be—neglected by the most respectable Class of Society, [they] are forced to intermix with the lowest, and in what that must end—we would wish to draw a Veil—all the Care that can be taken of them cant prevent it, it arrises from our peculiar situation in regard to these people." Clay went on to recommend as "the most eligible plan" that the children be sent to Europe if his correspondent would accept them as wards. "The Boy might be Bound to some business . . . and the Girl might make a very good Wife to some honest Tradesman." It was essential that they cross the Atlantic: "this alone can save them . . . I think they might both be made usefull Members of Society no such distinctions interfere with their happiness on your side the Water."[8] Clay added finally that several of his friends endorsed his proposal. Apparently America offered little opportunity for blacks to become whites through intermixture. American society, wedded as it was to Negro slavery, drew a rigid line which did not exist in Europe: this was indeed "our peculiar situation in regard to these people."

The existence of a rigid barrier between whites and those of Negro blood necessarily required a means by which the barrier could on occasion be passed. Some accommodation had to be made for those persons with so little Negro blood that they appeared to be white, for one simply could not go around calling apparently white persons Negroes. Once the stain was washed out visibly it was useless as a means of identification. Thus there developed the silent mechanism of "passing." Such a device would have been unnecessary if those of mixed ancestry and appearance had been regarded as midway between white and black. It was the existence of a broad chasm which necessitated the sudden leap which passing represented.

Fortunately it is possible to catch a glimpse of this process as it operated in the colonial period by following the extraordinary career of a family named Gibson in South Carolina. In 1731 a member of the Commons House of Assembly announced in the chamber that several free colored men with their white wives had immigrated from Virginia with the intention of settling on the Santee River. Free Negroes were undesirable enough, but white wives made the case exceptionally disturbing. "The house apprehending [this prospect] to be of ill Consequence to this Province," appointed a committee to inquire into the matter. Governor Robert Johnson had already sent for what seemed to be the several families involved, and the committee asked him to report his findings to the house.

"The people lately come into the Settlements having been sent for," Johnson duly reported, "I have had them before me in Council and upon Examination find that they are not Negroes nor Slaves but Free people, That the Father of them here is named Gideon Gibson and his Father was also free, I have been informed by a person who has lived in Virginia that this Gibson has lived there Several Years in good Repute and by his papers that he has produced before me that his transactions there have been very regular, That he has for several years paid Taxes for two tracts of Land and had seven Negroes of his own, That he is a Carpenter by Trade and is come hither for the support of his Family." This evident respectability so impressed the governor that he allowed the Gibson family to remain in the colony. "The account he has given of himself," Johnson declared, "is so Satisfactory that he is no Vagabond that I have in Consideration of his Wifes being a white woman and several White women Capable of working and being Serviceable in the Country permitted him to Settle in this Country upon entering into Recognizance for his good behaviour which I have taken accordingly."[9]

The meaning of Johnson's statement that "they are not Negroes nor Slaves but Free people" is not entirely clear. Certainly Gideon Gibson himself was colored; it seems likely that he was mulatto rather than Negro, but it is impossible to tell surely. At any rate Gideon Gibson prospered very nicely: by 1736 either he or a son of the same name owned 450 acres of Carolina land. He continued to own Negroes, and in 1757 he was described as owning property in two widely separated counties. By 1765 the status of Gideon Gibson (by this time definitely the son of the original carpenter) was such that he was appointed administrator of an estate.[10] His sister married a wealthy planter, and there is no evidence to indicate that Gibson himself was regarded by his neighbors as anything but white.[11] In 1768 he was leading a band of South Carolina Regulators on the field of battle. The commander dispatched to arrest Gibson was a planter and colonel in the militia, George Gabriel Powell, who ignominiously resigned his commission when his men sided with the Regulators. This latter worthy, apparently a kind master to his own Negroes, sought vindication by attacking Gibson's ancestry.[12] The exact nature of the attack is unclear, but the matter came up on the floor of the Commons, of which Powell was a member. The prominent merchant-patriot of Charles Town, Henry Laurens, recorded the conflict in a letter written some years later. Laurens was writing from England of his own conviction that slavery ought to be brought to an end, a conviction that inevitably raised the question of color.

> Reasoning from the colour carries no conviction. By perseverance the black may be blanched and the "stamp of Providence" effectually effaced. Gideon Gibson escaped the penalties of the negro law by producing upon comparison more red and white in his face than could be discovered in the faces of half the descendants of the French refugees in our House of Assembly, including your old acquaintance the Speaker. I challenged them all to the trial. The children of this same Gideon, having passed through another stage of whitewash were of fairer complexion than their prosecutor George Gabriel [Powell].—But to confine them to their original clothing will be best. They may and ought to continue a separate people, may be subjected by special

laws, kept harmless, made useful and freed from the tyranny and arbitrary power of individuals; but as I have already said, this difficulty cannot be removed by arguments on this side of the water.[13]

Laurens showed both sides of the coin. He defended an individual's white status on the basis of appearance and at the same time expressed the conviction that colored persons "may and ought to continue a separate people." Once an Ethiopian always an Ethiopian, unless he could indeed change his skin.

Gideon Gibson's successful hurdling of the barrier was no doubt an unusual case; it is of course impossible to tell how unusual. Passing was difficult but not impossible, and it stood as a veiled, unrecognized monument to the American ideal of a society open to all comers. One Virginia planter advertised in the newspaper for his runaway mulatto slave who he stated might try to pass for free or as a "white man." An English traveler reported calling upon a Virginia lawyer who was "said to be" and who looked like a mulatto.[14] But the problem of evidence is insurmountable. The success of the passing mechanism depended upon its operating in silence. Passing was a conspiracy of silence not only for the individual but for a biracial society which had drawn a rigid color line based on visibility. Unless a white man was a white man, the gates were open to endless slander and confusion.

That the existence of such a line in the continental colonies was not predominantly the effect of the English cultural heritage is suggested by even a glance at the English colonies in the Caribbean. The social accommodation of racial intermixture in the islands followed a different pattern from that on the continent. It was regarded as improper, for example, to work mulattoes in the fields — a fundamental distinction. Apparently they were preferred as tradesmen, house servants, and especially as concubines.[15] John Luffman wrote that mulatto slaves "fetch a lower price than blacks, unless they are tradesmen, because the purchasers cannot employ them in the drudgeries to which negroes are put too; the colored men, are therefore mostly brought up to trades or employed as house slaves, and the women of this description are generally prostitutes."[16] Though the English in the Caribbean thought of their society in terms of white, colored, and black, they employed a complicated battery of names to distinguish persons of various racial mixtures. This terminology was borrowed from the neighboring Spanish, but words are not acquired unless they fulfill a need. While the English settlers on the continent borrowed one Spanish word to describe all mixtures of black and white, the islanders borrowed at least four — *mulatto, sambo, quadroon,* and *mestize* — to describe differing degrees.[17] And some West Indians were prepared to act upon the logic which these terms implied. The respected Jamaican historian, Bryan Edwards, actually proposed extension of civil privileges to mulattoes in proportion to their admixture of white blood.[18] Such a proposition was unheard of on the continent.

The difference between the two regions on this matter may well have been connected with another pronounced divergence in social practice. The attitude toward interracial sex was far more genial in the islands than in the continental colonies. In the latter, miscegenation very rarely met with anything but disapproval in principle, no matter how avid the practice. Sexual intimacy between any white person and any Negro (that "unnatural and inordinate copulation") was utterly condemned. Protests against the practice were frequent.[19] A traveler in New York reported that the citizens of Albany possessed a particular "moral delicacy" on one point: "they were from infancy in habits of familiarity with these humble friends [the Negroes], yet being early taught that nature had placed between them a barrier, which it was in a high degree criminal and disgraceful to pass, they considered a mixture of such distinct races with abhorrence, as a violation of her laws."[20] About 1700 the Chester County Court in Pennsylvania ordered a Negro "never more to meddle with any white woman more uppon paine of his life." Public feeling on this matter was strong enough to force its way over the hurdles of the legislative process into the statute books of many colonies. Maryland and Virginia forbade cohabitation of whites and Negroes well before the end of the seventeenth century. Similar prohibitions were adopted by Massachusetts, North and South Carolina, and Pennsylvania during the next quarter-century and by Georgia when Negroes were admitted to that colony in 1750. Thus two Northern and all Southern colonies legally prohibited miscegenation.[21] Feeling against intercourse with Negroes was strengthened by the fact that such activity was generally illicit; Americans had brought from England certain standards of marital fidelity which miscegenation flagrantly violated.

The contrast offered by the West Indies is striking. Protests against interracial sex relations were infrequent. Colored mistresses were kept openly. "The Planters are in general rich," a young traveler wrote, "but a set of dissipating, abandoned, and cruel people. Few even of the married ones, but keep a Mulatto or Black Girl in the house or at lodgings for certain purposes."[22] Edward Long of Jamaica put the matter this way: "He who should presume to shew any displeasure against such a thing as simple fornication, would for his pains be accounted a simple blockhead; since not one in twenty can be persuaded, that there is either sin; or shame in cohabiting with his slave."[23] Perhaps most significant of all, no island legislature prohibited extramarital miscegenation and only one declared against intermarriage.[24] The reason, of course, was that white men so commonly slept with Negro women that to legislate against the practice would have been merely ludicrous. Concubinage was such an integral part of island life that one might just as well attempt to abolish the sugar cane.

Mulattoes in the West Indies, then, were products of accepted practice, something they assuredly were not in the continental colonies. In the one area they were the fruits of a desire which society tolerated and almost institutionalized; in the other they represented an illicit passion which public morality unhesitatingly condemned. On the continent, unlike the West Indies, mulattoes represented a practice about which men could only feel guilty. To reject and despise the productions of one's own guilt was only natural.

If such difference in feeling about miscegenation has any connection with the American attitude toward mulattoes, it only raises the question of what caused that difference. Since the English settlers in both the West Indies and the continental colonies brought with them the same cultural baggage, something in their colonial experiences must have caused the divergence in their attitudes toward miscegenation. Except perhaps for climatic disimilarity, a factor of very doubtful importance, the most fundamental difference lay in the relative numbers of whites and Negroes in the two areas. On the continent the percentage of Negroes in the total population reached its peak in the period 1730–65 and has been declining since. It ranged from about 3 per cent in New England, 8 to 15 per cent in the middle colonies, 30 to 40 in Maryland and Virginia, 25 in North Carolina, 40 in Georgia, to a high of some 60 per cent in South Carolina. The proportion of Negroes in the islands was far higher: 75 per cent in Barbados, 80 in the Leeward Islands, and over 90 in Jamaica.[25]

These figures strongly suggest a close connection between a high proportion of Negroes and open acceptance of miscegenation. South Carolina, for example, where Negroes formed a majority of the population, was alone among the continental colonies in tolerating even slightly conspicuous interracial liaisons.[26] Thoroughly disparate proportions of Negroes, moreover, made it inevitable that the West Indies and the continental colonies would develop dissimilar societies. The West Indian planters were lost not so much in the Caribbean as in a sea of blacks. They found it impossible to re-create English culture as they had known it. They were corrupted by living in a police state, though not themselves the objects of its discipline. The business of the islands was business, the production of agricultural staples; the islands were not where one really lived, but where one made one's money. By contrast, the American colonists maintained their hold on the English background, modifying it not so much to accommodate slavery as to winning the new land. They were numerous enough to create a new culture with a validity of its own, complete with the adjustments necessary to absorb non-English Europeans. Unlike the West Indians, they felt no need to be constantly running back to England to reassure themselves that they belonged to civilization. Because they were conscious of the solid worth of their own society, forged with their own hands, they vehemently rejected any trespass upon it by a people so alien as the Negroes. The islanders could hardly resent trespass on something which they did not have. By sheer weight of numbers their society was black and slave.

This fundamental difference was perhaps reinforced by another demographic factor. In the seventeenth century the ratio of men to women had been high in America and higher still in the West Indies, where the ratio was about three to two, or, as the sex ratio is usually expressed, 150 (males per 100 females). In the following century it dropped drastically. New England's sex ratio went below 100 as a result of emigration which was as usual predominantly male. Elsewhere on the continent the bounding birth rate nearly erased the differential: in 1750, except on the edge of the frontier, it was probably no more than 110 and in most places less. Perhaps not so well known is the fact that the same process occurred in most of the English islands. Emigration sapped their male strength until Barbados had a sex ratio in the 80's and the various Leeward Islands were balanced in the neighborhood of 100. A significant exception was Jamaica, where in mid-eighteenth century a plentiful supply of land maintained a sex ratio of nearly two to one.[27]

Male numerical predomination was surely not without effect on interracial sexual relations. Particularly where the white population was outnumbered by the black, white women formed a small group. Their scarcity rendered them valuable. The natural reaction on the part of white men was to place them protectively upon a pedestal and then run off to gratify passions elsewhere. For their part white women, though they might propagate children, inevitably held themselves aloof from the world of lust and passion, a world associated with infidelity and Negro slaves. Under no circumstances would they have attempted, nor would they have been allowed, to clamber down from their pedestal to seek pleasures of their own across the racial line. In fact the sexual union of white women with Negro men was uncommon in all colonies. When it did occur (and it did more often than is generally supposed) it was in just those areas to which the demographic factors point—America north of South Carolina, especially in New England, where white women even married Negroes. Such a combination, legitimized or not, was apparently unknown in the West Indies.[28]

If a high sex ratio contributed to the acceptability of miscegenation, it may well have enhanced the acceptability of mulatto offspring. For example, there is the striking fact that Jamaica, the only colony where the sex ratio continued high, was the only colony to give legislative countenance to the rise of mulattoes. In 1733 the legislature provided that "no Person who is not above Three Degrees removed in a lineal Descent from the Negro Ancestor exclusive, shall be allowed to vote or poll in Elections; and no one shall be deemed a Mulatto after the Third Generation, as aforesaid, but that they shall have all the Privileges and Immunities of His Majesty's white Subjects of this Island, provided they are brought up in the Christian Religion."[29] In this same period Barbados was barring any person "whose original Extract shall be proved to have been from a Negro" from voting and from testifying against whites.[30] Beginning in the 1730's the Jamaican legislature passed numerous private acts giving the colored offspring (and sometimes the colored mistress) of such and such a planter the rights and privileges of white persons, especially the right to inherit the planter's estate. There was objection to this blanching of mulattoes, however, for in 1761 the Assembly restricted the amount of property a planter might leave to his mulatto children, saying that "such bequests tend greatly to destroy the distinction requisite, and absolutely necessary to be kept up in this island, between white persons and negroes, their issue and offspring. . . . " The law failed to destroy the acceptability of the practice, however, for the private acts continued.[31] It was in Jamaica, too, that Bryan Edwards called for extension of civil privileges to mulattoes. And Edward Long, in his history of the island, wrote that those beyond the third generation were "called English, and consider themselves as free from all taint of the Negroe race."[32] Thus Jamaica, with the highest proportion of Negroes and highest sex ratio of all the English colonies, was unique in its practice of publicly transforming Negroes into white men.

The American continental colonist refused to make this extension of privilege. He remained firm in his rejection of the mulatto, in his categorization of mixed-bloods as belonging to the lower caste. It was an unconscious decision dictated perhaps in large part by the weight of Negroes on his society, heavy enough to be a burden, yet not so heavy as to make him abandon all hope of maintaining his own identity, physically and culturally. Interracial propagation was a constant reproach that he was failing to be true to himself. Sexual intimacy strikingly symbolized a union he wished to avoid. If he could not restrain his sexual nature, he could at least reject its fruits and thus solace himself that he had done no harm. Perhaps he sensed as well that continued racial intermixture would eventually undermine the logic of the racial slavery upon which his society was based. For the separation of slaves from free men depended on a clear demarcation of the races, and the presence of mulattoes blurred this essential distinction. Accordingly he made every effort to nullify the effects of racial intermixture: by classifying the mulatto as a Negro he was in effect denying that intermixture had occurred at all.

Notes

1. See, for example, Irene Diggs, "Color in Colonial Spanish America," *Journal of Negro History*, XXXVIII (1953), 403–27.

2. These statements are based on an examination of what I believe to be nearly all the colonial and state statutes concerning Negroes and slaves through 1807. For the use of *mulatto* see the *Oxford English Dictionary* and the private petition to the Virginia Assembly in "The Randolph Manuscript," *Virginia Magazine of History and Biography*, XVII (1909), 232. The word was first used in a statute in 1678: William Hand Browne and others, eds., *Archives of Maryland* (Baltimore, 1883–), VII, 76. Maryland actually created a legally separate class of persons known as "Mulattoes born of white women," and in doing so developed a severe case of legislative stuttering. The difficulty originated in 1664 when the Assembly declared that children were to follow the condition of the father (rather than the mother as in other colonies). It took 35 years to straighten out this matter, but meanwhile some provision had to be made for mulatto children of white mothers, for no one really wanted them to be slaves. The Assembly provided that they should serve until age 31. This group was sometimes treated legally as white and sometimes as Negro, a procedure which seems to have been followed only about through the 1730's. (Virginia in 1691 enacted similar provisions for this class, but apparently abandoned them five years later.) The underlying intention was that mulatto children of white mothers should be free in status, though punished for their illegitimate origin. This was not discrimination between mulattoes and Negroes but between mulattoes of two different kinds of mothers, white and black. The legal confusion and inconsistencies on this matter may be followed in Browne and others, eds., *Archives of Md.*, I, 526–27, 533–34; VII, 176, 177, 203–05; XIII, 290, 292, 304, 306–07, 308, 323, 380, 394, 529, 546–49; XIX, 428; XXII, 551–52; XXVI, 254–61; XXX, 289–90; XXXIII, 111–12; XXXVI, 275–76; XXXVIII, 39; William Kilty, ed., *The Laws of Maryland* (Annapolis, 1799–1800), II, chap. 67, sec. 14. None of the standard secondary sources on the Negro in Maryland offer a satisfactory account of this matter. For Virginia, see William Waller Hening, ed., *The Statutes at Large: Being a Collection of All the Laws of Virginia* . . . (New York, Philadelphia, Richmond, 1819–23), II, 170; III, 87, 137–40, 252. A Virginia militia act of 1777 declared that free mulattoes might serve as "drummers, fifers, or pioneers" (Hening, ed., *Statutes of Va.*, V, 268), but this failure to refer to "negroes and mulattoes" was so unusual that one must suspect inadvertent omission. See also a clear case of such omission in Massachusetts: George H. Moore, *Notes on the History of Slavery in Massachusetts* (New York, 1866), 228–37.

3. Duc de La Rochefoucault Liancourt, *Travels through the United States of North America* . . . (London, 1799), I, 568; Kenneth and Anna M. Roberts, trans., *Moreau de St. Méry's American Journey, 1793–1798* (Garden City, N.Y., 1947), 301–02.

4. Hening, ed., *Statutes of Va.*, III, 252; Walter L. Clark, ed., *The State Records of North Carolina* (Goldsboro, N.C., 1886–1910), XXIII, 106, 160, 262, 345, 526, 559, 700, 882; XXIV, 61; XXV, 283, 445; William L. Saunders, ed., *The Colonial Records of North Carolina* (Raleigh, 1886–90), VII, 605, 608, 645. In 1785–87 Virginia altered the definition to one-quarter Negro, but there was no general trend in this direction during the 19th century; see Hening, ed., *Statutes of Va.*, XII, 184; Samuel Shepard, ed., *The Statutes at Large of Virginia, from October Session 1792, to December Session 1806, Inclusive*, New Ser., being a continuation of Hening (Richmond, 1835–36), I, 123.

5. See, for example, Hugh Jones, *The Present State of Virginia from Whence Is Inferred a Short View of Maryland and North Carolina*, ed. Richard L. Morton (Chapel Hill, 1956), 50; John Brickell, *The Natural History of North-Carolina* . . . (Dublin, 1737), 263, 273; Anne Grant, *Memoirs of an American Lady; With Sketches of Manners and Scenes in America as They Existed Previous to the Revolution*, ed. James G. Wilson (New York, 1901), I, 134; [George Milligen-Johnston], *A Short Description of the Province of South-Carolina* (London, 1770), in Chapman J. Milling, ed., *Colonial South Carolina; Two Contemporary Descriptions by Governor James Glen and Doctor George Milligen-Johnston*, South Caroliniana, Sesquicentennial Series, No. 1 (Columbia, 1951), 136; Parish Transcripts, Box III, bundle: Minutes of Council in Assembly (1755), 3, New-York Historical Society, New York City. See also Kenneth W. Porter, "Relations between Negroes and Indians within the Present Limits of the United States," *Jour. of Negro Hist.*, XVII (1932), 298–306, 322–27.

6. Allen D. Candler, comp., *The Colonial Records of the State of Georgia* (Atlanta, 1904–16), XVIII, 659. The wording of the act is ambiguous, and though free Negroes might have fallen under its provisions, the legislature was apparently thinking only of mulattoes and mustees.

7. *South-Carolina Gazette* (Charleston), Mar. 22, 1735.

8. Joseph Clay to John Wright, Savannah, Feb. 17, 1784, in *Letters of Joseph Clay, Merchant of Savannah, 1776–1793* . . . (Georgia Historical Society, *Collections*, VIII [1913]), 203–04. Further testimony that mulattoes considered themselves superior to Negroes may be found in William Logan to Lord Granville, London, Aug. 13, 1761, Logan Papers, XI, 60, Historical Society of Pennsylvania, Philadelphia.

9. Parish Transcripts, Box II, bundle: S.C., Minutes of House of Burgesses (1730–35), 9.

10. *South-Carolina Gazette*, Aug. 29, 1743, supplement; Nov. 26, Dec. 10, 1750; Mar. 3, 1757, supplement; "Abstracts of Records of the Proceedings in the Court of Ordinary, 1764–1771," *South Carolina Historical and Genealogical Magazine*, XXII (1921), 97, 127; see also XXIII (1922), 35; [Prince Frederick Parish], *The Register Book for the Parish Prince Frederick, Winyaw* (Baltimore, 1916), 15, 20, 32, 34.

11. For this point I am indebted to Dr. Richard M. Brown, of Rutgers University, who is currently publishing a study of the South Carolina Regulators. He also provided information and references on the younger Gideon Gibson's regulating activities and kindly pointed out to me a useful local history: Alexander Gregg, *History of the Old Cheraws* [2nd ed.] (Columbia, 1905). See this source, 72n, for the marriage of Gibson's sister.

12. For the Regulators' battle, see Gregg, *Old Cheraws*, 73–74, 139–56; Charles Woodmason, *The Carolina Backcountry on the Eve of the Revolution; The Journal and Other Writings of Charles Woodmason, Anglican Itinerant*, ed. Richard J. Hooker (Chapel Hill, 1953), 176–77. For biographical information on Powell and his kind-

ness to his slaves, A. S. Salley, ed., "Diary of William Dillwyn during a Visit to Charles Town in 1772," *S.C. Hist. and Genea. Mag.*, XXXVI (1935), 35, and n.

13. Henry Laurens to William Drayton, Feb. 15, 1783, in David Duncan Wallace, *The Life of Henry Laurens; With a Sketch of the Life of Lieutenant-Colonel John Laurens* (New York and London, 1915), 454. The speaker was Peter Manigault.

14. Rind, *Virginia Gazette* (Williamsburg), Apr. 23, 1772; J[ohn] F. D. Smyth, *A Tour in the United States of America: Containing an Account of the Present Situation of That Country . . .* (London, 1784), I, 123.

15. [Thomas Tryon], *Friendly Advice to the Gentlemen-Planters of the East and West Indies* ([London], 1684), 140–41; John Singleton, *A General Description of the West-Indian Islands, as far as Relates to the British, Dutch, and Danish Governments . . .* (Barbados, 1767), 152–53; [Janet Schaw], *Journal of a Lady of Quality; Being the Narrative of a Journey to the West Indies, North Carolina, and Portugal, in the Years 1774 to 1776,* ed. Evangeline Walker Andrews, in collaboration with Charles M. Andrews, 3rd ed. (New Haven, 1939), 112; [Edward Long], *The History of Jamaica . . .* (London, 1774), II, 328–30, 332–35; William Beckford, *A Descriptive Account of the Island of Jamaica* (London, 1790), II, 322; Bryan Edwards, *The History, Civil and Commercial, of the British Colonies in the West Indies,* 3rd ed. (London, 1801), II, 18–31. The only place in the United States ever to develop an established institution of mulatto concubinage was New Orleans, where the influence of the Spanish and of French refugees from the West Indies was strong.

16. John Luffman, *A Brief Account of the Island of Antigua, together with the Customs and Manners of Its Inhabitants, as Well White as Black* (London, 1789), 115.

17. *Mulatto* meant one-half white; *sambo*, one-fourth white; *quadroon*, three-fourths white; and *mestize* (which did not imply Indian mixture as it did on the continent), seven-eighths white. Long, *Jamaica*, II, 260–61; Edwards, *History*, II, 18; J[ohn] G. Stedman, *Narrative of a Five Years' Expedition, against the Revolted Negroes of Surinam, in Guiana* (London, 1796), II, plate opposite p. 98; *Jamaica, a Poem, in Three Parts* (London, 1777), 22–23.

18. Edwards, *History,* II, 24n.

19. For a few examples: James Fontaine, *Memoirs of a Huguenot Family,* trans. and ed. Ann Maury (New York, 1872), 350; Eugene P. Chase, trans. and ed., *Our Revolutionary Forefathers; The Letters of François, Marquis de Barbé-Marbois during His Residence in the United States as Secretary of the French Legation, 1779–1785* (New York, 1929), 74; *South-Carolina Gazette*, Mar. 18, 1732; Mar. 28, 1743; May 22, 1749; Elhanan Winchester, *The Reigning Abominations, Especially the Slave Trade, Considered as Causes of Lamentation* (London, 1788), 22n; Klaus G. Loewald, Beverly Starika, and Paul S. Taylor, trans. and eds., "Johann Martin Bolzius Answers a Questionnaire on Carolina and Georgia," *William and Mary Quarterly*, 3rd Ser., XIV (1957), 235.

20. Grant, *Memoirs,* I, 85.

21. Hening, ed., *Statutes of Va.,* II, 170; III, 86–87, 452–54; Browne and others, eds., *Archives of Md.,* I, 533–34; VII, 204–05; XIII, 546–49; XXII, 552; XXVI, 259–60; XXX, 289–90; XXXIII, 112; XXXVI, 275–76; Edward R. Turner, *The Negro in Pennsylvania, Slavery — Servitude — Freedom, 1639–1861* (Washington, 1911), 30n; *The Acts and Resolves, Public and Private, of the Province of the Massachusetts Bay* (Boston, 1869–1922), I, 578–79; *Acts and Laws of the Commonwealth of Massachusetts* (Boston, 1890–98), IV, 10; Clark, ed., *State Recs. of N.C.,* XXIII, 65, 106, 160, 195; Thomas Cooper and David J. McCord, eds., *Statutes at Large of South Carolina* (Columbia, 1836–41), III, 20; James T. Mitchell and others, eds., *Statutes at Large of*

Pennsylvania from 1682 to 1809 (Harrisburg, 1896–1915), IV, 62–63; also X, 67–73, and the *Pennsylvania Packet* (Philadelphia), Mar. 4, 1779; Candler, comp., *Col. Recs. of Ga.,* I, 59–60. Delaware, not considered a Southern colony or state by contemporaries, passed no outright prohibition until 1807 (repealed the next year) but provided for heavier fines in interracial bastardy cases than in such cases where only whites were involved; *Laws of the State of Delaware* (New Castle and Wilmington, 1797–1816), I, 105–09; IV, 112–13, 221.

22. Samuel Thornely, ed., *The Journal of Nicholas Cresswell, 1774–1777* (New York, 1924), 39.

23. Long, *Jamaica*, II, 328.

24. The exception was Montserrat; the law was probably disallowed: Colonial Office Papers, Ser. 391, LXIX, 51 (Feb. 16, 1762), Public Record Office, London, for which reference I am indebted to Frank W. Pitman, *The Development of the British West Indies, 1700–1763* (New Haven, 1917), 27, where the citation is given as C.O. 391/70, p. 51 (Feb. 16, 1762). This statement on the absence of anti-miscegenation laws is based on a reading of the statutes of the various islands which, from the nature of the sources, is probably less complete than for the continental colonies. For obvious reasons only those islands settled primarily by Englishmen have been included: those captured from the French had a different cultural heritage. An act applying to all the Leeward Islands declared that no "Free Person" should be married to "any Slave," but this provision was in a section regulating the conduct of free Negroes and almost certainly applied only to them; *Acts of Assembly, Passed in the Charibbee Leeward Islands. From 1690, to 1730* (London, 1734), 138–39. Bermuda in 1663 acted against miscegenation, but this fact merely gives additional confirmation to the pattern outlined above, since the island at the time had fairly close contact with Virginia and never became like the Caribbean islands in economic structure, proportion of Negroes, or social atmosphere. See J. H. Lefroy, comp., *Memorials of the Discovery and Early Settlement of the Bermudas or Somers Islands, 1515–1685* (London, 1877–79), II, 190.

25. Population statistics for the colonial period are at best merely rough estimates in most cases. I have compiled tables showing the proportion of Negroes in the total population for the principal colonies settled by Englishmen, with figures drawn largely from the following sources: U.S. Bureau of the Census, *A Century of Population Growth, from the First Census of the United States to the Twelfth, 1799–1900* (Washington, 1909); Evarts B. Greene and Virginia D. Harrington, *American Population before the Federal Census of 1790* (New York, 1932); *Calendar of State Papers, Colonial Series, America and West Indies*, 37 vols. (London, 1860–); Alan Burns, *History of the British West Indies* (London, 1954), 401, 454, 461, 465, 499, 500, 510, 511, 514, 515; Vincent T. Harlow, *A History of Barbados, 1625–1685* (Oxford, 1926), 338; C. S. S. Higham, *The Development of the Leeward Islands under the Restoration, 1660–1688; A Study of the Foundations of the Old Colonial System* (Cambridge, Eng., 1921), 145, 148; Pitman, *West Indies*, 48, 370, 374, 378; Edwards, *History*, II, 2. My figures are in substantial agreement with those which may be calculated from a table recently compiled by Stella H. Sutherland in U.S., Bureau of the Census, *Historical Statistics of the United States, Colonial Times to 1957* (Washington, 1960), 756, except in the case of North Carolina where her figures yield a proportion nearly 10 per cent higher than mine.

26. For a New Englander's comment on miscegenation in South Carolina see Mark Anthony DeWolfe Howe, ed., "Journal of Josiah Quincy, Junior, 1773," *Massachusetts Historical Society, Proceedings*, XLIX (Boston, 1916), 463.

27. Tables of the sex ratios in the various colonies have been calculated from the sources given in the previous note and, in addition, Pitman, *West Indies,* 371–82; Long, *Jamaica,* I, 376.

28. I have found no cases of white women sleeping with colored men in the West Indies. For this combination on the continent, see extracts from the Court of General Sessions of the Peace [Suffolk County, Mass.], Apr. 4, 1704, Oct. 2, 1705, Apr. 6, 1708, July 4, 1710, Apr. 6, 1714, in Parish Transcripts, Box XVI; James Bowdoin to George Scott, Boston, Oct. 14, 1763, in Bowdoin-Temple Papers, XXVIII, 56, Mass. Hist. Soc., Boston, in which Bowdoin wrote that "My Man Caesar has been engaged in an amour with some of the white ladies of the Town. . . . " so he was sending him to Grenada in exchange for produce or another Negro boy; W. H. Morse, "Lemuel Haynes," *Jour. of Negro Hist.,* IV (1919), 22; [Daniel Horsmanden], *A Journal of the Proceedings in the Detection of the Conspiracy Formed by Some White People, in Conjunction with Negro and Other Slaves, for Burning the City of New-York in America, and Murdering the Inhabitants* (New York, 1744), 2, 4; *Boston News-Letter,* June 25, 1741; Arthur W. Calhoun, *A Social History of the American Family from Colonial Times to the Present* (Cleveland, 1917–19), I, 211; Helen T. Catterall, ed., *Judicial Cases Concerning American Slavery and the Negro* (Washington, 1926), I, 89–91; II, 12; IV, 28, 32; *Maryland Gazette* (Annapolis), Aug. 19, 1746; James H. Johnston, Race Relations in Virginia and Miscegenation in the South, 1776–1860 (unpubl. Ph.D. diss., University of Chicago, 1937), 199–202; John H. Franklin, *The Free Negro in North Carolina, 1790–1860* (Chapel Hill, 1943), 37, 39; Saunders, *Col. Recs. of N.C.,* II, 704; "Johann Martin Bolzius," 235. For this combination in actual marriage, see Lorenzo J. Greene, *The Negro in Colonial New England, 1620–1776* (New York, 1942), 201–02; Morse, "Lemuel Haynes," 26; Grant, *Memoirs,* I, 86; Calhoun, *Family,* I, 211; Catterall, ed., *Judicial Cases,* II, 11; La Rochefoucault Liancourt, *Travels,* I, 602; *Maryland Gazette,* July 31, 1794; and the case of Gideon Gibson discussed above. A causal connection between the sex ratio and miscegenation has been suggested by Herbert Moller, "Sex Composition and Correlated Culture Patterns of Colonial America," *William and Mary Quarterly,* 3rd Ser., II (1945), 131–37, but some of his conclusions must be treated with caution.

29. *Acts of Assembly, Passed in the Island of Jamaica; from 1681, to 1737, inclusive* (London, 1738), 260–61; see also Long, *Jamaica,* II, 261, 321. This same definition of a mulatto was retained in 1780; *Acts of Assembly, Passed in the Island of Jamaica; from 1770, to 1783, inclusive* (Kingston, 1786), 174.

30. *Acts of Assembly, Passed in the Island of Barbadoes, from 1648, to 1718* (London, 1721), 112, 153, 171, 213, 226, 267; Richard Hall, comp., *Acts, Passed in the Island of Barbados. From 1643, to 1762, inclusive* (London, 1764), 256.

31. *Acts of Assembly, Passed in the Island of Jamaica, from the Year 1681 to the Year 1769 Inclusive.* 2 vols. in 1, with an *Appendix: Containing Laws respecting Slaves* (Kingston, 1787), I, Table of Acts, 18, 20–25, 30–31; II, Table of Acts, 3, 7–11, 14–15; II, 36–39; *Acts of Assembly, Passed in the Island of Jamaica; from 1770, to 1783, Inclusive,* Table of Acts, 8, 11, 13, 16, 18, 20, 22, 24, 26, 28, 30–31; *Acts of Assembly, Passed in the Island of Jamaica, from the Year 1784 to the Year 1788 Inclusive* (Kingston, 1789), Table of Acts, vi–viii, xi, xv–xvi; *The Laws of Jamaica: Comprehending All the Acts in Force, Passed between the Thirty-Second Year of the Reign of King Charles the Second, and the Thirty-Third Year of the Reign of King George the Third* (St. Jago de la Vega, 1792), I, Table of Acts, no pagination; *The Laws of Jamaica, Passed in the Thirty-Third Year of the Reign of King George the Third* (St. Jago de la Vega, 1793), Table of Acts, no

pagination; *The Laws of Jamaica, Passed in the Thirty-Fourth Year of the Reign of King George the Third* (St. Jago de la Vega, 1794), Table of Acts, no pagination. See also Long, *Jamaica*, II, 320–23; Edwards, *History*, II, 22–23.

32. Long, *Jamaica*, II, 332. This general picture of Jamaica is borne out by a work on a somewhat later period; Philip D. Curtin, *Two Jamaicas: The Role of Ideas in a Tropical Colony, 1830–1865* (Cambridge, Mass., 1955), chaps. 1–3.

Edmund S. Morgan

Slavery and Freedom: The American Paradox

The final selection is Edmund S. Morgan's presidential address to the Organization of American Historians in 1972. Such an occasion offers a highly regarded scholar the chance to reflect on large questions. Morgan chose to ask how to turn slavery from a deplorable exception into a central part of the American story, bound up closely with freedom itself. His book about that problem, *American Slavery, American Freedom,* was three years away from publication but in "Slavery and Freedom: The American Paradox" he presents his large argument. The essay shakes the origins-of-slavery debate away from sectional differences and deep roots, relocating it in relation to the undoubted fact that late-eighteenth-century Virginia gave America its foremost exemplars of liberty. The link between what they proclaimed and how they lived was not, he suggests, mere happenstance or a regrettable but minor contradiction. It was fundamental.

Although Morgan begins in the eighteenth century, he takes the reader back to slavery's beginnings in the Chesapeake. As of 1670, slavery did not define black Virginians' condition, and most plantation field labor was done by whites. As of 1700, precisely the reverse was true on both counts. Morgan does not investigate the demographic price to the slaves of the transition (although Allan Kulikoff does so in *Tobacco and Slaves: The Development of Southern Cultures in the Chesapeake, 1680–1800* [1986]). He does suggest that if freedom includes different kinds of people acting together without turning their differences into civil war, black slavery gave white Virginians what they needed to be free. Colonial Virginia was not the first human society in which slavery and freedom coexisted. The ancient and medieval worlds offer ample precedent. Yet unlike any Athenian, Roman, or Florentine, one famous slaveholding Virginian did proclaim the equality of all men. As Thomas Jefferson understood himself, that implied the inadmissibility of any form of slavery. There, perhaps, beats the heart of an American paradox that still is not completely worked out.

Edmund S. Morgan received his Ph.D. from Harvard University and enjoyed a long teaching career at Brown University and Yale University, where he is now Sterling Professor of History, Emeritus. He is one of the foremost scholars of early American history.

Questions for a Closer Reading

1. Why does Morgan assert that the development of American slavery and of American freedom need to be considered together?

2. Is racism the only explanation for slavery's continuing place in "the republican vision of the eighteenth century"?

3. Does Morgan's argument help us understand the particular difficulties posed by Thomas Jefferson's attitude toward slavery?

4. What reasons did the very earliest English colonizers have for thinking that Virginia would be "a spearhead of English liberty in an oppressed world"? When, why, and how did that vision fail?

5. In what ways did the switch from servitude to slavery resolve the problems that seventeenth-century white Virginians had created for themselves?

Slavery and Freedom:
The American Paradox

American historians interested in tracing the rise of liberty, democracy, and the common man have been challenged in the past two decades by other historians, interested in tracing the history of oppression, exploitation, and racism. The challenge has been salutary, because it has made us examine more directly than historians have hitherto been willing to do, the role of slavery in our early history. Colonial historians, in particular, when writing about the origin and development of American institutions have found it possible until recently to deal with slavery as an exception to everything they had to say. I am speaking about myself but also about most of my generation. We owe a debt of gratitude to those who have insisted that slavery was something more than an exception, that one-fifth of the American population at the time of the Revolution is too many people to be treated as an exception.[1]

We shall not have met the challenge simply by studying the history of that one fifth, fruitful as such studies may be, urgent as they may be. Nor shall we have met the challenge if we merely execute the familiar maneuver of turning our old interpretations on their heads. The temptation is already apparent to argue that slavery and oppression were the dominant features of American history and that efforts to advance liberty and equality were the exception, indeed no more than a device to divert the masses while their chains were being fastened. To dismiss the rise of liberty and equality in American history as a mere sham is not only to ignore hard facts, it is also to evade the problem presented by those facts. The rise of liberty and equality in this country was accompanied by the rise of slavery. That two such contradictory developments were taking place simultaneously over a long period of our history, from the seventeenth century to the nineteenth, is the central paradox of American history.

Edmund S. Morgan, "Slavery and Freedom: The American Paradox," *Journal of American History* 59 (1972): 5–29.

The challenge, for a colonial historian at least, is to explain how a people could have developed the dedication to human liberty and dignity exhibited by the leaders of the American Revolution and at the same time have developed and maintained a system of labor that denied human liberty and dignity every hour of the day.

The paradox is evident at many levels if we care to see it. Think, for a moment, of the traditional American insistence on freedom of the seas. "Free ships make free goods" was the cardinal doctrine of American foreign policy in the Revolutionary era. But the goods for which the United States demanded freedom were produced in very large measure by slave labor. The irony is more than semantic. American reliance on slave labor must be viewed in the context of the American struggle for a separate and equal station among the nations of the earth. At the time the colonists announced their claim to that station they had neither the arms nor the ships to make the claim good. They desperately needed the assistance of other countries, especially France, and their single most valuable product with which to purchase assistance was tobacco, produced mainly by slave labor. So largely did that crop figure in American foreign relations that one historian has referred to the activities of France in supporting the Americans as "King Tobacco Diplomacy," a reminder that the position of the United States in the world depended not only in 1776 but during the span of a long lifetime thereafter on slave labor.[2] To a very large degree it may be said that Americans bought their independence with slave labor.

The paradox is sharpened if we think of the state where most of the tobacco came from. Virginia at the time of the first United States census in 1790 had 40 percent of the slaves in the entire United States. And Virginia produced the most eloquent spokesmen for freedom and equality in the entire United States: George Washington, James Madison, and above all, Thomas Jefferson. They were all slaveholders and remained so throughout their lives. In recent years we have been shown in painful detail the contrast between Jefferson's pronouncements in favor of republican liberty and his complicity in denying the benefits of that liberty to blacks.[3] It has been tempting to dismiss Jefferson and the whole Virginia dynasty as hypocrites. But to do so is to deprive the term "hypocrisy" of useful meaning. If hypocrisy means, as I think it does, deliberately to affirm a principle without believing it, then hypocrisy requires a rare clarity of mind combined with an unscrupulous intention to deceive. To attribute such an intention, even to attribute such clarity of mind in the matter, to Jefferson, Madison, or Washington is once again to evade the challenge. What we need to explain is how such men could have arrived at beliefs and actions so full of contradiction.

Put the challenge another way: how did England, a country priding itself on the liberty of its citizens, produce colonies where most of the inhabitants enjoyed still greater liberty, greater opportunities, greater control over their own lives than most men in the mother country, while the remainder, one fifth of the total, were deprived of virtually all liberty, all opportunities, all control over their own lives? We may admit that the Englishmen who colonized America and their revolutionary descendants were racists, that consciously or unconsciously they believed liberties and rights should be confined to persons of a light complexion. When we have said as much, even when we have probed the depths of racial prejudice, we will not have fully accounted for the paradox. Racism was surely an essential element in it, but I should like to suggest another element, that I believe to have influenced the development of both slavery and freedom as we have known them in the United States.

Let us begin with Jefferson, this slaveholding spokesman of freedom. Could there have been anything in the kind of freedom he cherished that would have made him acquiesce, however reluctantly, in the slavery of so many Americans? The answer, I think, is yes. The freedom that Jefferson spoke for was not a gift to be conferred by governments, which he mistrusted at best. It was a freedom that sprang from the independence of the individual. The man who depended on another for his living could never be truly free. We may seek a clue to Jefferson's enigmatic posture toward slavery in his attitude toward those who enjoyed a seeming freedom without the independence needed to sustain it. For such persons Jefferson harbored a profound distrust, which found expression in two phobias that crop up from time to time in his writings.

The first was a passionate aversion to debt. Although the entire colonial economy of Virginia depended on the willingness of planters to go into debt and of British merchants to extend credit, although Jefferson himself was a debtor all his adult life—or perhaps because he was a debtor—he hated debt and hated anything that made him a debtor. He hated it because it limited his freedom of action. He could not, for example, have freed his slaves so long as he was in debt. Or so at least he told himself. But it was the impediment not simply to their freedom but to his own that bothered him. "I am miserable," he wrote, "till I shall owe not a shilling. . . . "[4]

The fact that he had so much company in his misery only added to it. His Declaration of Independence for the United States was mocked by the hold that British merchants retained over American debtors, including himself.[5] His hostility to Alexander Hamilton was rooted in his recognition that Hamilton's pro-British foreign policy would tighten the hold of British creditors, while his domestic policy would place the government in the debt of a class of native American creditors, whose power might become equally pernicious.

Though Jefferson's concern with the perniciousness of debt was almost obsessive, it was nevertheless altogether in keeping with the ideas of republican liberty that he shared with his countrymen. The trouble with debt was that by undermining the independence of the debtor it threatened republican liberty. Whenever debt brought a man under another's power, he lost more than his own freedom of action. He also weakened the capacity of his country to survive as a republic. It was an axiom of current political thought that republican government required a body of free, independent, property-owning citizens.[6] A nation of men, each of whom owned enough property to support his family, could be a republic. It would follow that a nation of debtors, who had lost their property or mortgaged it to creditors, was ripe for tyranny. Jefferson accordingly favored every means of keeping men out of debt and keeping property widely distributed. He insisted on the abolition of primogeniture and entail; he declared that the earth belonged to the living and should not be kept from them by the debts or credits of the dead; he would have given fifty acres of land to every American who did not have it—all because he believed the citizens of a republic must be free from the control of other men and that they could be free only if they were economically free by virtue of owning land on which to support themselves.[7]

If Jefferson felt so passionately about the bondage of the debtor, it is not surprising that he should also have sensed a danger to the republic from another class of men who, like debtors, were nominally free but whose independence was illusory. Jefferson's second phobia was his distrust of the landless urban workman who labored in manufactures. In Jefferson's view, he was a free man in name only. Jefferson's hostility to artificers is well known and is generally attributed to his romantic preference for the rural life. But both his distrust for artificers and his idealization of small landholders as "the most precious part of a state" rested on his concern for individual independence as the basis of freedom. Farmers made the best citizens because they were "the most vigorous, the most independant, the most virtuous. . . . " Artificers, on the other hand, were dependent on "the casualties and caprice of customers." If work was scarce, they had no land to fall back on for a living. In their dependence lay the danger. "Dependance," Jefferson argued, "begets subservience and venality, suffocates the germ of virtue, and prepares fit tools for the designs of ambition." Because artificers could lay claim to freedom without the independence to go with it, they were "the instruments by which the liberties of a country are generally overturned."[8]

In Jefferson's distrust of artificers we begin to get a glimpse of the limits—and limits not dictated by racism—that defined the republican vision of the eighteenth century. For Jefferson was by no means unique among republicans in his distrust of the landless laborer. Such a distrust was a necessary corollary of the widespread eighteenth-century insistence on the independent, property-holding individual as the only bulwark of liberty, an insistence originating in James Harrington's republican political philosophy and a guiding principle of American colonial politics, whether in the aristocratic South Carolina assembly or in the democratic New England town.[9] Americans both before and after 1776 learned their republican lessons from the seventeenth- and eighteenth-century British commonwealthmen; and the commonwealthmen were uninhibited in their contempt for the masses who did not have the propertied independence required of proper republicans.

John Locke, the classic explicator of the right of revolution for the protection of liberty, did not think about extending that right to the landless poor. Instead, he concocted a scheme of compulsory labor for them and their children. The children were to begin at the age of three in public institutions, called working schools because the only subject taught would be work (spinning and knitting). They would be paid in bread and water and grow up "inured to work." Meanwhile the mothers, thus relieved of the care of their offspring, could go to work beside their fathers and husbands. If they could not find regular employment, then they too could be sent to the working school.[10]

It requires some refinement of mind to discern precisely how this version of women's liberation from child care differed from outright slavery. And many of Locke's intellectual successors, while denouncing slavery in the abstract, openly preferred slavery to freedom for the lower ranks of laborers. Adam Ferguson, whose works were widely read in America, attributed the overthrow of the Roman republic, in part at least, to the emancipation of slaves, who "increased, by their numbers and their vices, the weight of that dreg, which, in great and prosperous cities, ever sinks, by the tendency of vice and misconduct to the lowest condition."[11]

That people in the lowest condition, the dregs of society, generally arrived at that position through their own vice and misconduct, whether in ancient Rome or modern Britain, was an unexamined article of faith among eighteenth-century republicans. And the vice that was thought to afflict the lower ranks most severely was idleness. The eighteenth-century's preferred cure for idleness lay in the religious and ethical doctrines which R. H. Tawney described as the New Medicine for Poverty, the doctrines in which Max Weber discerned the origins of the spirit of capitalism. But in every society a stubborn mass of men and women refused the medicine. For such persons the commonwealthmen did not hesitate to prescribe slavery. Thus Francis Hutcheson, who could argue eloquently against the enslavement of Africans, also argued that perpetual slavery should be "the ordinary punishment of such idle vagrants as, after proper admonitions and tryals of temporary servitude, cannot be engaged to support themselves and their families by any useful labours."[12] James Burgh, whose *Political Disquisitions* earned the praises of many American revolutionists, proposed a set of press gangs "to seize all idle and disorderly persons, who have been three times complained of before a magistrate, and to set them to work during a certain time, for the benefit of great trading, or manufacturing companies, &c."[13]

The most comprehensive proposal came from Andrew Fletcher of Saltoun. Jefferson hailed in Fletcher a patriot whose political principles were those "in vigour at the epoch of the American emigration [from England]. Our ancestors brought them here, and they needed little strengthening to make us what we are. . . . "[14] Fletcher, like other commonwealthmen, was a champion of liberty, but he was also a champion of slavery. He attacked the Christian church not only for having promoted the abolition of slavery in ancient times but also for having perpetuated the idleness of the freedmen thus turned loose on society. The church by setting up hospitals and almshouses had enabled men through the succeeding centuries to live without work. As a result, Fletcher argued, his native Scotland was burdened with 200,000 idle rogues, who roamed the country, drinking, cursing, fighting, robbing, and murdering. For a remedy he proposed that they all be made slaves to men of property. To the argument that their masters might abuse them, he answered in words which might have come a century and a half later from a George Fitzhugh: that this would be against the master's own interest, "That the most brutal man will not use his beast ill only out of a humour; and that if such Inconveniences do sometimes fall out, it proceeds, for the most part, from the perverseness of the Servant."[15]

In spite of Jefferson's tribute to Fletcher, there is no reason to suppose that he endorsed Fletcher's proposal. But he did share Fletcher's distrust of men who were free in name while their empty bellies made them thieves, threatening the property of honest men, or else made them slaves in fact to anyone who would feed them. Jefferson's own solution for the kind of situation described by Fletcher was given in a famous letter to Madison, prompted by the spectacle Jefferson encountered in France in the 1780s, where a handful of noblemen had engrossed huge tracts of land on which to hunt game, while hordes of the poor went without work and without bread. Jefferson's proposal, characteristically phrased in terms of natural right, was for the poor to appropriate the uncultivated lands of the nobility. And he drew for the United States his usual lesson of the need to keep land widely distributed among the people.[16]

Madison's answer, which is less well known than Jefferson's letter, raised the question whether it was possible to eliminate the idle poor in any country as fully populated as France. Spread the land among them in good republican fashion and there would still be, Madison thought, "a great surplus of inhabitants, a greater by far than will be employed in cloathing both themselves and those who feed them. . . . " In spite of those occupied in trades and as mariners, soldiers, and so on, there would remain a mass of men without work. "A certain degree of misery," Madison concluded, "seems inseparable from a high degree of populousness."[17] He did not, however, go on to propose, as Fletcher had done, that the miserable and idle poor be reduced to slavery.

The situation contemplated by Madison and confronted by Fletcher was not irrelevant to those who were planning the future of the American republic. In a country where population grew by geometric progression, it was not too early to think about a time when there might be vast numbers of landless poor, when there might be those mobs in great cities that Jefferson feared as sores on the body politic. In the United States as Jefferson and Madison knew it, the urban labor force as yet posed no threat, because it was small; and the agricultural labor force was, for the most part, already enslaved. In Revolutionary America, among men who spent their lives working for other men rather than working for themselves, slaves probably constituted a majority.[18] In Virginia they constituted a large majority.[19] If Jefferson and Madison, not to mention Washington, were unhappy about that fact and yet did nothing to alter it, they may have been restrained, in part at least, by thoughts of the role that might be played in the United States by a large mass of free laborers.

When Jefferson contemplated the abolition of slavery, he found it inconceivable that the freed slaves should be allowed to remain in the country.[20] In this attitude he was probably moved by his or his countrymen's racial prejudice. But he may also have had in mind the possibility that when slaves ceased to be slaves, they would become instead a half million idle poor, who would create the same problems for the United States that the idle poor of Europe did for their states. The slave, accustomed to compulsory labor, would not work to support himself when the compulsion was removed. This was a commonplace among Virginia planters before the creation of the republic and long after. "If you free the slaves," wrote Landon Carter, two days after the Declaration of Independence, "you must send them out of the country or they must steal for their support."[21]

Jefferson's plan for freeing his own slaves (never carried out) included an interim educational period in which they would have been half-taught, half-compelled to support themselves on rented land; for without guidance and preparation for self-support, he believed, slaves could not be expected to become fit members of a republican society.[22] And St. George Tucker, who drafted detailed plans for freeing Virginia's slaves, worried about "the possibility of their becoming idle, dissipated, and finally a numerous banditti, instead of turning their attention to industry and labour." He therefore included in his plans a provision for compelling the labor of the freedmen on an annual basis. "For we must not lose sight of this important consideration," he said, "that these people must be *bound* to labour, if they do not *voluntarily* engage therein. . . . In absolving them from the yoke of slavery, we must not forget the interests of society. Those interests require the exertions of every individual in some mode or other; and those who have not wherewith to support themselves honestly without corporal labour, whatever be their complexion, ought to be compelled to labour."[23]

It is plain that Tucker, the would-be emancipator, distrusted the idle poor regardless of color. And it seems probable that the Revolutionary champions of liberty who acquiesced in the continued slavery of black labor did so not only because of racial prejudice but also because they shared with Tucker a distrust of the poor that was inherent in eighteenth-century conceptions of republican liberty. Their historical guidebooks had made them fear to enlarge the free labor force.

That fear, I believe, had a second point of origin in the experience of the American colonists, and especially of Virginians, during the preceding century and a half. If we turn now to the previous history of Virginia's labor force, we may find, I think, some further clues to the distrust of free labor among Revolutionary republicans and to the paradoxical rise of slavery and freedom together in colonial America.

The story properly begins in England with the burst of population growth there that sent the number of Englishmen from perhaps three million in 1500 to four-and-one-half million by 1650.[24] The increase did not occur in response to any corresponding growth in the capacity of the island's economy to support its people. And the result was precisely that misery which Madison pointed out to Jefferson as the consequence of "a high degree of populousness." Sixteenth-century England knew the same kind of unemployment and poverty that Jefferson witnessed in eighteenth-century France and Fletcher in seventeenth-century Scotland. Alarming numbers of idle and hungry men drifted about the country looking for work or plunder. The government did what it could to make men of means hire them, but it also adopted increasingly severe measures against their wandering, their thieving, their roistering, and indeed their very existence. Whom the workhouses and prisons could not swallow the gallows would have to, or perhaps the army. When England had military expeditions to conduct abroad, every parish packed off its most unwanted inhabitants to the almost certain death that awaited them from the diseases of the camp.[25]

As the mass of idle rogues and beggars grew and increasingly threatened the peace of England, the efforts to cope with them increasingly threatened the liberties of Englishmen. Englishmen prided themselves on a "gentle government,"[26] a government that had been releasing its subjects from old forms of bondage and endowing them with new liberties, making the "rights of Englishmen" a phrase to conjure with. But there was nothing gentle about the government's treatment of the poor; and as more Englishmen became poor, other Englishmen had less to be proud of. Thoughtful men could see an obvious solution: get the surplus Englishmen out of England. Send them to the New World, where there were limitless opportunities for work. There they would redeem themselves, enrich the mother country, and spread English liberty abroad.

The great publicist for this program was Richard Hakluyt. His *Principall Navigations, Voiages and Discoveries of the English Nation*[27] was not merely the narrative of voyages by Englishmen around the globe, but a powerful suggestion that the world ought to be English or at least ought to be ruled by Englishmen. Hakluyt's was a dream of empire, but of benevolent empire, in which England would confer the blessings of her own free government on the less fortunate peoples of the world. It is doubtless true that Englishmen, along with other Europeans, were already imbued with prejudice against men of darker complexions than their own. And it is also true that the principal beneficiaries of Hakluyt's empire would be Englishmen. But Hakluyt's dream cannot be dismissed as mere hypocrisy any more than Jefferson's affirmation of human equality can be so dismissed. Hakluyt's compassion for the poor and oppressed was not confined to the English poor, and in Francis Drake's exploits in the Caribbean Hakluyt saw, not a thinly disguised form of piracy, but a model for English liberation of men of all colors who labored under the tyranny of the Spaniard.

Drake had gone ashore at Panama in 1572 and made friends with an extraordinary band of runaway Negro slaves. "Cimarrons" they were called, and they lived a free and hardy life in the wilderness, periodically raiding the Spanish settlements to carry off more of their people. They discovered in Drake a man who hated the Spanish as much as they did and who had the arms and men to mount a stronger attack than they could manage by themselves. Drake wanted Spanish gold, and the Cimarrons wanted Spanish iron for tools. They both wanted Spanish deaths. The alliance was a natural one and apparently untroubled by racial prejudice. Together the English and the Cimarrons robbed the mule train carrying the annual supply of Peruvian treasure across the isthmus. And before Drake sailed for England with his loot, he arranged for future meetings.[28] When Hakluyt heard of this alliance, he concocted his first colonizing proposal, a scheme for seizing the Straits of Magellan and transporting Cimarrons there, along with surplus Englishmen. The straits would be a strategic strong point for England's world empire, since they controlled the route from Atlantic to Pacific. Despite the severe climate of the place, the Cimarrons and their English friends would all live warmly together, clad in English woolens, "well lodged and by our nation made free from the tyrannous Spanyard, and quietly and courteously governed by our nation."[29]

The scheme for a colony in the Straits of Magellan never worked out, but Hakluyt's vision endured, of liberated natives and surplus Englishmen, courteously governed in English colonies around the world. Sir Walter Raleigh caught the vision. He dreamt of wresting the treasure of the Incas from the Spaniard by allying with the Indians of Guiana and sending Englishmen to live with them, lead them in rebellion against Spain, and govern them in the English manner.[30] Raleigh also dreamt of a similar colony in the country he named Virginia. Hakluyt helped him plan it.[31] And Drake stood ready to supply Negroes and Indians, liberated from Spanish tyranny in the Caribbean, to help the enterprise.[32]

Virginia from the beginning was conceived not only as a haven for England's suffering poor, but as a spearhead of English liberty in an oppressed world. That was the dream; but when it began to materialize at Roanoke Island in 1585, something went wrong. Drake did his part by liberating Spanish Caribbean slaves, and carrying to Roanoke those who wished to join him.[33] But the English settlers whom Raleigh sent there proved unworthy of the role assigned them. By the time Drake arrived they had shown themselves less than courteous to the Indians on whose assistance they depended. The first group of settlers murdered the chief who befriended them, and then gave up and ran for home aboard Drake's returning ships. The second group simply disappeared, presumably killed by the Indians.[34]

What was lost in this famous lost colony was more than the band of colonists who have never been traced. What was also lost and never quite recovered in subsequent ventures was the dream of Englishman and Indian living side by side in peace and liberty. When the English finally planted a permanent colony at Jamestown they came as conquerors, and their government was far from gentle. The Indians willing to endure it were too few in numbers and too broken in spirit to play a significant part in the settlement.

Without their help, Virginia offered a bleak alternative to the workhouse or the gallows for the first English poor who were transported there. During the first two decades of the colony's existence, most of the arriving immigrants found precious little English liberty in Virginia.[35] But by the 1630s the colony seemed to be working out, at least in part, as its first planners had hoped. Impoverished Englishmen were arriving every year in large numbers, engaged to serve the existing planters for a term of years, with the prospect of setting up their own households a few years later. The settlers were spreading up Virginia's great rivers, carving out plantations, living comfortably from their corn fields and from the cattle they ranged in the forests, and at the same time earning perhaps ten or twelve pounds a year per man from the tobacco they planted. A representative legislative assembly secured the traditional liberties of Englishmen and enabled a larger proportion of the population to participate in their own government than had ever been the case in England. The colony even began to look a little like the cosmopolitan haven of liberty that Hakluyt had first envisaged. Men of all countries appeared there: French, Spanish, Dutch, Turkish, Portuguese, and African.[36] Virginia took them in and began to make Englishmen out of them.

It seems clear that most of the Africans, perhaps all of them, came as slaves, a status that had become obsolete in England, while it was becoming the expected condition of Africans outside Africa and of a good many inside.[37] It is equally clear that a substantial number of Virginia's Negroes were free or became free. And all of them, whether servant, slave, or free, enjoyed most of the same rights and duties as other Virginians. There is no evidence during the period before 1660 that they were subjected to a more severe discipline than other servants. They could sue and be sued in court. They did penance in the parish church for having illegitimate children. They earned money of their own, bought and sold and raised cattle of their own. Sometimes they bought their own freedom. In other cases, masters bequeathed them not only freedom but land, cattle, and houses.[38] Northampton, the only county for which full records exist, had at least ten free Negro households by 1668.[39]

As Negroes took their place in the community, they learned English ways, including even the truculence toward authority that has always been associated with the rights of Englishmen. Tony Longo, a free Negro of Northampton, when served a warrant to appear as a witness in court, responded with a scatological opinion of warrants, called the man who served it an idle rascal, and told him to go about his business. The man offered to go with him at any time before a justice of the peace so that his evidence could be recorded. He would go with him at night, tomorrow, the next day, next week, any time. But Longo was busy getting in his corn. He dismissed all pleas with a "Well, well, Ile goe when my Corne is in," and refused to receive the warrant.[40]

The judges understandably found this to be contempt of court; but it was the kind of contempt that free Englishmen often showed to authority, and it was combined with a devotion to work that English moralists were doing their best to inculcate more widely in England. As England had absorbed people of every nationality over the centuries and turned them into Englishmen, Virginia's Englishmen were absorbing their own share of foreigners, including Negroes, and seemed to be successfully moulding a New World community on the English model.

But a closer look will show that the situation was not quite so promising as at first it seems. It is well known that Virginia in its first fifteen or twenty years killed off most of the men who went there. It is less well known that it continued to do so. If my estimate of the volume of immigration is anywhere near correct, Virginia must have been a death trap for at least another fifteen years and probably for twenty or twenty-five. In 1625 the population stood at 1,300 or 1,400; in 1640 it was about 8,000.[41] In the fifteen years between those dates at least 15,000 persons must have come to the colony.[42] If so, 15,000 immigrants increased the population by less than 7,000. There is no evidence of a large return migration. It seems probable that the death rate throughout this period was comparable only to that found in Europe during the peak years of a plague. Virginia, in other words, was absorbing England's surplus laborers mainly by killing them. The success of those who survived and rose from servant to planter must be attributed partly to the fact that so few did survive.

After 1640, when the diseases responsible for the high death rate began to decline and the population began a quick rise, it became increasingly difficult for an indigent immigrant to pull himself up in the world. The population probably passed 25,000 by 1662,[43] hardly what Madison would have called a high degree of populousness. Yet the rapid rise brought serious trouble for Virginia. It brought the engrossment of tidewater land in thousands and tens of thousands of acres by speculators, who recognized that the demand would rise.[44] It brought a huge expansion of tobacco production, which helped to depress the price of tobacco and the earnings of the men who planted it.[45] It brought efforts by planters to prolong the terms of servants, since they were now living longer and therefore had a longer expectancy of usefulness.[46]

It would, in fact, be difficult to assess all the consequences of the increased longevity; but for our purposes one development was crucial, and that was the appearance in Virginia of a growing number of freemen who had served their terms but who were now unable to afford land of their own except on the frontiers or in the interior. In years when tobacco prices were especially low or crops especially poor, men who had been just scraping by were obliged to go back to work for their larger neighbors simply in order to stay alive. By 1676 it was estimated that one fourth of Virginia's freemen were without land of their own.[47] And in the same year Francis Moryson, a member of the governor's council, explained the term "freedmen" as used in Virginia to mean "persons without house and land," implying that this was now the normal condition of servants who had attained freedom.[48]

Some of them resigned themselves to working for wages; others preferred a meager living on dangerous frontier land or a hand-to-mouth existence, roaming from one county to another, renting a bit of land here, squatting on some there, dodging the tax collector, drinking, quarreling, stealing hogs, and enticing servants to run away with them.

The presence of this growing class of poverty-stricken Virginians was not a little frightening to the planters who had made it to the top or who had arrived in the colony already at the top, with ample supplies of servants and capital. They were caught in a dilemma. They wanted the immigrants who kept pouring in every year. Indeed they needed them and prized them the more as they lived longer. But as more and more turned free each year, Virginia seemed to have inherited the problem that she was helping England to solve. Virginia, complained Nicholas Spencer, secretary of the colony, was "a sinke to drayen England of her filth and scum."[49]

The men who worried the uppercrust looked even more dangerous in Virginia than they had in England. They were, to begin with, young, because it was young persons that the planters wanted for work in the fields; and the young have always seemed impatient of control by their elders and superiors, if not downright rebellious. They were also predominantly single men. Because the planters did not think women, or at least English women, fit for work in the fields, men outnumbered women among immigrants by three or four to one throughout the century.[50] Consequently most of the freedmen had no wife or family to tame their wilder impulses and serve as hostages to the respectable world.

Finally, what made these wild young men particularly dangerous was that they were armed and had to be armed. Life in Virginia required guns. The plantations were exposed to attack from Indians by land and from privateers and petty-thieving pirates by sea.[51] Whenever England was at war with the French or the Dutch, the settlers had to be ready to defend themselves. In 1667 the Dutch in a single raid captured twenty merchant ships in the James River, together with the English warship that was supposed to be defending them; and in 1673 they captured eleven more. On these occasions Governor William Berkeley gathered the planters in arms and at least prevented the enemy from making a landing. But while he stood off the Dutch he worried about the ragged crew at his back. Of the ablebodied men in the colony he estimated that "at least one third are Single freedmen (whose Labour will hardly maintaine them) or men much in debt, both which wee may reasonably expect upon any Small advantage the Enemy may gaine upon us, wold revolt to them in hopes of bettering their Condicion by Shareing the Plunder of the Country with them."[52]

Berkeley's fears were justified. Three years later, sparked not by a Dutch invasion but by an Indian attack, rebellion swept Virginia. It began almost as Berkeley had predicted, when a group of volunteer Indian fighters turned from a fruitless expedition against the Indians to attack their rulers. Bacon's Rebellion was the largest popular rising in the colonies before the American Revolution. Sooner or later nearly everyone in Virginia got in on it, but it began in the frontier counties of Henrico and New Kent, among men whom the governor and his friends consistently characterized as rabble.[53] As it spread eastward, it turned out that there were rabble everywhere, and Berkeley understandably raised his estimate of their numbers. "How miserable that man is," he exclaimed, "that Governes a People wher six parts of seaven at least are Poore Endebted Discontented and Armed."[54]

Virginia's poor had reason to be envious and angry against the men who owned the land and imported the servants and ran the government. But the rebellion produced no real program of reform, no ideology, not even any revolutionary slogans. It was a search for plunder, not for principles. And when the rebels had redistributed whatever wealth they could lay their hands on, the rebellion subsided almost as quickly as it had begun.

It had been a shattering experience, however, for Virginia's first families. They had seen each other fall in with the rebels in order to save their skins or their possessions or even to share in the plunder. When it was over, they eyed one another distrustfully, on the lookout for any new Bacons in their midst, who might be tempted to lead the still restive rabble on more plundering expeditions. When William Byrd and Laurence Smith proposed to solve the problems of defense against the Indians by establishing semi-independent buffer settlements on the upper reaches of the rivers, in each of which they would engage to keep fifty men in arms, the assembly at first reacted favorably. But it quickly occurred to the governor and council that this would in fact mean gathering a crowd of Virginia's wild bachelors and furnishing them with an abundant supply of arms and ammunition. Byrd had himself led such a crowd in at least one plundering foray during the rebellion. To put him or anyone else in charge of a large and permanent gang of armed men was to invite them to descend again on the people whom they were supposed to be protecting.[55]

The nervousness of those who had property worth plundering continued throughout the century, spurred in 1682 by the tobacco-cutting riots in which men roved about destroying crops in the fields, in the desperate hope of producing a shortage that would raise the price of the leaf.[56] And periodically in nearby Maryland and North Carolina, where the same conditions existed as in Virginia, there were tumults that threatened to spread to Virginia.[57]

As Virginia thus acquired a social problem analagous to England's own, the colony began to deal with it as England had done, by restricting the liberties of those who did not have the proper badge of freedom, namely the property that government was supposed to protect. One way was to extend the terms of service for servants entering the colony without indentures. Formerly they had served until twenty-one; now the age was advanced to twenty-four.[58] There had always been laws requiring them to serve extra time for running away; now the laws added corporal punishment and, in order to make habitual offenders more readily recognizable, specified that their hair be cropped.[59] New laws restricted the movement of servants on the highways and also increased the amount of extra time to be served for running away. In addition to serving two days for every day's absence, the captured runaway was now frequently required to compensate by labor for the loss to the crop that he had failed to tend and for the cost of his apprehension, including rewards paid for his capture.[60] A three week's holiday might result in a year's extra service.[61] If a servant struck his master, he was to serve another year.[62] For killing a hog he had to serve the owner a year and the informer another year. Since the owner of the hog, and the owner of the servant, and the informer were frequently the same man, and since a hog was worth at best less than one tenth the hire of a servant for a year, the law was very profitable to masters. One Lancaster master was awarded six years extra service from a servant who killed three of his hogs, worth about thirty shillings.[63]

The effect of these measures was to keep servants for as long as possible from gaining their freedom, especially the kind of servants who were most likely to cause trouble. At the same time the engrossment of land was driving many back to servitude after a brief taste of freedom. Freedmen who engaged to work for wages by so doing became servants again, subject to most of the same restrictions as other servants.

Nevertheless, in spite of all the legal and economic pressures to keep men in service, the ranks of the freedmen grew, and so did poverty and discontent. To prevent the wild bachelors from gaining an influence in the government, the assembly in 1670 limited voting to landholders and householders.[64] But to disfranchise the growing mass of single freemen was not to deprive them of the weapons they had wielded so effectively under Nathaniel Bacon. It is questionable how far Virginia could safely have continued along this course, meeting discontent with repression and manning her plantations with annual importations of servants who would later add to the unruly ranks of the free. To be sure, the men at the bottom might have had both land and liberty, as the settlers of some other colonies did, if Virginia's frontier had been safe from Indians, or if the men at the top had been willing to forego some of their profits and to give up some of the lands they had engrossed. The English government itself made efforts to break up the great holdings that had helped to create the problem.[65] But it is unlikely that the policy makers in Whitehall would have contended long against the successful.

In any case they did not have to. There was another solution, which allowed Virginia's magnates to keep their lands, yet arrested the discontent and the repression of other Englishmen, a solution which strengthened the rights of Englishmen and nourished that attachment to liberty which came to fruition in the Revolutionary generation of Virginia statesmen. But the solution put an end to the process of turning Africans into Englishmen. The rights of Englishmen were preserved by destroying the rights of Africans.

I do not mean to argue that Virginians deliberately turned to African Negro slavery as a means of preserving and extending the rights of Englishmen. Winthrop Jordan has suggested that slavery came to Virginia as an unthinking decision.[66] We might go further and say that it came without a decision. It came automatically as Virginians bought the cheapest labor they could get. Once Virginia's heavy mortality ceased, an investment in slave labor was much more profitable than an investment in free labor; and the planters bought slaves as rapidly as traders made them available. In the last years of the seventeenth century they bought them in such numbers that slaves probably already constituted a majority or nearly a majority of the labor force by 1700.[67] The demand was so great that traders for a time found a better market in Virginia than in Jamaica or Barbados.[68] But the social benefits of an enslaved labor force, even if not consciously sought or recognized at the time by the men who bought the slaves, were larger than the economic benefits. The increase in the importation of slaves was matched by a decrease in the importation of indentured servants and consequently a decrease in the dangerous number of new freedmen who annually emerged seeking a place in society that they would be unable to achieve.[69]

If Africans had been unavailable, it would probably have proved impossible to devise a way to keep a continuing supply of English immigrants in their place. There was a limit beyond which the abridgment of English liberties would have resulted not merely in rebellion but in protests from England and in the cutting off of the supply of further servants. At the time of Bacon's Rebellion the English commission of investigation had shown more sympathy with the rebels than with the well-to-do planters who had engrossed Virginia's lands. To have attempted the enslavement of English-born laborers would have caused more disorder than it cured. But to keep as slaves black men who arrived in that condition *was* possible and apparently regarded as plain common sense.

The attitude of English officials was well expressed by the attorney who reviewed for the Privy Council the slave codes established in Barbados in 1679. He found the laws of Barbados to be well designed for the good of his majesty's subjects there, for, he said, "although Negros in that Island are punishable in a different and more severe manner than other Subjects are for Offences of the like nature; yet I humbly conceive that the Laws there concerning Negros are reasonable Laws, for by reason of their numbers they become dangerous, and being a brutish sort of People and reckoned as goods and chattels in that Island, it is of necessity or at least convenient to have Laws for the Government of them different from the Laws of England, to prevent the great mischief that otherwise may happen to the Planters and Inhabitants in that Island."[70] In Virginia too it seemed convenient and reasonable to have different laws for black and white. As the number of slaves increased, the assembly passed laws that carried forward with much greater severity the trend already under way in the colony's labor laws. But the new severity was reserved for people without white skin. The laws specifically exonerated the master who accidentally beat his slave to death, but they placed new limitations on his punishment of "Christian white servants."[71]

Virginians worried about the risk of having in their midst a body of men who had every reason to hate them.[72] The fear of a slave insurrection hung over them for nearly two centuries. But the danger from slaves actually proved to be less than that which the colony had faced from its restive and armed freedmen. Slaves had none of the rising expectations that so often produce human discontent. No one had told them that they had rights. They had been nurtured in heathen societies where they had lost their freedom; their children would be nurtured in a Christian society and never know freedom.

Moreover, slaves were less troubled by the sexual imbalance that helped to make Virginia's free laborers so restless. In an enslaved labor force women could be required to make tobacco just as the men did; and they also made children, who in a few years would be an asset to their master. From the beginning, therefore, traders imported women in a much higher ratio to men than was the case among English servants,[73] and the level of discontent was correspondingly reduced. Virginians did not doubt that discontent would remain, but it could be repressed by methods that would not have been considered reasonable, convenient, or even safe, if applied to Englishmen. Slaves could be deprived of opportunities for association and rebellion. They could be kept unarmed and unorganized. They could be subjected to savage punishments by their owners without fear of legal reprisals. And since their color disclosed their probable status, the rest of society could keep close watch on them. It is scarcely surprising that no slave insurrection in American history approached Bacon's Rebellion in its extent or in its success.

Nor is it surprising that Virginia's freedmen never again posed a threat to society. Though in later years slavery was condemned because it was thought to compete with free labor, in the beginning it reduced by so much the number of freedmen who would otherwise have competed with each other. When the annual increment of freedmen fell off, the number that remained could more easily find an independent place in society, especially as the danger of Indian attack diminished and made settlement safer at the heads of the rivers or on the Carolina frontier. There might still remain a number of irredeemable, idle, and unruly freedmen, particularly among the convicts whom England exported to the colonies. But the numbers were small enough, so that they could be dealt with by the old expedient of drafting them for military expeditions.[74] The way was thus made easier for the remaining freedmen to acquire property, maybe acquire a slave or two of their own, and join with their superiors in the enjoyment of those English liberties that differentiated them from their black laborers.

A free society divided between large landholders and small was much less riven by antagonisms than one divided between landholders and landless, masterless men. With the freedman's expectations, sobriety, and status restored, he was no longer a man to be feared. That fact, together with the presence of a growing mass of alien slaves, tended to draw the white settlers closer together and to reduce the importance of the class difference between yeoman farmer and large plantation owner.[75]

The seventeenth century has sometimes been thought of as the day of the yeoman farmer in Virginia; but in many ways a stronger case can be made for the eighteenth century as the time when the yeoman farmer came into his own, because slavery relieved the small man of the pressures that had been reducing him to continued servitude. Such an interpretation conforms to the political development of the colony. During the seventeenth century the royally appointed governor's council, composed of the largest property-owners in the colony, had been the most powerful governing body. But as the tide of slavery rose between 1680 and 1720 Virginia moved toward a government in which the yeoman farmer had a larger share. In spite of the rise of Virginia's great families on the black tide, the power of the council declined; and the elective House of Burgesses became the dominant organ of government. Its members nurtured a closer relationship with their yeoman constituency than had earlier been the case.[76] And in its chambers Virginians developed the ideas they so fervently asserted in the Revolution: ideas about taxation, representation, and the rights of Englishmen, and ideas about the prerogatives and powers and sacred calling of the independent, property-holding yeoman farmer—commonwealth ideas.

In the eighteenth century, because they were no longer threatened by a dangerous free laboring class, Virginians could afford these ideas, whereas in Berkeley's time they could not. Berkeley himself was obsessed with the experience of the English civil wars and the danger of rebellion. He despised and feared the New Englanders for their association with the Puritans who had made England, however briefly, a commonwealth.[77] He was proud that Virginia, unlike New England, had no free schools and no printing press, because books and schools bred heresy and sedition.[78] He must have taken satisfaction in the fact that when his people did rebel against him under Bacon, they generated no republican ideas, no philosophy of rebellion or of human rights. Yet a century later, without benefit of rebellions, Virginians had learned republican lessons, had introduced schools and printing presses, and were as ready as New Englanders to recite the aphorisms of the commonwealthmen.

It was slavery, I suggest, more than any other single factor, that had made the difference, slavery that enabled Virginia to nourish representative government in a plantation society, slavery that transformed the Virginia of Governor Berkeley to the Virginia of Jefferson, slavery that made the Virginians dare to speak a political language that magnified the rights of freemen, and slavery, therefore, that brought Virginians into the same commonwealth political tradition with New Englanders. The very institution that was to divide North and South after the Revolution may have made possible their union in a republican government.

Thus began the American paradox of slavery and freedom, intertwined and interdependent, the rights of Englishmen supported on the wrongs of Africans. The American Revolution only made the contradictions more glaring, as the slaveholding colonists proclaimed to a candid world the rights not simply of Englishmen but of all men. To explain the origin of the contradictions, if the explanation I have suggested is valid, does not eliminate them or make them less ugly. But it may enable us to understand a little better the strength of the ties that bound freedom to slavery, even in so noble a mind as Jefferson's. And it may perhaps make us wonder about the ties that bind more devious tyrannies to our own freedoms and give us still today our own American paradox.

Notes

1. Particularly Staughton Lynd, *Class Conflict, Slavery, and the United States Constitution: Ten Essays* (Indianapolis, 1967).

2. Curtis P. Nettels, *The Emergence of a National Economy 1775–1815* (New York, 1962), 19. See also Merrill Jensen, "The American Revolution and American Agriculture," *Agricultural History*, XLIII (Jan. 1969), 107–24.

3. William Cohen, "Thomas Jefferson and the Problem of Slavery," *Journal of American History*, LVI (Dec. 1969), 503–26; D. B. Davis, *Was Thomas Jefferson an Authentic Enemy of Slavery?* (Oxford, 1970); Winthrop D. Jordan, *White over Black: American Attitudes toward the Negro, 1550–1812* (Chapel Hill, 1968), 429–81.

4. Julian P. Boyd, ed., *The Papers of Thomas Jefferson* (18 vols., Princeton, 1950–), X, 615. For other expressions of Thomas Jefferson's aversion to debt and distrust of credit, both private and public, see *ibid.*, II, 275–76, VIII, 398–99, 632–33, IX, 217–18, 472–73, X, 304–05, XI, 472, 633, 636, 640, XII, 385–86.

5. Jefferson's career as ambassador to France was occupied very largely by unsuccessful efforts to break the hold of British creditors on American commerce.

6. See Caroline Robbins, *The Eighteenth-Century Commonwealthman: Studies in the Transmission, Development and Circumstance of English Liberal Thought from the Restoration of Charles II until the War with the Thirteen Colonies* (Cambridge, Mass., 1959); J. G. A. Pocock, "Machiavelli, Harrington, and English Political Ideologies in the Eighteenth Century," *William and Mary Quarterly*, XXII (Oct. 1965), 549–83.

7. Boyd, ed., *Papers of Thomas Jefferson*, I, 344, 352, 362, 560, VIII, 681–82.

8. *Ibid.*, VIII, 426, 682; Thomas Jefferson, *Notes on the State of Virginia*, William Peden, ed. (Chapel Hill, 1955), 165. Jefferson seems to have overlooked the dependence of Virginia's farmers on the casualties and caprice of the tobacco market.

9. See Robbins, *The Eighteenth-Century Commonwealthmen;* Pocock, "Machiavelli, Harrington, and English Political Ideologies," 549–83; Michael Zuckerman, "The Social Context of Democracy in Massachusetts," *William and Mary Quarterly*, XXV (Oct. 1968), 523–44; Robert M. Weir, "'The Harmony We Were Famous For': An Interpretation of Pre-Revolutionary South Carolina Politics," *ibid.*, XXVI (Oct. 1969), 473–501.

10. C. B. Macpherson, *The Political Theory of Possessive Individualism* (Oxford, 1962), 221–24; H. R. Fox Bourne, *The Life of John Locke* (2 vols., London, 1876), II, 377–90.

11. Adam Ferguson, *The History of the Progress and Termination of the Roman Republic* (5 vols., Edinburgh, 1799), I, 384. See also Adam Ferguson, *An Essay on the History of Civil Society* (London, 1768), 309–11.

12. Francis Hutcheson, *A System of Moral Philosophy* (2 vols., London, 1755), II, 202; David B. Davis, *The Problem of Slavery in Western Culture* (Ithaca, 1966), 374–78. I am indebted to David B. Davis for several valuable suggestions.

13. James Burgh, *Political Disquisitions: Or, An ENQUIRY into public Errors, Defects, and Abuses* . . . (3 vols., London, 1774–1775), III, 220–21. See the proposal of Bishop George Berkeley that "sturdy beggars should . . . be seized and made slaves to the public for a certain term of years." Quoted in R. H. Tawney, *Religion and the Rise of Capitalism: A Historical Essay* (New York, 1926), 270.

14. E. Millicent Sowerby, ed., *Catalogue of the Library of Thomas Jefferson* (5 vols., Washington, 1952–1959), I, 192.

15. Andrew Fletcher, *Two Discourses Concerning the Affairs of Scotland; Written in the Year 1698* (Edinburgh, 1698). See second discourse (separately paged), 1–33, especially 16.

16. Boyd, ed., *Papers of Thomas Jefferson*, VIII, 681–83.

17. *Ibid.*, IX, 659–60.

18. Jackson Turner Main, *The Social Structure of Revolutionary America* (Princeton, 1965), 271.

19. In 1755, Virginia had 43,329 white tithables and 60,078 black. Tithables included white men over sixteen years of age and black men and women over sixteen. In the census of 1790, Virginia had 292,717 slaves and 110,936 white males over sixteen, out of a total population of 747,680. Evarts B. Greene and Virginia D. Harrington, *American Population before the Federal Census of 1790* (New York, 1932), 150–55.

20. Jefferson, *Notes on the State of Virginia*, 138.

21. Jack P. Greene, ed., *The Diary of Colonel Landon Carter of Sabine Hall, 1752–1778* (2 vols., Charlottesville, 1965), II, 1055.

22. Boyd, ed., *Papers of Thomas Jefferson*, XIV, 492–93.

23. St. George Tucker, *A Dissertation on Slavery with a Proposal for the Gradual Abolition of It, in the State of Virginia* (Philadelphia, 1796). See also Jordan, *White over Black*, 555–60.

24. Joan Thirsk, ed., *The Agrarian History of England and Wales*, Vol. IV: *1500–1640* (Cambridge, England, 1967), 531.

25. See Edmund S. Morgan, "The Labor Problem at Jamestown, 1607–18," *American Historical Review*, 76 (June 1971), 595–611, especially 600–06.

26. This is Richard Hakluyt's phrase. See E. G. R. Taylor, ed., *The Original Writings & Correspondence of the Two Richard Hakluyts* (2 vols., London, 1935), I, 142.

27. Richard Hakluyt, *The Principall Navigations, Voiages and Discoveries of the English Nation*... (London, 1589).

28. The whole story of this extraordinary episode is to be found in I. A. Wright, ed., *Documents concernings English Voyages to the Spanish Main 1569–1580* (London, 1932).

29. Taylor, ed., *Original Writings & Correspondence*, I, 139–46.

30. Walter Raleigh, *The Discoverie of the large and bewtiful Empire of Guiana*, V. T. Harlow, ed. (London, 1928), 138–49; V. T. Harlow, ed., *Ralegh's Last Voyage: Being an account drawn out of contemporary letters and relations*... (London, 1932), 44–45.

31. Taylor, ed., *Original Writings & Correspondence*, II, 211–377, especially 318.

32. Irene A. Wright, trans. and ed., *Further English Voyages to Spanish America, 1583–1594: Documents from the Archives of the Indies at Seville*... (London, 1951), lviii, lxiii, lxiv, 37, 52, 54, 55, 159, 172, 173, 181, 188–89, 204–06.

33. The Spanish reported that "Although their masters were willing to ransom them the English would not give them up except when the slaves themselves desired to go." *Ibid.*, 159. On Walter Raleigh's later expedition to Guiana, the Spanish noted that the English told the natives "that they did not desire to make them slaves, but only to be their friends; promising to bring them great quantities of hatchets and knives, and especially if they drove the Spaniards out of their territories." Harlow, ed., *Ralegh's Last Voyage*, 179.

34. David Beers Quinn, ed., *The Roanoke Voyages 1584–1590* (2 vols., London, 1955).

35. Morgan, "The Labor Problem at Jamestown, 1607–18," pp. 595–611; Edmund S. Morgan, "The First American Boom: Virginia 1618 to 1630," *William and Mary Quarterly*, XXVIII (April 1971), 169–98.

36. There are no reliable records of immigration, but the presence of persons of these nationalities is evident from county court records, where all but the Dutch are commonly identified by name, such as "James the Scotchman," or "Cursory the Turk." The Dutch seem to have anglicized their names at once and are difficult to identify except where the records disclose their naturalization. The two counties for which the most complete records survive for the 1640s and 1650s are Accomack-Northampton and Lower Norfolk. Microfilms are in the Virginia State Library, Richmond.

37. Because the surviving records are so fragmentary, there has been a great deal of controversy about the status of the first Negroes in Virginia. What the records do make clear is that not all were slaves and that not all were free. See Jordan, *White over Black*, 71–82.

38. For examples, see Northampton County Court Records, Deeds, Wills, etc., Book III, f. 83, Book V, ff. 38, 54, 60, 102, 117–19; York County Court Records, Deeds, Orders, Wills, etc., no. 1, ff. 232–34; Surry County Court Records, Deeds, Wills, etc., no. 1, f. 349; Henrico County Court Records, Deeds and Wills 1677–1692, f. 139.

39. This fact has been arrived at by comparing the names of householders on the annual list of tithables with casual identifications of persons as Negroes in the court records. The names of householders so identified for 1668, the peak year during the period for which the lists survive (1662–1677) were: Bastian Cane, Bashaw Ferdinando, John Francisco, Susan Grace, William Harman, Philip Mongum, Francis Pane, Manuel Rodriggus, Thomas Rodriggus, and King Tony.

The total number of households in the county in 1668 was 172; total number of tithables 435; total number of tithable free Negroes 17; total number of tithable unfree Negroes 42. Thus nearly 29 percent of tithable Negroes and probably of all Negroes were free; and about 13.5 percent of all tithables were Negroes.

40. Northampton Deeds, Wills, etc., Book V, 54–60 (Nov. 1, 1654).

41. The figure for 1625 derives from the census for that year, which gives 1,210 persons, but probably missed about 10 percent of the population. Morgan, "The First American Boom," 170n–71n. The figure for 1640 is derived from legislation limiting tobacco production per person in 1639–1640. The legislation is summarized in a manuscript belonging to Jefferson, printed in William Waller Hening, *The Statutes at Large; Being a Collection of All the Laws of Virginia, from the First Session of the Legislature, in the Year 1619* (13 vols., New York, 1823), I, 224–25, 228. The full text is in "Acts of the General Assembly, Jan. 6, 1639–40," *William and Mary Quarterly*, IV (Jan. 1924), 17–35, and "Acts of the General Assembly, Jan. 6, 1639–40," ibid. (July 1924), 159–62. The assembly calculated that a levy of four pounds of tobacco per tithable would yield 18,584 pounds, implying 4,646 tithables (men over sixteen). It also calculated that a limitation of planting to 170 pounds per poll would yield 1,300,000, implying 7,647 polls. Evidently the latter figure is for the whole population, as is evident also from Hening, *Statutes*, I, 228.

42. In the year 1635, the only year for which such records exist, 2,010 persons embarked for Virginia from London alone. See John Camden Hotten, ed., *The Original Lists of Persons of Quality* . . . (London, 1874), 35–145. For other years casual estimates survive. In February 1627/8 Francis West said that 1,000 had been "lately received." Colonial Office Group, Class 1, Piece 4, folio 109 (Public Record Office, London). Hereafter cited CO 1/4, f. 109. In February 1633/4 Governor John Harvey said that "this yeares newcomers" had arrived "this yeare." Yong to Sir Tobie Matthew, July 13, 1634, "Aspinwall Papers," *Massachusetts Historical Society Collections*, IX (1871), 110. In May 1635, Samuel Matthews said that 2,000 had arrived "this yeare." Mathews to   ?, May 25, 1635, "The Mutiny in Virginia, 1635," *Virginia Magazine of History and Biography*, I (April 1894), 417. And in March 1636, John West said that 1,606 persons had arrived "this yeare." West to Commissioners for Plantations, March 28, 1636, "Virginia in 1636," ibid., IX (July 1901), 37.

43. The official count of tithables for 1662 was 11,838. Clarendon Papers, 82 (Bodleian Library, Oxford). The ratio of tithables to total population by this time was probably about one to two. (In 1625 it was 1 to 1.5; in 1699 it was 1 to 2.7.) Since the official count was almost certainly below the actuality, a total population of roughly 25,000 seems probable. All population figures for seventeenth-century Virginia should be treated as rough estimates.

44. Evidence of the engrossment of lands after 1660 will be found in CO 1/39, f. 196; CO 1/40, f. 23; CO 1/48, f. 48; CO 5/1309, numbers 5, 9, and 23; Sloane Papers, 1008, ff. 334–35 (British Museum, London). A recent count of headrights in patents issued for land in Virginia shows 82,000 headrights claimed in the years from 1635 to 1700. Of these nearly 47,000 or 57 percent (equivalent to 2,350,000 acres) were claimed in the twenty-five years after 1650. W. F. Craven, *White, Red, and Black: The Seventeenth-Century Virginian* (Charlottesville, 1971), 14–16.

45. No continuous set of figures for Virginia's tobacco exports in the seventeenth century can now be obtained. The available figures for English imports of American tobacco (which was mostly Virginian) are in United States Bureau of the Census, *Historical Statistics of the United States, Colonial Times to 1957* (Washington, D.C., 1960), series Z 238–40, p. 766. They show for 1672 a total of 17,559,000

pounds. In 1631 the figure had been 272,300 pounds. Tobacco crops varied heavily from year to year. Prices are almost as difficult to obtain now as volume. Those for 1667–1675 are estimated from London prices current in Warren Billings, "Virginia's Deploured Condition, 1660–1676: The Coming of Bacon's Rebellion" (doctoral dissertation, Northern Illinois University, 1969), 155–59.

46. See below.

47. Thomas Ludwell and Robert Smith to the king, June 18, 1676, vol. LXXVII, f. 128, Coventry Papers Longleat House, American Council of Learned Societies British Mss. project, reel 63 (Library of Congress).

48. Ibid., 204–05.

49. Nicholas Spencer to Lord Culpeper, Aug. 6, 1676, ibid., 170. See also CO 1/49, f. 107.

50. The figures are derived from a sampling of the names of persons for whom headrights were claimed in land patents. Patent Books I–IX (Virginia State Library, Richmond). Wyndham B. Blanton found 17,350 women and 75,884 men in "a prolonged search of the patent books and other records of the times . . . ," a ratio of 1 woman to 4.4 men. Wyndham B. Blanton, "Epidemics, Real and Imaginary, and other Factors Influencing Seventeenth Century Virginia's Population," *Bulletin of the History of Medicine,* XXXI (Sept.–Oct. 1957), 462. See also Craven, *White, Red, and Black,* 26–27.

51. Pirates were particularly troublesome in the 1680s and 1690s. See CO 1/48, f. 71; CO 1/51, f. 340; CO 1/52, f. 54; CO 1/55, ff. 105–06; CO 1/57, f. 300; CO 5/1311, no. 10.

52. CO 1/30, ff. 114–15.

53. CO 1/37, ff. 35–40.

54. Vol. LXXVII, 144–46, Coventry Papers.

55. Hening, *Statutes,* II, 448–54; CO 1/42, f. 178; CO 1/43, f. 29; CO 1/44, f. 398; CO 1/47, ff. 258–60, 267; CO 1/48, f. 46; vol. LXXVIII, 378–81, 386–87, 398–99, Coventry Papers.

56. CO 1/48 passim.

57. CO 1/43, ff. 359–65; CO 1/44, ff. 10–62; CO 1/47, f. 261; CO 1/48, ff. 87–96, 100–02, 185; CO 5/1305, no. 43; CO 5/1309, no. 74.

58. Hening, *Statutes,* II, 113–14, 240.

59. Ibid., II, 266, 278.

60. Ibid., II, 116–17, 273–74, 277–78.

61. For example, James Gray, absent twenty-two days, was required to serve fifteen months extra. Order Book 1666–1680, p. 163, Lancaster County Court Records.

62. Hening, *Statutes,* II, 118.

63. Order Book 1666–1680, p. 142, Lancaster County Court Records.

64. Hening, *Statutes,* II, 280. It had been found, the preamble to the law said, that such persons "haveing little interest in the country doe oftner make tumults at the election to the disturbance of his majesties peace, then by their discretions in their votes provide for the conservasion thereof, by makeing choyce of persons fitly qualifyed for the discharge of soe greate a trust. . . . "

65. CO 1/39, f. 196; CO 1/48, f. 48; CO 5/1309, nos. 5, 9, 23; CO 5/1310, no. 83.

66. Jordan, *White over Black,* 44–98.

67. In 1700 they constituted half of the labor force (persons working for other men) in Surry County, the only county in which it is possible to ascertain the numbers. Robert Wheeler, "Social Transition in the Virginia Tidewater, 1650–1720: The

Laboring Household as an Index," paper delivered at the Organization of American Historians' meeting, New Orleans, April 15, 1971. Surry County was on the south side of the James, one of the least wealthy regions of Virginia.

68. See the letters of the Royal African Company to its ship captains, Oct. 23, 1701; Dec. 2, 1701; Dec. 7, 1704; Dec. 21, 1704; Jan. 25, 1704//5, T70 58 (Public Record Office, London).

69. Abbot Emerson Smith, *Colonists in Bondage: White Servitude and Convict Labor in America 1607–1776* (Chapel Hill, 1947), 335. See also Thomas J. Wertenbaker, *The Planters of Colonial Virginia* (Princeton, 1922), 130–31, 134–35; Craven, *White, Red, and Black*, 17.

70. CO 1/45, f. 138.

71. Hening, *Statutes*, II, 481–82, 492–93; III, 86–88, 102–03, 179–80, 333–35, 447–62.

72. For example, see William Byrd II to the Earl of Egmont, July 12, 1736, in Elizabeth Donnan, ed., *Documents Illustrative of the History of the Slave Trade to America* (4 vols., Washington, 1930–1935), IV, 131–32. But compare Byrd's letter to Peter Beckford, Dec. 6, 1735, "Letters of the Byrd Family," *Virginia Magazine of History and Biography*, XXXVI (April 1928), 121–23, in which he specifically denies any danger. The Virginia assembly at various times laid duties on the importation of slaves. See Donnan, ed., *Documents Illustrative of the History of the Slave Trade*, IV, 66–67, 86–88, 91–94, 102–17, 121–31, 132–42. The purpose of some of the acts was to discourage imports, but apparently the motive was to redress the colony's balance of trade after a period during which the planters had purchased far more than they could pay for. See also Wertenbaker, *The Planters of Colonial Virginia*, 129.

73. The Swiss traveler Francis Ludwig Michel noted in 1702 that "Both sexes are usually bought, which increase afterwards." William J. Hinke, trans. and ed., "Report of the Journey of Francis Louis Michel from Berne Switzerland to Virginia, October 2, (1) 1701–December 1, 1702: Part II," *Virginia Magazine of History and Biography*, XXIV (April 1916), 116. A sampling of the names identifiable by sex, for whom headrights were claimed in land patents in the 1680s and 1690s shows a much higher ratio of women to men among blacks than among whites. For example, in the years 1695–1699 (Patent Book 9) I count 818 white men and 276 white women, 376 black men and 220 black women (but compare Craven, *White, Red, and Black*, 99–100). In Northampton County in 1677, among seventy-five black tithables there were thirty-six men, thirty-eight women, and one person whose sex cannot be determined. In Surry County in 1703, among 211 black tithables there were 132 men, seventy-four women, and five persons whose sex cannot be determined. These are the only counties where the records yield such information. Northampton County Court Records, Order Book 10, 189–91; Surry County Court Records, Deeds, Wills, etc., No. 5, part 2, 287–90.

74. Virginia disposed of so many this way in the campaign against Cartagena in 1741 that a few years later the colony was unable to scrape up any more for another expedition. Fairfax Harrison, "When the Convicts Came," *Virginia Magazine of History and Biography*, XXX (July 1922), 250–60, especially 256–57; John W. Shy, "A New Look at Colonial Militia," *William and Mary Quarterly*, XX (April 1963), 175–85. In 1736, Virginia had shipped another batch of unwanted freedmen to Georgia because of a rumored attack by the Spanish. Byrd II to Lord Egmont, July 1736, "Letters of the Byrd Family," *Virginia Magazine of History and Biography*, XXXVI (July 1928), 216–17. Observations by an English traveler who embarked on the same ship suggest that they did not go willingly: "our Lading consisted of all

the Scum of Virginia, who had been recruited for the Service of Georgia, and who were ready at every Turn to mutiny, whilst they belch'd out the most shocking Oaths, wishing Destruction to the Vessel and every Thing in her." "Observations in Several Voyages and Travels in America in the Year 1736," *William and Mary Quarterly,* XV (April 1907), 224.

75. Compare Lyon G. Tyler, "Virginians Voting in the Colonial Period," *William and Mary Quarterly,* VI (July 1897), 7–13.

76. John C. Rainbolt, "The Alteration in the Relationship between Leadership and Constituents in Virginia, 1660 to 1720," *William and Mary Quarterly,* XXVII (July 1970), 411–34.

77. William Berkeley to Richard Nicolls, May 20, 1666, May 4, 1667, Additional Mss. 28, 218, ff. 14–17 (British Museum, London).

78. Hening, *Statutes,* II, 517.

Making Connections

The questions that precede each selection are intended to help students deal with that particular piece of writing. But all the selections here are in dialogue with one another around one large problem. That problem is how we can best understand the emergence of slavery as a fundamental aspect of early American life. As the selections show, there are many possibilities for addressing that problem. They may be mutually exclusive. Or they may complement one another. It is certainly the case that each of these selections makes much more sense if it is read as part of a discussion rather than standing alone. The questions that follow should aid students to realize that the discussion is not finished and that everyone is free to join in.

1. Ira Berlin's essay is built around the process that turned African Creoles into enslaved Africans. How do the other selections expand Berlin's insight?

2. Berlin's subjects are Creoles, meaning people who draw upon two different cultures. So are Washington's. How did the two groups differ?

3. In the light of this collection, was there ever a realistic prospect that Virginia would not become a "slave society"?

4. In what ways can we see Africans and their offspring as among the founders of early America as well as among its victims?

5. The readings in this book discuss specific places, times, and situations rather than generalized "slavery." How do they complicate our picture of American slavery's beginnings?

6. What is the relative balance of culture, demography, and economics in the emergence of Western Hemisphere slavery?

7. How did being of African descent become the only characteristic absolutely necessary for being considered a slave in America?

8. On balance, are you persuaded by Higginbotham's argument that early American whites saw black people as inferior from the very start?

9. In the light of these readings, how might you reconstruct the forces that caused twenty black servants to arrive in Virginia in 1619?

10. What is the place of gender and sexuality in the emergence of American slavery?

11. Does the argument of Berlin and Washington that Africans were involved in enslavement absolve white enslavers from responsibility?

12. Was African slavery an unfortunate exception to early American freedom? Or, in the light of these readings, do you think that freedom and slavery went together?

Suggestions for Further Reading

This volume is not intended to provide a massive bibliography, but any interested student will want to delve into the subject more deeply. For a selection drawn from a book, the best way to start is to go to that book and place the selection within the author's larger argument. Each selection is reproduced with full annotation, as originally published, to allow interested students to go to the author's original sources, study them, and compare their own readings with what the author has made of the same material.

To start going beyond what is here, see W. E. B. Du Bois, *The Suppression of the African Slave Trade to the United States of America, 1638–1870* (1896; reprint, New York: Schocken, 1969) and Oscar Handlin and Mary Flug Handlin, "Origins of the Southern Labor System," *William and Mary Quarterly*, 3rd ser., 7 (1950), 199–222. Others, mentioned in Part One, include Richard S. Dunn, *Sugar and Slaves: the Rise of the Planter Class in the English West Indies, 1624–1713* (Chapel Hill: University of North Carolina Press, 1972); Winthrop D. Jordan, *White over Black: American Attitudes toward the Negro, 1550–1812* (Chapel Hill: University of North Carolina Press, 1968); and Edmund S. Morgan, *American Slavery, American Freedom: The Ordeal of Colonial Virginia* (New York: Norton, 1975). Very important studies that place the issue in a much larger context include David Brion Davis, *The Problem of Slavery in Western Culture* (Ithaca: Cornell University Press, 1967), and *Slavery and Human Progress* (New York: Oxford University Press, 1984); Orlando Patterson, *Slavery and Social Death* (Cambridge: Harvard University Press, 1982); Robin Blackburn, *The Making of New World Slavery, from the Baroque to the Modern* (London: Verso, 1997), and Ira Berlin, *Many Thousands Gone: The First Two Centuries of Slavery in North America* (Cambridge, Mass.: Harvard University Press, 1998). In January 1997 the *William and Mary Quarterly* published a special issue (3rd, ser., 54) titled "Constructing Race" with a major article by Blackburn, "The Old World Background to European Colonial Slavery," as well as eight other essays.

Peter H. Wood has reflected on how understanding of early African American history has developed in "'I Did the Best I Could for My Day':

The Study of Early Black History during the Second Reconstruction, 1960–1976," *William and Mary Quarterly,* 3rd ser., 35 (1978): 185–225. More recently, the British scholar Betty Wood (no relation) has also brought the subject together with her short synthesis *The Origins of American Slavery: Freedom and Bondage in the English Colonies* (New York: Hill and Wang, 1997). The best discussion of the African slave trade remains Philip D. Curtin, *The African Slave Trade: A Census* (Madison: University of Wisconsin Press, 1969), on which I have relied here. There is an enormous literature on the subject. Herbert S. Klein, *The Middle Passage: Comparative Studies in the Atlantic Slave Trade* (Princeton: Princeton University Press, 1978), and Hugh Thomas, *The Slave Trade: The Story of the Atlantic Slave Trade, 1440–1870* (New York: Simon and Schuster, 1997), open the way to deeper exploration. On the issue of white servitude, I have relied on Morgan, *American Slavery, American Freedom.* For arguments to the contrary, see David W. Galenson, *White Servitude in Colonial America: An Economic Analysis* (Cambridge: Cambridge University Press, 1981).

Daniel C. Littlefield, *Rice and Slaves: Ethnicity and the Slave Trade in Colonial South Carolina* (Baton Rouge: Louisiana State University Press, 1981), enriches our understanding of African culture's transplantation to South Carolina. So do Allan Kulikoff, *Tobacco and Slaves: The Development of Southern Cultures in the Chesapeake, 1680–1800* (Chapel Hill: University of North Carolina Press, 1986); Albert Raboteau, *Slave Religion: The "Invisible Institution" in the Ante-Bellum South* (New York: Oxford University Press, 1978); and Sterling Stuckey, *Slave Culture: Nationalist Theory and the Foundations of Black America* (New York: Oxford University Press, 1987). The most recent addition to the list is Philip D. Morgan, *Slave Counterpoint: Black Culture in the Eighteenth-Century Chesapeake and Low Country* (Chapel Hill: University of North Carolina Press, 1998). On the development of the law of slavery, the pioneering work of Leon Higginbotham Jr., excerpted here, is supplemented now by Thomas D. Morris, *Slavery and the Law, 1619–1860* (Chapel Hill: University of North Carolina Press, 1996); Philip J. Schwarz, *Slave Laws in Virginia* (Athens: University of Georgia Press, 1996); Jenny Wahl Bourne, *The Bondsman's Burden: An Economic Analysis of the Common Law of Southern Slavery* (Cambridge: Cambridge University Press, 1998); and an ever-expanding body of scholarship by Paul Finkelman. Yet another illustration of what we are learning is Kathleen Brown, *Good Wives, Nasty Wenches, and Anxious Patriarchs* (Chapel Hill: University of North Carolina Press, 1996), which looks at Colonial Virginia through the eyes of both elite white women and enslaved black women. The questions of slave health that are raised in the volumes by Richard Dunn and Peter Wood already noted are explored more deeply in Richard B. Sheridan, *Doctors and Slaves: A Medical and Demographic History of Slavery in the British West Indies,*

1680–1834 (Cambridge: Cambridge University Press, 1985), and Todd Savitt, *Medicine and Slavery: The Diseases and Health Care of Blacks in Ante-Bellum Virginia* (Urbana: University of Illinois Press, 1978). Contact between Africans and Native Americans is studied by Jack D. Forbes, *Black Africans and Native Americans: Color, Race, and Caste in the Evolution of Red-Black Peoples* (Oxford: Basil Blackwell, 1988).

Finally, there are many studies that explore how slavery took shape in particular places. Some are already mentioned. Among noteworthy others are T. H. Breen and Stephen Innes, *"Myne Owne Ground": Race and Freedom on Virginia's Eastern Shore, 1640–1676* (New York: Oxford University Press, 1980); Joyce D. Goodfriend, *Before the Melting Pot: Society and Culture in Colonial New York City, 1664–1730* (Princeton: Princeton University Press, 1992); Gwendolyn Midlo Hall, *Africans in Colonial Louisiana: The Development of Afro-Creole Culture in the Eighteenth Century* (Baton Rouge: Louisiana State University Press, 1992); Marvin L. Michael Kay and Lorin Lee Cary, *Slavery in North Carolina, 1748–1775* (Chapel Hill: University of North Carolina Press, 1995); Gary B. Nash, *Forging Freedom: The Formation of Philadelphia's Black Community, 1720–1840* (Cambridge: Harvard University Press, 1988); Orlando Patterson, *The Sociology of Slavery: An Analysis of the Origins, Development, and Structure of Negro Slave Society in Jamaica* (Rutherford, N.J.: Fairleigh Dickinson University Press, 1967); William D. Pierson, *Black Yankees: The Development of an Afro-American Subculture in Eighteenth-Century New England* (Amherst: University of Massachusetts Press, 1988); and Daniel H. Usner Jr., *Indians: Settlers, and Slaves in a Frontier Exchange Economy, The Lower Mississippi Valley before 1783* (Chapel Hill: University of North Carolina Press, 1992).